UNHOLY ALLIANCE

The Agenda Iran, Russia, and Jihadists
Share for Conquering the World

JAY SEKULOW

HOWARD BOOKS
AN IMPRINT OF SIMON & SCHUSTER, INC.

New York Nashville London Toronto Sydney New Delhi

Howard Books
An Imprint of Simon & Schuster, Inc.
1230 Avenue of the Americas
New York, NY 10020

First Howard Books hardcover edition September 2016

HOWARD and colophon are trademarks of Simon & Schuster, Inc.

For information about special discounts for bulk purchases, please contact Simon & Schuster Special Sales at 1-866-506-1949 or business@simonandschuster.com.

The Simon & Schuster Speakers Bureau can bring authors to your live event. For more information, or to book an event, contact the Simon & Schuster Speakers Bureau at 1-866-248-3049 or visit our website at www.simonspeakers.com.

Interior design by Jaime Putorti

Manufactured in the United States of America

10 9 8 7 6 5 4 3 2 1

Library of Congress Cataloging-in-Publication Data

Names: Sekulow, Jay, author.
Title: Unholy alliance : The Agenda Iran, Russia, and Jihadists share for conquering the world / Jay Sekulow.
Description: Nashville, TN : Howard Books, 2016. | Includes bibliographical references and index.
Identifiers: LCCN 2016016348 | ISBN 9781501141027 (hardcover : alk. paper)
Subjects: LCSH: Islam. | Terrorism—Religious aspects—Islam. | Iran—History—Revolution, 1979—Influence. | Iran—Foreign relations—Russia (Federation) | Russia (Federation)—Foreign relations—Iran. | Iran—Foreign relations—Syria. | Syria—Foreign relations—Iran. | Russia (Federation)—Foreign relations—Syria. | Syria—Foreign relations—Russia (Federation) | United States—Foreign relations—Middle East. | Middle East—Foreign relations—United States.
Classification: LCC BP161.3 .S455 2016 | DDC 327.1/17—dc23 LC record available at https://lccn.loc.gov/2016016348

ISBN 978-1-5011-4102-7
ISBN 978-1-5011-4103-4 (ebook)

"Nothing is too difficult for the brave."

CONTENTS

PREFACE

This book is the second in a series (that began with #1 *New York Times* bestseller *Rise of ISIS*) published with our Oxford Centre for the Study of Law & Public Policy. Much of the research for this book took place during my summers at the University of Oxford at the historic and world-renowned Bodleian Library. Three years ago, I undertook an extensive study of the former prime minister of Great Britain Benjamin Disraeli. I was privileged to have access to his private papers. Interestingly, Disraeli faced challenges eerily similar to the ones addressed in this book. During Disraeli's time, Russia caused much commotion throughout Europe and especially with Turkey. Not much has changed in the ensuing 150 years. Disraeli famously said, "Questions between Russia and England are not questions that can be settled by arbitration. They are questions in which power is involved; and power can only be met by power. Questions of this kind can only be settled by force. I do not mean necessarily by war. I mean by diplomacy or war; because in my opinion, diplomacy is force without violence."

The next year at the University of Oxford, I studied former British prime minister Winston Churchill, who prophetically warned, "Unsuccessful intervention in the affairs of another country is generally agreed to be a mistake." Churchill was correct and we should heed his admonition even today.

Last year, I did a comprehensive study of T. E. Lawrence—Lawrence of Arabia. Lawrence played a pivotal role in the development of the modern Arab world. He was both pro-Arab *and* a Zionist. Unlike today, during this time period, this was not a contradiction. I read the entirety of Lawrence's tome, *Seven Pillars of Wisdom*, as well as his personal letters. Colonel Lawrence had a comprehensive and personal relation with the emerging Arab political leaders during World War I. He also encountered the Persians (the Iranians of today). He made an interesting and important observation regarding their unique view of Islam. Lawrence observed that the "Shia Mohammedans from Pershia . . . were surly and fanatical, refusing to eat or drink with infidels; holding the Sunni as bad as Christians; following only their own priests and notables."

Each of these three leaders provides valuable insight into the intrigue that is the Middle East today, because the lessons they learned from their leadership in their eras can instruct us on the challenges we face in our own time.

A new alliance has developed in the last few years that has created what I call an unholy alliance. History often repeats itself. We no longer have the luxury of simply letting history unfold. We must change the course of events, rewriting the history if needed, to preserve our constitutional republic.

In this volume, I discuss and analyze the history and suggest a path of engagement to end what is the latest in a history-spanning line of attempts to export Sharia law and radical jihad around the world. We will win. We must win. We have no option.

1

Exporting Terrorism

Every day. Every single day.

We turn on the news, check our phones, or start our computers, and we see the horrific headlines. Tragically, they've become commonplace now. We expect them. Terrorists burn entire villages to the ground, with the children's wailing heard miles away. Christian men are forced to kneel above explosives that are detonated by jihadists. Crucifixions. Beheadings. Christians are buried alive. Missionaries' sons and daughters are slaughtered. Women are sold into sex slavery—the younger the girl, the higher the price. Radical Islamic terrorists even distribute pamphlets explaining how Islamic law does not forbid the rape of young girls.

It breaks our hearts. It makes our stomachs churn. We crave justice.

But the slaughter of Christians and other religious minorities and desecration of these religions' heritages aren't restricted to villages in the middle of nowhere. Nor has radical Islam stopped at cities in Iraq and Syria. The entire world is at war with radical Islam, whether President Barack Obama and progressives in the

ivory towers of academia and the powerful halls of our federal government are willing to admit it or not. One thing is certain: radical
Islam is at war with us.

Terrorist attacks are now a reality for everyone around the
world. No one is safe. No city, town, or village is out of the reach
of the radical jihadists. No one and no place is terrorist-proof. On
November 13, 2015, the world was shocked by several coordinated
attacks in Paris, France.[1] Two explosions erupted outside a stadium
filled with fans enjoying a soccer game.[2] At the exact same time,
gunmen armed with assault rifles engaged in shooting sprees at four
different locations in Paris, and a suicide bomber detonated a bomb
inside a restaurant.[3] Altogether, 130 people were killed in a single
hour, and hundreds more were injured.[4] Daesh, more commonly
known as the Islamic State of Iraq and Syria, or ISIS, claimed credit
for the massacre.[5] I still remember watching the news, glued to the
TV, talking with the American Center for Law & Justice's affiliate offices in Europe and around the world. When would the next
attack happen? How many more would die? I prayed for the victims,
the families, and the law enforcement and military officials working
to find the evil men and women targeting all of us. The Paris attacks
weren't the beginning, and they certainly would not be the end.

In modern history, the norm has been for terror cells to disperse
after a major attack like Paris. The surviving jihadists normally
scatter around the world and the cell is done. But tragically and
unfortunately, after Paris, the ISIS cell in Europe stayed alive and
carried out another large-scale attack in Brussels.[6] This network of
ISIS-linked cells in Europe included many jihadists who had spent
time fighting in Syria.

> Interviews and confidential court documents seen by *The
> Wall Street Journal* define the fugitives as part of an exten-
> sive web of young men who developed a deep hatred of the
> West after embracing radical Islam at underground mosques

and clandestine meetings in Molenbeek, a heavily Muslim populated district in the heart of Brussels. They have since become central to Islamic State's plans to strike the West, according to investigators, who suspect the Brussels network is behind the movement of battle-hardened operatives from Syria to Europe.[7]

When this cell struck again, on March 22, 2016, they attacked the ticketing and baggage area of the Brussels airport and one of the main subway stations, resulting in the death of at least thirty-five people, including three Americans.[8] More than three hundred others were injured.[9] On June 28, 2016, jihadists using a similar strategy attacked Istanbul's airport in Turkey, killing forty-one and injuring more than two hundred thirty.[10] And once again in Europe, on July 14, 2016, as Bastille Day celebrations commenced in Nice, France, a jihadist drove a large truck down a street, leaving at least eighty-four dead and more than two hundred injured.[11] Another attack could strike the heart of Europe at any moment. Meanwhile, miles of ocean aren't enough to keep the United States safe from jihadists.

In fact, only a month after the Paris attacks, in the United States, Tashfeen Malik and her husband, Syed Rizwan Farook, opened fire on colleagues with whom Syed had worked. The attack took place during a holiday party being held at a county convention center in San Bernardino, California.[12] In fact, just weeks before the terrorist attack, Syed's coworkers had thrown a baby shower for them. This couple killed the very people who had celebrated the birth of their child. This is beyond horrific. Again, as the news broke, I suspected jihad had once again come to our homeland. Sure enough, the FBI officially classified the massacre as a terrorist attack. On the day of the shooting, Tashfeen Malik posted on her Facebook page a pledge of allegiance to ISIS.[13]

In the early-morning hours of June 12, 2016, at a nightclub in

Orlando, Florida, Omar Mir Seddique Mateen—an American citizen born to Afghan parents—carried out the largest terrorist attack on U.S. soil since 9/11, slaughtering at least forty-nine of our fellow Americans and injuring dozens more.[14] He called 911 during the attack and pledged allegiance to ISIS.[15] Once again, terrorism had struck on our shores. And sadly, reports showed that Mateen had been under FBI investigation numerous times previously, and had been cleared.

But not all terrorist attacks on America get the same news coverage. Whenever possible, politicians work with the media to downplay terrorist attacks by ignoring their Islamist causes, calling them instead routine crimes. This most recently happened in early January 2016 when a gunman ambushed a police officer in Philadelphia, Pennsylvania, firing multiple close-range shots into his patrol car.[16] While in custody, the gunman openly confessed to being a follower of Allah, committing the act "in the name of Islam," and pledged allegiance to ISIS.[17] The same thing happened immediately after a terrorist openly fired on military recruiting offices in Chattanooga, Tennessee, in July 2015.[18] In both of these cases, the media and many politicians went out of their way to avoid talking about possible Islamist connections, including disregarding—until it was unavoidable—the ties to radicals or the audible pledges to Allah.[19]

Sadly, while media reports of tragic attacks in Paris, San Bernardino, and Brussels remind us of the threat we face, it's impossible to comprehend just how often jihadists shed innocent blood and butcher men, women, and children around the world. On November 12, 2015, two suicide bombers killed forty-three people in the streets of Beirut, Lebanon, and injured at least 239 others.[20] One surviving attacker claimed to have been working for ISIS, and an online statement purporting to be from the organization claimed responsibility.[21] On January 12, 2016, a suicide bomber blew himself up in Istanbul, Turkey, choosing to attack an area frequented by tourists and filled with innocent families.[22] Ten people died in the attack and fifteen others were injured.[23] Although no terror group officially claimed responsibility, the Turkish government identified the bomber as Syrian and believed that ISIS committed the attack.[24]

This is just a small sampling of the alarming attacks that have occurred around the world. As this sample suggests, ISIS has been establishing a name for itself as a primary perpetrator of Islamic terrorism globally, reaching even to American soil. But what is ISIS, and perhaps more important, what is the cause or inspiration that has led to its development? Is ISIS truly the primary terror threat in the world today, or is it simply the most visible face of a deeper problem, a single sprout growing from a much more ominous and extensive root system?

The Many Faces of Terror

As we know, ISIS is not the only group responsible for acts of terrorism around the world. Many other terrorist groups, both new and old, join ISIS by pledging fidelity to its Caliphate or, at the very least, express similar goals—to conquer the world by destroying anyone who refuses to bow to its radical ideology and anything that threatens its radical apocalyptic worldview. The groups use many different names and consist of many different nationalities. Yet they are inspired by the same religious zeal. They are known as Boko Haram in Nigeria and other African countries, the al-Nusra Front in Syria, Hamas in Palestine, Hezbollah in Lebanon, the Taliban in Afghanistan, and al-Qaeda throughout the world.

On December 16, 2014, seven Taliban militants attacked a school in Peshawar, Pakistan, killing at least 145 people, the vast majority of whom were children between the ages of twelve and sixteen.[25] Hamas constantly carries out its campaign of terror against Israel and Jewish people everywhere. For decades Hamas has indiscriminately and deliberately fired thousands of rockets at Israeli civilians.[26] In 2014, Palestinian terrorists as well as civilians started a stabbing campaign (that continues today) against innocent Jewish men, women, and children, killing and wounding scores of Israelis.[27]

So what are these terrorists' goals? Who is their primary target? The vast majority of the targets are Western, with attacks in Europe and the United States being the unholy grail for these jihadists. Whether we are willing to admit it or even realize it, they are determined to eliminate us. No amount of posturing or political correctness will make this any less true. If we are to stop this terrible pattern of death and terror, we must understand the underlying motivation that has galvanized groups such as ISIS and spurred them into action. We must diagnose the disease before we can truly eradicate the symptoms.

The Historical Roots of Terror

So how did we get here? Where did ISIS come from? The origin and motivating force of ISIS—the latest radical Islamic effort to establish a worldwide Caliphate—is tied directly to the tumultuous situation in Iraq and Syria in particular, and the Middle East in general. Understanding it requires a foundational knowledge of modern history.

Prior to World War II, the United States' involvement in the Middle East was minimal. But after the war, the world was radically different. With Europe in ruins, the Soviet Union flexing its muscle, and the United States emerging as the preeminent world power, balance shifted, leading to substantial growth in the Middle East's strategic importance. Thus, the United States became more heavily involved there.[28] Two global superpowers emerged, competing for geopolitical influence and the future of human civilization. On one side was the Soviet Union, promoting communism and authoritarianism. On the other was the United States, standing up for freedom and the historic values prized by Western civilization.[29] This was in fact the beginning of a proxy war between the United States and the USSR, the Cold War, with some of the most significant and potentially dangerous conflicts in the Middle East.[30] Battles and wars erupted in Egypt and other countries as well. One such battle—the Suez Canal Crisis—involved Israel, Egypt, and other countries. The Soviet Union sought to gain control over oil resources in the Middle East in order to oppose the United States and other Western powers, and the United States began to move into the region in order to counter Soviet interests.[31] American and Western forces established military bases in the region as a crucial part of the contingency strategy should the Cold War erupt into actual armed conflict, and also for security and intelligence-gathering purposes.[32] Thus, for many years, the Middle East was a theater of crucial strategic importance, as the Soviet Union and the United States vied for global supremacy.

World balance shifted again after the fall of the Soviet Union and the United States established itself as the hegemon, the world's primary superpower. Even in the absence of the Soviet Union, however, the Middle East remained a tumultuous region in which the United States remained heavily involved throughout the 1990s, especially because of the need to counter and contain the regional ambitions of Saddam Hussein in Iraq.[33] Encouraged by the 1979 Islamic Revolution in Iran, Islamic terrorist organizations increased their opposition to America and U.S.-backed secular regimes in the region.[34] The pinnacle of anti-American terror occurred on September 11, 2001, and it ignited the Global War on Terrorism and spurred further U.S. involvement in the Middle East.[35] After the terrorist attacks on 9/11, the United States decided it had to root out terrorist threats around the world so that radical jihadists could never again strike us at home. Through the brave sacrifice of hundreds of thousands of Americans and other allies who fought evil jihadists in Afghanistan and Iraq, al-Qaeda

Our enemies no longer fear us and our allies don't trust us.

was weakened. It cost us lives and money, but the United States believed that the battle was necessary and continued its decades-long commitment to destroy terrorists throughout the Middle East.[36]

Recently, however, a change has occurred in U.S. policy toward the Middle East, as we have begun to withdraw from the region under President Obama.[37] According to Ryan Crocker, dean and executive professor of the Bush School of Government & Public Service at Texas A&M University and a former U.S. ambassador to Afghanistan, Iraq, Syria, Lebanon, and Pakistan, we are now seeing "the lowest ebb since World War II for U.S. influence and engagement in the region."[38] The United States has substantially withdrawn its troops from Iraq and Afghanistan and has, for the most part, chosen not to involve itself in the civil war raging in Syria, due to the Obama administration's foreign policy decisions.[39] This departure has created a vacuum in the Middle East, a void waiting to be filled by some other country.[40] Our enemies no longer fear us and our allies don't trust us.

Power abhors a vacuum. As Crocker explains, "[I]f you look at the heart of the Middle East, where the U.S. once was, we are now gone—and in our place, we have Iran, Iran's Shiite proxies [e.g., Hezbollah], Islamic State [i.e., ISIS] and the Russians."[41] Strangely, some Muslim sects that normally war with one another are even joining forces in some of these unlikely alliances. For example, Shia Iran is supporting Sunni Hamas because they both want to see Israel wiped off the face of the planet. Eager to spread its vision of Islamic revolution throughout the Islamic world, Iran has been strategically expanding its reach through proxy terror organizations ever since it overthrew the Shah in 1979 and established the Islamic Republic of Iran. At the same time, Russia's activity in the Middle East has greatly increased[42] as our former Cold War foe attempts to regain a foothold in the region and assert control over lucrative oil resources.[43] As Iran seeks to fill the vacuum and oppose American interests around the world, it has cultivated an alliance with Russia, a nation led by a former Cold War intelligence officer who dreams of returning Russia to its Soviet-level influence in the region and throughout the world. In February 2016, Iran's defense minister, Brigadier General Hossein Dehghan, traveled to Moscow to meet with Russian president Vladimir Putin to arrange for the purchase and delivery of Russian weaponry to Iran.[44] Despite a United Nations (UN) resolution banning Iran from purchasing tanks and combat aircraft without UN approval,[45] Iran is eager to purchase Russia's most advanced tanks and fighter jets.[46] During the same visit, Dehghan met with Russian defense minister Sergei Shoigu, who then stated, "I am convinced that our meeting is going to contribute toward reinforcing friendly relations between Russian and Iranian armed forces."[47] This is the formation of the unholy alliance in which numerous enemies of freedom join together to fight America and our allies.

This is not shocking to even the most rudimentary student of world history. We recognize human nature, and we know how evil works. If the United States is unwilling to sacrifice and stand up against dictators and terrorists, then the dictators and terrorists will work together to ensure more people around the world are oppressed, and they will oppose the United States at every turn. When we show weakness, they show strength. When we withdraw, they advance. When we lack

> And let there be no doubt, this will result in more terrorist attacks, more aggression, more lives lost, and a reshaping of the world order.

strategy, they execute their strategy. And let there be no doubt, this will result in more terrorist attacks, more aggression, more lives lost, and a reshaping of the world order.

The Syrian Civil War: A Case Study

Nowhere is the unholy alliance between Russia and Iran more clearly displayed than in their partnership with Syrian president Bashar al-Assad against the rebel forces attempting to overthrow his regime.[48] Both Russia and Iran have supported Assad's regime as part of a strategic alliance. Also embroiled in that conflict, positioning itself against both the pro-Assad forces as well as many of the rebel forces, is ISIS.[49] Despite the danger of this conflict, the Obama administration has done very little to intervene.

To understand this conflict in Syria, one must understand the intra-Muslim conflict between Sunni and Shia Muslims. ISIS adheres to a jihadist Sunni strand of Islam while Assad is Alawite, a sect belonging to Shia Islam. Later in this book, I'll discuss these branches at greater length, laying out how these conflicts have led to proxy wars, unlikely coalitions, and ultimately, the unholy alliance between Iran and Russia. Thus it becomes clear that America's withdrawal from the Middle East has allowed Iran, Russia, and ISIS the opportunity to grow in strength and expand their control of the region. This in turn has led to the growth and spread of terrorism in every part of the world.

> **America's withdrawal from the Middle East has allowed Iran, Russia, and ISIS the opportunity to grow in strength and expand their control of the region.**

As Iran increases in strength, the Middle East becomes increasingly unstable, especially as other Middle Eastern countries react to oppose Iranian hegemony. After an Iranian mob attacked the Saudi Arabian embassy in Tehran in early 2016 in response to Saudi Arabia's execution of an outspoken Shiite cleric, Saudi Arabia severed its diplomatic ties with Iran.[50] Sudan and Bahrain followed the Saudis' lead, completely severing relations with Iran. The United Arab Emirates also downgraded its diplomatic ties with Iran.[51] As tensions grew between Iran and Saudi Arabia, the Saudis, interestingly, turned to Pakistan for help.[52] All of this sets the stage for further conflict and turbulence in this pivotal region of the world.

Recent U.S. foreign policy has done more than simply allow these dangerous forces to multiply and to gain control of an increasingly unstable Middle East. It has also actively compounded the problem through the disastrous Iran nuclear deal, formally known as the Joint Comprehensive Plan of Action.[53] The JCPOA, announced in 2015, came about after years of negotiations between Iran and the United States, the United Kingdom, France, Russia, China, and Germany, the so-called P5+1.[54] President Obama entered office wanting to negotiate with Iran, making clear he was willing to do whatever it took. As soon as the Obama administration sent senior advisor Valerie Jarrett to negotiate through back channels, Iran knew how desperate the Obama administration was. The Iranians sensed this desperation, which allowed them to get everything they wanted while giving up virtually nothing in return.

The deal completely capitulates to Iran, providing very broad relief from existing sanctions in coming years as well as the ability to recover billions of dollars' worth of hard currency presently frozen abroad in foreign banks.[55] Frozen Iranian assets based in the United States, including oil, petrochemical, and investment companies, will also be lifted.[56] Estimates suggest that loosening sanctions will provide Iran up to $150 billion in assets currently tied up.[57]

That's billions to terrorists around the world who hate America. That's billions to President Assad in Syria to kill his own citizens and use chemical weapons on children. That's billions to Hamas to launch rockets toward innocent Israeli civilians. That's billions to Hezbollah. That's billions in payments to Russia for weapons that violate international sanctions, money that Russia can, in violation of international law, use to attack its neighbors.

What has Iran promised the United States and the world in return? Iran has agreed to relax its uranium enrichment efforts and repurpose some of its nuclear facilities for peaceful operations.[58] Yet there is considerable fear that Iran will leverage the removal of trade restrictions and the $150 billion it is receiving to build nuclear weapons and to support terrorism worldwide.

Several years before the Iran nuclear deal was finalized, Lieutenant Colonel Oliver L. North said,

It will change the world as we know it today, if the
Iranians . . . put on the end of one of those North Korean–
provided missiles anything that looks like a warhead. . . .
[T]he Iranians are building not only the warheads, they
have the means of delivering it, and I'm telling you target
number one is Israel. The Israelis cannot abide that; it is
truly an existential threat.[59]

Dani Yatom, Mossad's former director, said that

a nuclear Iran is going to be an existential threat [for
Israel]. . . . The main reason for trying to achieve a nuclear
capability is to be able to cope with Israel and probably to
destroy Israel, because once they will have such a bomb,
they will face a very very huge temptation to use it. And I
think they might use it.[60]

Essentially, by agreeing to the Iran nuclear deal, the Obama
administration has added fuel to the already dangerous fire of the
ayatollahs' revolutionary Iran, which in turn will certainly continue
to sponsor terrorism worldwide and export its revolution to other
Muslim countries and terrorist organizations.

How Radical Islam and Russia
Endanger Our Way of Life

I wrote this book for a very simple reason: we will soon reach a point
at which it's too late. Civilizations aren't destroyed in an instant, but
rather by a series of cowardly capitulations and gradual erosion of
strength. If we don't act soon, then the world as we know it could
cease to exist. Our enemies who historically have been fighting each
other are now teaming up not only to take down the United States,

but also to eradicate Christians and Jewish people in every part of the world.

This book explores the causes and consequences of Iran's dangerous increase in strength and aggression as it reacts to the dwindling presence of the United States in the Middle East and takes advantage of the favorable treatment the Iran nuclear deal provided. It will expose Iran's role as an exporter of terror worldwide and its ultimate ambition to fulfill Shiite Islam's apocalyptic prophecies of taking over Jerusalem for the arrival of the Mahdi. It will explore the implications of Islam, its tenets and its mind-sets, and will provide an overview of Sharia law, which controls the radical Muslim's mind, whether he is the Grand Ayatollah of Iran or a foot soldier in ISIS's jihadist army. Ultimately, however, this book's goal is to reveal the existence, nature, and danger of the unholy alliance that has developed between Iran, Syria, Russia, and terror organizations around the globe.

> If we don't act soon, then the world as we know it could cease to exist.

President Obama has consistently failed to name our enemy. He desires to create a modern international community based on mutual respect, international security, and global prosperity. This is a false narrative, plain and simple. How can these things be achieved when the United States faces a serious security threat? Only after we understand the true nature of the enemy we are facing will we be in a position to effectively combat it.

It's a sad day when even Hollywood understands these truths that the U.S. president refuses to acknowledge. Like many Americans, I enjoy *Homeland*, a fictional television series about the CIA that rips plotlines from our real-life headlines. In the season-five premiere, a CIA agent is asked by bureaucrats and politicians why ISIS and radical terrorists continue to succeed. He's asked whether the U.S. strategy is working. He answers:

What strategy? Tell me what the strategy is and I'll tell you if it's working. [Silence] See, that right there is the problem because they—they have a strategy. They're gathering right now in Raqqa by the tens of thousands, hidden in the civilian population, cleaning their weapons and they know exactly why they're there. They call it the end times. What do you think the beheadings are about? The crucifixions in Deir Hafer, the revival of slavery? Do you think they make this [stuff] up? It's all in the book. Their . . . book. The only book they ever read—they read it all the time. They never stop. They're there for one reason and one reason only: to die for the Caliphate and usher in a world without infidels. That's their strategy and it's been that way since the seventh century. So do you really think that a few special forces teams are going to put a dent in that?[61]

Winston Churchill, one of the greatest leaders of the twentieth century, gave one of his most famous speeches after the Battle of Dunkirk in the summer of 1940. The Allied troops had retreated and the United States was still not entering the war; so to inspire the troops and draw U.S. support, Churchill gave a stirring speech about the resolve of the freedom-loving people to stand up to evil. He concluded:

The British Empire and the French Republic, linked together in their cause and in their need, will defend to the death their native soil, aiding each other like good comrades to the utmost of their strength. Even though large tracts of Europe and many old and famous States have fallen or may fall into the grip of the Gestapo and all the odious apparatus of Nazi rule, we shall not flag or fail. We shall go on to the end, we shall fight in France, we shall fight on the seas and oceans, we shall fight with growing confidence and growing strength in the air, we shall defend our Island, whatever the cost may be, we shall fight on the beaches, we shall fight on the landing grounds, we shall fight in the fields and in the streets, we shall fight in the hills; we shall never surrender, and even if, which I do not for a moment believe, this Island or a large part of it were subjugated and starving, then our Empire beyond the seas, armed and guarded by the British Fleet, would carry on the struggle, until, in God's good time, the New World, with all its power and might, steps forth to the rescue and the liberation of the old.[62]

This is the type of leadership and resolve we need today. Though the Nazis have been vanquished and communism has been diminished, we now fight a more ancient and ideological foe. A foe that wants each and every single one of us dead.

The stakes could not be any higher.

2

Rising from the Ashes of the Ottoman Empire

The history of the Middle East is essentially as long as recorded history itself. From the earliest days of human civilization, Mesopotamia[1]—the cradle of civilization—has been a location of pivotal importance. The nations and states in the Middle East today, however, are relative newcomers to the scene. Just a hundred years ago, the geopolitical landscape of the Middle East was very different. The Arab states that we know today came into being at the end of World War I with the disintegration of the Ottoman Empire.

The Ottoman nation first entered into history as a small tribal state at the end of the thirteenth century, filling the void left by the weakness of the Byzantine Empire and the destruction of Seljuk Turkish power by the Mongols.[2] Over the course of the next two centuries, it grew into an impressive empire in its own right.[3] The Ottoman Empire controlled the entire Middle East for more than four hundred years, from the mid-fifteenth century until the early twentieth century.[4] At its peak in 1683, the empire stretched from Budapest to Iran and the Persian Gulf, down both sides of the

Red Sea, and across North Africa to Algiers.[5] The Ottomans were Turks, not Arabs, so for those four-plus centuries the Middle East was dominated by a non-Arab power. The last wholly Arab power had been the Umayyad Caliphate circa AD 750.[6]

Until the end of the nineteenth century, the Ottoman Empire had ruled its subjects with a relatively soft hand.[7] The sultans allowed ethnic and religious minorities to remain autonomous as long as they paid their taxes to Constantinople.[8] However, with the rise of nationalism, modern communications, and global commerce, such rule became increasingly difficult in the late nineteenth and early twentieth centuries.[9] The world had become a smaller place, and the Ottomans' traditional methods no longer worked satisfactorily to rule over the empire's minority populations.[10]

Just a hundred years ago, the geopolitical landscape of the Middle East was very different.

Throughout the nineteenth century, the nations of Europe grew more powerful while the Ottoman Empire steadily declined.[11] In the 1870s, Czarist Russia destroyed an Ottoman army in the Balkans, leading to the independence of Romania, Serbia, and Montenegro.[12] In 1881, the Ottomans lost Tunisia to the French; in 1882, the British took Egypt; and in 1908, the Austro-Hungarians annexed Bosnia-Herzegovina.[13] In the period leading up to World War I, the Ottomans suffered defeat in the First Balkan War and lost most of their remaining European territories.[14] The British, taking advantage of the Ottoman decline, seized the Suez Canal in 1882.[15] Collectively, these events worsened relations between the Ottomans and the European continent.

Beginning in the late nineteenth century, the Zionist movement began to gain traction in Europe.[16] While the Europeans and the Ottomans were each attempting to solidify their respective political holds on the Middle East, Jews around the world started a serious discussion about creating a Jewish state in Palestine. The return to Zion (the Holy Land) had been an aspiration of Jews in the Diaspora for millennia. However, it was Theodor Herzl, a Hungarian writer, who helped create the modern political movement aimed at establishing a Jewish state in Palestine.[17] In his 1896 book, *The Jewish State*, Herzl argued that Jews would never be safe from anti-Semitic persecution until they had their own state.[18]

A prime example of the pervasive anti-Semitism occurring in Europe at this time was the Dreyfus Affair, a French espionage trial that took place in 1894.[19] Alfred Dreyfus was a French-Jewish army captain who was accused of selling military secrets to Germany, for which he was subjected to a court-martial and convicted of treason.[20] Fueled by anti-Semitic rhetoric that framed French Jews as disloyal and untrustworthy, the public was quick to condemn Dreyfus as a traitor.[21] In 1896, evidence began to surface showing that the crime had actually been committed by Ferdinand Walsin-Esterhazy, another French officer. However, a court-martial of Esterhazy acquitted him of the crime.[22] The controversy grew to such proportions that France was split between "Dreyfusards" and "anti-Dreyfusards." In 1898, evidence surfaced that indicated a document critical to Dreyfus's conviction had been forged, strengthening the Dreyfusard cause.[23] Nevertheless, a subsequent court-martial convicted Dreyfus again in 1899.[24] The president of the French republic then pardoned the captain and a civilian court of appeals set aside the judgment in 1906, but it was not until 1995 that the French army acknowledged Dreyfus's exoneration.[25]

In 1897 Theodor Herzl presided over the World Zionist Congress in Basel, Switzerland, where he tried to spur the Jewish global audience to action.[26] Somewhat surprisingly, Herzl experienced opposition from many European and American Jewish leaders.[27] These leaders were afraid that Zionism would fuel the long-standing view that Jews were not completely loyal to their birth countries.[28] Additionally, there were fears that the harsh climate of Palestine would not support a large Jewish population.[29] Aaron Aaronsohn, an agronomist and amateur archaeologist, worked to dispel the climate fears.[30] He examined similar climates, such as the American West, and argued that the prosperity in those locations could be repeated in Palestine.[31] Aaronsohn's work encouraged many Jews to support the Zionist movement, resulting in the raising of nearly $20,000 in 1909 toward the Jewish state's creation.[32]

A Collapsing Empire and Great Britain

As the Zionist movement grew early in the twentieth century, the already declining Ottoman Empire began to suffer further from internal conflicts. The Committee of Union and Progress (CUP), a group of young military officers who later became known as the "Young Turks," staged a reformist coup in 1908 and forced the sultan to reinstate the parliamentary constitution that had been discarded thirty years earlier.[33] By 1911, the Young Turks had become a stronger reform movement that sought to modernize the declining Ottoman Empire, calling for the extension of full rights to women and minorities.[34] In its attempt to gain the favor of Turks, as well as Jews, Christians, and other non-Turkish minorities, this movement attempted to simultaneously embrace three conflicting goals: modernization, the defense of Islam, and Turanism (a return to Turkic cultural unity).[35] Instead of reviving the empire, this mixed-bag progressive movement had the effect of alienating both Muslim traditionalists and the non-Turkish population.[36]

The Young Turks also found no support from the European powers. What seemed at first like a promising reform movement actually hastened the decay of the empire.[37] When World War I began, the Ottoman Empire joined the Central Powers of Germany and Austria-Hungary against the Allied Powers of Great Britain, France, and the Russian Empire, due primarily to the Russian Empire's desire to control the Bosphorus and the Dardanelles.[38] The Allied Powers went on to win the war, handing the Ottoman Empire a severe defeat.[39]

Even before the outbreak of the First World War in 1914, a movement had begun in the Arab provinces to establish a national Arab political identity separate and independent from the Ottoman Empire.[40] In 1908, Hussein ibn Ali was appointed Sharif[41] of the Hejaz, a province within the Ottoman Empire that essentially existed to rule the two Islamic holy cities of Mecca and Medina.[42] Hussein was appointed by the Turkish government in the hopes that his long prior residence would make him sympathetic to the Ottomans.[43]

Sharif and caliph were two religio-political offices intertwined.[44] As long as the sharif acknowledged the sultan of the Ottoman Empire as "caliph," the sultan could claim supremacy over all other Muslim princes.[45] The sharifs had recognized the Ottoman sultans as caliphs since 1517, when Sultan Selim the Grim had conquered the Hejaz (generally present-day Saudi Arabia).[46] The Ottoman claim to the Caliphate was based, first, upon its "protection" of the holy cities of Mecca and Medina and, second, on its "military supremacy in Arabia."[47]

When the secular Young Turk revolt in 1909 overthrew the Islamic regime of Sultan Abdul Hamid,[48] Hussein did not approve.[49] Hussein was by nature conservative and viewed Arab nationalism as inconsistent with Islam.[50] He claimed descent from Hashem, the great-grandfather of the Prophet Muhammad.[51] This genealogy gave him legitimacy with the Arabs[52] and his family the name of Hashemite.[53] While most Muslim jurists agreed that the ruler of Mecca had a superior legal claim to the Caliphate, the legal argument could not defeat the Ottomans' superior army.[54]

At the beginning of World War I, Hussein saw a chance to increase his power and actively sought to obtain the loyalty of local tribes.[55] He initially sought recognition from the Turks of a hereditary kingship over the Hejaz.[56] The Turks' rejection of a hereditary kingship for Sharif Hussein led him to seek an alliance with the British.[57]

Great Britain was eager to encourage Hussein's ambitions, foreseeing that an Arab revolt would significantly weaken the Ottoman Empire. While the Ottoman *vilayets* (provinces) of Damascus, Beirut, Basra, and Baghdad were agricultural and, with the city of Jerusalem, subject to typical Ottoman administration,[58] in the Arabian Peninsula (what we know today as Saudi Arabia), Turkish authority was minimal and, so long as the nomadic Arab chieftains feigned respect, little exercised.[59] Hussein had ample opportunity to rebel.

What we call Saudi Arabia today was not a country in 1914 as we understand it. The minimal Turkish rule did not extend to the interior.[60] The Arabian Peninsula had three families vying for power in the desert and others in the Yemen hills.[61] The three desert powers were the Hashemites, the Rashid, and the Saud. The Rashid were agricultural, at war with the Saud, in the north of the peninsula and sympathetic to the Turks (who had aided them against the Saud). The Saud were not sympathetic to the Turks or even the Hashemites.[62] When the First World War started, the British began negotiations with both the Saud and Sharif Hussein of the Hashemites. Both parties, at different times, aided the British against the Ottomans.[63]

> What we call Saudi Arabia today was not a country in 1914 as we understand it.

Additionally, Britain's demand for oil was growing greater than then-current world supply, and the British feared that without a stable supply, their industries and modernization would grind to a halt.[64] With its recently discovered vast oil fields, the Middle East offered the perfect solution to Britain's oil problem.[65] Britain could use Hussein to weaken the Ottoman Empire and thereby expand British control over its own oil supply.[66]

Hussein's ambitions were filled with Islamic and pan-Arabic rhetoric,[67] but it is hard to tell if he was motivated by a desire for an independent Hashemite kingdom or dreams of pan-Arab independence. [68] His "nationalism was based on the traditional concept of tribal and family unity whereas Abdullah's [Hussein's son] was based on the theory of Arab preeminence among Muslims."[69]

Over a period of three years, Sharif Hussein communicated via letters with Sir Henry McMahon, the British high commissioner in Egypt.[70] The first of these letters was sent in 1914, soon after Britain declared war on Germany and its ally, the Ottoman Empire.[71] In his initial letter, Hussein asked Britain to grant him control over the Arab territories, based on his assertion that "the whole of the Arab nation without any exception have decided in these last years to accomplish their freedom, and grasp the reins of their administration both in theory and practice."[72]

With its recently discovered vast oil fields, the Middle East offered the perfect solution to Britain's oil problem.

Hussein further requested that Britain "approve the proclamation of an Arab [Caliphate] of Islam" that would rule these lands.[73] Hussein's goals were to dismantle the Ottoman Empire and to build in its place an Islamic Arab empire.[74] His desire was to rule the entire Middle East area that was then under Ottoman control, though he was willing to make exceptions for those places with large British populations, such as the port of Aden, in what is now Yemen.[75]

Hussein continually maintained that it was not out of selfish interest that he made these requests: "[I]t is not I personally who am demanding of these limits which include only our [Arab] race, but . . . they are all proposals of the people, who, in short, believe that they are necessary for economic life."[76] McMahon originally responded to Hussein ambiguously, stating, "[I]t would appear to be premature to consume our time discussing such details in the heat of war."[77]

After Hussein reiterated to McMahon the urgency of his request, McMahon communicated the request to the British government, which then tentatively agreed to recognize an independent Arab state with some modifications within the territorial boundaries as proposed by Hussein.[78]

Germany and Jihad

The British were not the only European nation with a keen interest in the Middle East. Kaiser Wilhelm II of Germany had also developed an intense interest in the region, largely due to the influence and ambitions of Max von Oppenheim, a wealthy explorer, writer, and later diplomat.[79] Oppenheim, who had spent twenty years in the Middle East,[80] had convinced the Kaiser that Germany should use its increasingly benevolent friendship with the Muslim world to combat the British Empire.[81] Oppenheim's plan was to use Islamic teachings on jihad to stir up the Muslims against the French in North Africa, the Russians in Central Asia, and the British in India.[82]

By 1907, Germany was seeking ways to assert itself as an imperial power.[83] Wilhelm saw the Middle East as an opportunity to expand Germany's political and economic influence abroad.[84] The newly formed German nation-state needed room to grow, and Europe was already largely controlled by the British, French, and Russians.[85] The Middle East, on the other hand, was still largely free from European control and offered tremendous opportunity for colonization.[86]

Because the Ottoman Empire was crumbling, Kaiser Wilhelm recognized an opportunity to create a powerful German Empire in the Middle East with Muslims as its loyal supporters.[87] Wilhelm even went so far as to call himself "Hajji Wilhelm," the protector of Islam.[88] Yet, whereas the British chose to use Sharif Hussein of the Hejaz to stir up Arab nationalism against the Ottomans, Oppenheim tried to use pan-Islamism to stir up the Muslim masses against the European colonial nations.[89] Oppenheim wanted to use religious fanaticism, as opposed to Arab nationalism, to turn the Muslim population against the British.[90] Oppenheim encouraged the German foreign ministry to forge an alliance with the Ottoman Empire, recognizing the strategic advantage Germany could gain in the war if the Ottoman government in Constantinople were to call for a holy war against the Christian occupiers of Ottoman lands.[91]

The idea of fragmenting the British Empire via jihad had some merit. The Kaiser had even advanced the idea to the Czar.[92] As recently as 1898, the British had crushed an Islamic revolt at the battle of Omdurman in the Sudan.[93]

Oppenheim, working as the head of the German Intelligence Bureau for the East (nicknamed "the jihad bureau"),[94] employed numerous avenues to try to sow the seeds of jihad in the Muslim world. He bribed Muslim jurists across the Middle East into issuing fatwa[95] rulings against all Europeans except Germans, Austrians, and Hungarians.[96] Echoing what we often hear from ISIS and other Islamists today, Oppenheim also ran a propaganda war against the British, claiming that the British were untrustworthy and anti-Muslim, and he even distributed pamphlets to stir up old ethnic and religious resentment toward Christians in the Middle East.[97] Such pamphlets frequently cited verses from the Quran, which stated that "[t]he blood of the infidels in the Islamic lands may be shed with impunity" and that Muslims should "slay [the unbelievers] wherever ye find them."[98]

Assisting Oppenheim was Curt Prüfer, who was a prodigy with respect to learning foreign languages. Prüfer developed an extreme fascination with the Middle East.[99] As Prüfer grew older, he mastered Turkish and Arabic.[100] In 1907, he took a position as interpreter at the German embassy in Cairo.[101] It was there that Prüfer met Oppenheim.[102] Over the years, Oppenheim mentored young Prüfer and instilled in him the idea of using jihad as a tool to further Germany's interests.[103] Oppenheim also helped organize small terrorist cells, composed of pious Muslims, to assassinate British, French, and Russian citizens.[104] Such cells even began employing suicide tactics.[105]

To endear the Arabs to Germany, Germany helped finance and engineer miles of railroads within the Ottoman Empire.[106] Germany spent around three billion marks on its Middle East jihadist efforts.[107]

Despite its investments and some successes, Germany's efforts were ultimately unsuccessful. An attack by Sanussi tribesmen on Egypt from the Libyan desert caused no end of concern to the English in Cairo but was quickly put down.[108] An attempted rebellion by Indian Muslims, the Silk Letter Conspiracy, was discovered by the British before it began.[109] The Shah of Iran agreed to declare war on the Allied Powers but ultimately backed out in November 1915.[110] These attempts were as close as Germany came to success.[111]

Lawrence of Arabia

By June 1916, Britain's seeming support for an independent Arab state, the financial and military support it promised, and the turning of the tide of war against the Germans in favor of the British and French helped persuade the Arabs to side with the British and to revolt against the Ottomans rather than fight against the British, French, and Russians.[112]

The man responsible for helping to lead the successful Arab revolt against the Ottomans was T. E. Lawrence, later known as "Lawrence of Arabia." Lawrence came from an aristocratic Anglo-Irish family that resided in England.[113] He attended Oxford University and wrote his thesis on the influence of the Crusades on European military architecture.[114] To research his thesis, Lawrence had traveled to Syria in 1909.[115] As a twenty-one-year-old student, Lawrence had trekked across Syria and surveyed Crusader castles.[116] During this trip, Lawrence developed a fascination with the Middle East, its people, and its culture.[117]

Throughout his trip, Arabs received Lawrence with great hospitality and kindness.[118] Lawrence later joined an excavation expedition to the ancient city of Carchemish.[119] There, Lawrence first realized his potential to lead, specifically his ability to lead Arab men.[120] Lawrence, unlike other Westerners, took time to learn the Arabic language, to visit the workmen in their homes, and to learn about their culture.[121] Additionally, Lawrence earned their respect because he worked along with the men.[122] Such conduct greatly impressed the local Arabs[123] and was a core element in his ability to successfully lead the Arab revolt against the Ottomans. Throughout his time in the Middle East, Lawrence became an apologist for the Arabs and often criticized British negotiating policies.[124]

Lawrence convinced the British government to rely on local Arabs exclusively rather than send British troops to fight the Ottomans.[125] By limiting the use of British troops, the British stood a better chance at retaining the loyalty and trust of the Arabs.[126] The British, then, agreed to bankroll and supply the Arab forces under Emir Feisal, the son of Sharif Hussein of Mecca, and a key leader in the Arab revolt against the Ottomans in World War I.[127]

By 1916, Britain had provided nearly one million pounds in gold to the Arab forces.[128] Lawrence, donning Arab clothing at the suggestion of Feisal so that the troops would identify Lawrence as one of their leaders, took command of the Arab troops and led them successfully against the Ottoman forces in the Aqaba campaign.[129] Lawrence's reputation grew tremendously after his capture of Aqaba. Acting without orders from the British military, Lawrence and forty-five Arabs made a nearly six-hundred-mile journey through the desert in order to attack Aqaba from the rear.[130] Upon reaching Aqaba, Lawrence learned of an Ottoman relief force nearby.[131] After careful preparation, Lawrence and his force of now one thousand newly recruited Arabs fell upon the Ottoman relief force and annihilated it.[132] Approximately 300 Ottomans were killed, and another 160 surrendered, at the cost of only two Arab rebels.[133] The city of Aqaba surrendered soon after without firing a shot.[134] The British decorated Lawrence with the Victoria Cross, the highest British military award, for his efforts.[135] Later, Lawrence received the Distinguished Service Order medal and was promoted to the rank of colonel.[136]

Dividing the Middle East: The Sykes-Picot Agreement

While the British were openly supporting the Arabs in 1916, Britain, France, and Russia met secretly and agreed to divide the Arab territories among themselves,[137] enshrined in a document that came to be known as the Sykes-Picot Agreement after the English and French negotiators.[138] The Sykes-Picot Agreement did not draw actual boundary lines, but simply established general zones over which each country would maintain influence.[139] According to the agreement, France would control the area that would eventually become Lebanon and Syria, Britain would control Mesopotamia (Iraq) and Jordan, and Russia would control the Turkish straits, Turkish Armenia, and Persian Azerbaijan. Palestine was to be placed under international control.[140]

The Sykes-Picot Agreement was wholly unknown to the Arabs.[141] In fact, the British purposefully kept the agreement a secret in order to curry Hussein's support and favor.[142] The British accord with Hussein contained a "modest clause" stating that the British agreed to "support the establishment of native governments in parts of Syria and Mesopotamia, 'saving the interests of [their] ally, France.'"[143] By reserving the "interests of [its] ally," Britain, unbeknownst to Hussein, was referencing the Sykes-Picot Agreement.[144] The Arabs' agreement to revolt against the Ottomans, then, was based upon false pretenses because the British promise to support the establishment of local Arab governments was secretly limited by the Sykes-Picot Agreement.[145] Moreover, the same territory that the British had "promised" to Hussein was also "promised" to rival Arab groups in Cairo.[146] The British were using the recently fallen Ottoman territories as bargaining chips in their desire for Middle East expansion.

Rumors of the Sykes-Picot Agreement eventually reached the Arabs from Turkey.[147] The Turkish government disliked Hussein, and Britain's seemingly underhanded conduct was the Turks' "strongest card" to play in trying to drive a wedge between the two.[148] The Turks learned of the Sykes-Picot Agreement from the Bolsheviks, who had recently overthrown the Czar and publicly released the agreement in November 1917.[149]

That same month, Great Britain's foreign secretary, Sir Arthur Balfour, sent to Lord Rothschild, a leader of the British Jewish community, a letter that has become known as the Balfour Declaration.[150] The letter contained a short but clear message directly approved by the British government:

> His Majesty's Government view with favour the establishment in Palestine of a national home for the Jewish people, and will use their best endeavours to facilitate the achievement of this object, it being clearly understood that nothing shall be done which may prejudice the civil and religious rights of existing non-Jewish communities in Palestine, or the rights and political status enjoyed by Jews in any other country.[151]

Despite the publication of the Sykes-Picot Agreement and the Balfour Declaration, the leadership of the revolutionary Arab nationalists maintained its loyalty to and cooperation with Great Britain through the final year of the war.[152]

By the end of 1917, the Ottomans had lost Jerusalem, Mecca, and Baghdad.[153] These losses dealt a severe blow to the legitimacy of the Ottomans and turned the tide against them.[154] By late 1918, the war had ended, and the Ottomans had been defeated. It was not until after the defeat of the Ottoman Empire and the end of the war that disagreements arose, as the conflicting claims to Middle Eastern lands became more widely known.[155]

The dismemberment of the Ottoman Empire, planned for in the Sykes-Picot Agreement, was then completed by the armistice between the powers of France and Britain with the Ottomans at Mudros, Greece.[156] The armistice of Mudros deliberately used geographic terms that did not correspond to any Ottoman administrative divisions.[157] In it, the Ottomans agreed to the occupation of much of the empire, through a diplomatic sleight of hand where the French and British could occupy any "strategic point."[158]

It is important to note that, in contrast to the often violent relationship that has arisen between the Arab people and the Jewish people in the Middle East that we know today, at this early stage of development, the leaders of both groups appeared ready to cooperate and unite their aims. At the end of World War I, in 1918, Feisal met with Zionist leader Chaim Weizmann.[159]

> In contrast to the often violent relationship that has arisen between the Arab people and the Jewish people in the Middle East that we know today, at this early stage of development, the leaders of both groups appeared ready to cooperate and unite their aims.

Feisal was recognized as the "spokesman of the Arab world" at the Paris Peace Conference directly following the war.[160] In 1918, when the Arab resistance forces occupied Damascus, Feisal declared himself king of Syria, believing that he would receive British support after the war to create a unified Arab nation covering most of Syria.[161] It was while Feisal entertained this belief that he met with Weizmann.

Weizmann recounted that, in his meeting with Feisal, he explained to the Emir the nature of his mission and tried to "allay Arab fears and susceptibilities" concerning the prospect of a Jewish Palestinian state.[162] Weizmann also asked Feisal for "his powerful moral support."[163] The two carried on a lengthy conversation in which Weizmann found Feisal "by no means uninformed" about the Zionist program.[164] Weizmann spoke to Feisal about how the presence of a Jewish state would greatly benefit the Arabs, and

Weizmann found that Feisal was in "full agreement" with Weizmann.[165] This meeting occurred at Emir Feisal's camp on the Trans-Jordan plateau, where T. E. Lawrence (Lawrence of Arabia) was operating.[166]

Weizmann related, "[t]his first meeting in the desert laid the foundations of a lifelong friendship" between him and Lawrence.[167] Their meetings eventually "crystallized into an agreement" drafted by T. E. Lawrence and signed by Weizmann and Feisal.[168] The agreement would ensure that "[a]ll necessary measures shall be taken to encourage and stimulate immigration of Jews into Palestine on a large scale" and allow for the peaceful establishment of both Jews and Arabs in various territories in Palestine.[169] The agreement also included a reservation by Feisal: "If the Arabs are established as I have asked in my manifesto of 4 January, addressed to the British Secretary of State for Foreign Affairs, I will carry out what is written in this agreement. If changes are made, I cannot be answerable for failing to carry out this agreement."[170]

"Thus," says Weizmann, "the leader of the Arab world against Turkey, who by his leadership initiated a new period of Arab revival, came to a complete understanding with us, and would no doubt have carried this understanding into effect if his destiny had shaped as we at that time expected it would."[171]

The goodwill undergirding this agreement was further demonstrated by a letter written by Feisal to a member of the American Zionist deputation in 1919, while both Feisal and Weizmann were attending the Paris Peace Conference:

We feel that the Arabs and Jews are cousins in race, suffering similar oppressions at the hands of powers stronger than themselves, and by a happy coincidence have been able to take the first step toward the attainment of their national ideals together.

We Arabs, especially the educated among us, look with

deepest sympathy on the Zionist movement. Our deputation here in Paris is fully acquainted with the proposals submitted by the Zionist Organization to the Peace Conference, and we regard them as moderate and proper. We will do our best, in so far as we are concerned, to help them through; we will wish the Jews a most hearty welcome home.

With the chiefs of your movement, especially with Dr. Weizmann, we have had, and continue to have, the closest relations. He has been a great helper of our cause, and I hope the Arabs may soon be in a position to make the Jews some return for their kindness. We are working together for a reformed and revived Near East, and our two movements complete one another. The Jewish movement is national and not imperialistic. Our movement is national and not imperialistic; and there is room in Syria for us both. Indeed, I think that neither can be a real success without the other.

People less informed and less responsible than our leaders, ignoring the need for co-operation of the Arabs and the Zionists, have been trying to exploit the local differences that must necessarily arise in Palestine in the early stages of our movements. Some of them have, I am afraid, misrepresented your aims to the Arab peasantry, and our aims to the Jewish peasantry, with the result that interested parties have been able to make capital out of what they call our differences.

I wish to give you my firm conviction that these differences are not on questions of principle, but on matters of detail, such as must inevitably occur in every contact with neighboring peoples, and as are easily dissipated by mutual good will. Indeed, nearly all of them will disappear with fuller knowledge.

I look forward, and my people with me look forward, to

a future in which we will help you and you will help us, so that the countries in which we are mutually interested may once again take their place in the community of civilized peoples of the world.[172]

Others besides Weizmann and Feisal assisted in fostering cooperation between the Jewish people and Arab people. One such pivotal character was T. E. Lawrence. In his autobiography, Weizmann recounted his personal relationship with Lawrence, and stated:

[Lawrence's] relationship to the Zionist movement was a very positive one, in spite of the fact that he was pro-Arab, and he has mistakenly been represented as anti-Zionist. It was his view—as it was Feisal's—that the Jews would be of great help to the Arabs, and that the Arab world stood to gain much from a Jewish Homeland in Palestine.[173]

Weizmann's account of the support and friendship that once existed between the Jewish people and Arab leaders is a remarkable and an important part of the modern Middle East's history that should not be discounted.

In the end, however, the plans for cooperation set forth in the Feisal-Weizmann Agreement did not come to fruition.[174] Feisal's ambition to unite the Arab world and establish an Arab state in Syria with British support never materialized. Instead, he learned soon after the war that France had its eyes set on establishing its influence over Syria and Lebanon, and Britain was eager to support its ally in that goal.[175] Although Feisal attempted to negotiate with France, tensions between France and other Arab leaders who did not want to concede anything to France

"[Lawrence's] relationship to the Zionist movement was a very positive one, in spite of the fact that he was pro-Arab."

eventually culminated in Feisal's exile from Syria.[176] Britain, in an effort to mend the breach, then supported Feisal's ascension to the throne of Iraq in 1921,[177] with the intention of ruling indirectly through him.[178]

With the support of Britain, Feisal became king of Iraq. His reign (lasting only just over a decade), however, was troubled and destined for failure.[179] Feisal faced the challenges of ruling an unsettled people still reeling from the disintegration of the four-hundred-year-old Ottoman Empire, filled with ethnic, social, and sectarian divisions, and building the political structure of a brand-new state.[180] Iraq was the joining of three Ottoman *vilayets*—Basra, Mosul, and Baghdad—whose governors had each reported directly to Istanbul.[181] The fact that Feisal was not a native of Iraq concerned the people who had no desire to be ruled by foreigners.[182] On top of this, Britain had placed Feisal on the throne in order to ease anti-British sentiments and maintain its own power in the country, but Feisal soon manifested his contrary desire for an independent Iraq.[183] This conflict of purposes led to continuing friction between Feisal and Britain that lasted for more than a decade.[184] In 1933, after only twelve years of ruling Iraq and soon after Britain finally yielded to him much of the independence he desired, Feisal died from ill health and exhaustion.[185]

Persistent tension with Britain was not Feisal's only disappointment. The Saud family had decisively defeated the Rashid family in 1921 and then turned their attention to the Hashemites.[186] In 1925, the Saud, under the leadership of their king, Ibn Saud, occupied Mecca and expelled Sharif Hussein.[187]

According to Weizmann, this change of fate beyond Feisal's own control, resulting ultimately in the death of his dream of Arab unity, made it impossible for the Weizmann-Feisal Agreement to be realized.[188] Once Feisal ceased to be the recognized voice of the unified Arab people, no one person or group took his place. Weizmann attributed many of the difficulties of relations between the Jewish people and the Arab people to this fact: "[P]erhaps the paramount trouble is the lack of a single personality or group of personalities capable of representing the Arab world and speaking in its behalf." [189]

The harsh terms of the Treaty of Sèvres divided up the recently defeated Ottoman Empire.[190] In that treaty, the Ottomans agreed to renounce all claims to non-Turkish territory and to demobilize their military.[191] Further, the treaty created an independent Armenia and an autonomous Kurdistan;[192] but Kurdistan, while autonomous, would be under British control.[193] Greece would also exercise control over the Aegean islands in the Dardanelles.[194] Finally, the treaty opened the straits between the Mediterranean Sea and the Black Sea for public shipping.[195] Sultan Mehmed VI, the Ottoman ruler, signed the treaty in April 1920.[196]

The Treaty of Sèvres was met with widespread opposition across the rump Ottoman Empire.[197] Mustafa Kemal Atatürk, a highly respected Ottoman military leader, split with the sultan, launched the Turkish National Movement, and refused to demobilize Ottoman troops.[198] Instead, Atatürk set up a Turkish National Assembly, which in turn refused to ratify the Treaty of Sèvres[199] and began organizing troops around the city of Ankara.[200] The Turkish War of Independence broke out soon after.[201] After over two years of fighting, Atatürk and his forces had defeated all foreign armies, including the Armenians, the Greeks, and the French, thereby ending the war.[202]

After the war, both sides met in Lausanne, Switzerland, to negotiate a replacement for the Treaty of Sèvres. The Treaty of Lausanne was signed on July 24, 1923.[203] By that point, the Turkish sultanate had been abolished and did not take part in the treaty negotiations.[204] It was Atatürk's Ankara government that attended.[205]

Under the Treaty of Lausanne's terms, the previous ideas of an independent Armenia and an autonomous Kurdistan were abandoned.[206] The Turks agreed to give up their Arab provinces, but, in return, there would be no European spheres of influence in Turkey.[207] Turkey would also not have to pay war reparations,[208] and the capitulations to Europe would be abolished.[209] The system of capitulations goes back to the 1500s, when the European powers obtained concessions from the sultans in Istanbul,[210] where European citizens were exempt from Ottoman law. Under the treaty's terms, the British and French would retain control in Iraq and Syria.[211] Finally, the treaty gave Turkey sovereignty over the straits on the condition that an international commission would supervise shipping and a demilitarized zone would be established.[212] The Treaty of Lausanne officially recognized Turkish independence, and Mustafa Kemal Atatürk became Turkey's first president.[213]

The Modern Middle East and the State of Israel

Once Turkey renounced all claims to its previous Arab provinces, it fell to the Europeans to decide what states to create and where to draw the boundaries. This task was given to a brand-new representative of the international community—the League of Nations.[214] The League of Nations was an outgrowth of World War I and the first true realization of a system operating at the supranational level for the purpose of promoting peace through international cooperation.[215] Article 22 of the Covenant of the League of Nations, agreed to in 1919, proposed a Mandate System for transferring control of the areas previously ruled by the Ottoman Empire.[216]

The idea behind the Mandates was that the formerly Ottoman-controlled territories were not yet capable of independent statehood and, therefore, those territories should be entrusted to the supervision of "advanced nations" to responsibly administer the territories on behalf of the League until the people of those territories had developed sufficiently to govern themselves.[217] Article 22 stated that "[c]ertain communities . . . have reached a stage of development where their existence as independent nations can be provisionally recognized subject to the rendering of administrative advice and assistance by a Mandatory until such time as they are able to stand alone."[218] The Covenant set forth the concept of this Mandate System but did not specify its precise details, noting that "[t]he character of the mandate must differ according to the stage of development of the people, the geographical situation of the territory, its economic conditions and other similar circumstances."[219]

The World War I Allied powers agreed to an early version of the Mandate System in 1920 in a conference at San Remo, Italy,[220] and it was later confirmed by the League of Nations.[221] The Mandates placed Syria and Lebanon under the control of France, Palestine under the control of Great Britain, and proposed a Mandate for Mesopotamia, which we know today as Iraq.[222] At the time of the Mandate, Palestine consisted of the geographical area that is now Israel, the West Bank, the Gaza Strip, a slice of the Golan Heights, and Jordan.[223]

The French divided their Mandate into Syria and Lebanon with regard for their administrative needs.[224] The borders of Lebanon announced on September 1, 1920, did not correspond to the program of any Lebanese party.[225] The French had just crushed an Arab army on July 24, 1920, at the Battle of Maysalun.[226] The army had been raised by Feisal, the son of Sharif Hussein, in an attempt to become king of Syria.[227] Christian and Muslim Arabs had both sought an independent Greater Syria under Feisal.[228] The part of the Mandate that is modern-day Syria was made into several different states that later joined.[229]

The Mandate for Palestine was unique.

The Mandate for Palestine was unique. Unlike the Mandates for Syria and Mesopotamia (Iraq), which called on the Mandatory powers to prepare the inhabitants for independence, under the Mandate for Palestine, Britain was given the responsibility to create a "Jewish national home" in Palestine.[230] The British administration was to "facilitate Jewish immigration" and settlement throughout the land as well as "facilitate the acquisition of Palestinian citizenship by Jews who take up their permanent residence in Palestine."[231] Until 1948, when Britain departed Palestine, Britain was under an international, legal obligation to help establish a Jewish homeland in Palestine.[232]

In 1922, under its authority as the Mandatory, Britain divided Palestine into two parts. The larger section (about 78 percent of the territory), located east of the Jordan River, was renamed Transjordan, which ultimately became the modern-day Hashemite Kingdom of Jordan in 1946.[233] The smaller section, located west of the Jordan River, retained the name Palestine.[234] Jewish settlement was limited to the western, smaller section; Jews were forbidden to settle in Transjordan.[235] Thus, the continued formation of the "Jewish national home" was limited to the territory that now comprises Israel, the West Bank, and the Gaza Strip, while Jordan was split off from Mandatory Palestine to become an exclusively Arab state.

Throughout the era of the British Mandate, both the Arab and Jewish populations in Palestine grew substantially. Britain tried to keep peace between these populations by proposing power-sharing plans for the Jews and the Arabs, but the Arab leaders rejected each plan and vowed to reject any such plan that called for them to share power with the Jewish people.[236]

After Britain announced its withdrawal from the region in 1947, the United Nations began tackling the problem of how to approach Palestine after Britain's departure.[237] In Resolution 181, the UN General Assembly voted to partition Palestine into three parts: a Jewish state, an Arab state, and a UN-controlled zone around Jerusalem in order to pro-

> **The Arab leaders rejected each plan and vowed to reject any such plan that called for them to share power with the Jewish people.**

tect the holy sites of Judaism, Christianity, and Islam.[238] The Arab Palestinians rejected the plan and the resolution was never implemented.[239] If both sides had agreed to the plan, the UN's plan would have created an Arab Palestinian state and a Jewish Palestinian state in 1948.[240] However, since the Arab Palestinians rejected the plan, no Arab state was ever created.[241] After the British withdrew, Jewish Palestinians proclaimed the creation of a Jewish Palestinian state called the State of Israel.[242]

The State of Israel was proclaimed on May 14, 1948. Within a day of proclaiming its statehood, Israel was invaded by neighboring Arab states with the help of Arab Palestinians who were already fighting Jewish Palestinians.[243] This began the First Arab-Israeli War.[244] By 1949, Israel had defeated the Arab coalition, and the resulting armistices gave Israel control over most of the land of the Mandate.[245] Only the Gaza Strip and so-called West Bank remained in Arab hands.

> Within a day of proclaiming its statehood, Israel was invaded by neighboring Arab states with the help of Arab Palestinians who were already fighting Jewish Palestinians.

The West Bank was occupied by Jordanian military forces, and the Gaza Strip was occupied by Egyptian forces until the Six-Day War in 1967, when those territories also came under Israeli control.[246] Jordan continued to formally claim control over the West Bank until 1988, when King Hussein granted the request of the Palestine Liberation Organization (PLO) to renounce any Jordanian claims to the West Bank, after which the PLO became the sole Arab claimant of that territory.[247]

It is important to note that from 1967 until today, neither the PLO, the current Palestinian Authority (PA), nor any other Arab Palestinian political entity has exercised sovereign control over the West Bank. Further, prior to Israel's acquisition of the territory in 1967, dating back to the rule of the Ottoman Turks, there had never been a lawfully recognized Arab Palestinian sovereign over the territory in the former Mandate for Palestine.[248]

Today, one can hardly talk about the Middle East without bringing up war, terror, and unrest. The region has become synonymous with geopolitical instability and territorial conflicts, specifically with regard to the ongoing Israeli-Palestinian issue. Despite the fact that Arab Palestinians have no greater historical claim to the territories for which they are fighting than do Jewish inhabitants of the land of Palestine, the majority of the international community continues to demand that Israel relinquish control of these territories to allow the establishment of an independent Arab state ruled by a political entity whose ultimate goal is the utter destruction of Israel.[249]

As history shows, the Middle East is a region occupied by relatively young nation-states, born from the flames of conflict after the First World War, rising from the ashes of a once-powerful empire that collapsed upon itself, created without respect to ethnic or religious loyalties, and reared in an environment of intense international scrutiny and involvement. Ever since the beginning of World War I, this region has been a focus of keen interest to the world's major powers and the international community, who have involved themselves in the region to pursue conflicting goals. Understanding these tumultuous origins and history is critical to understanding the culture, politics, and mind-set of the modern Middle Eastern world.

3

A Clash of Cultures

The United States of America is the greatest country on the face of the earth.

But we often fail to realize just how different our way of life and thinking is from the billions of people in other parts of the world. It's why far too many of our leaders refuse to acknowledge the threat of radical Islam and call it out by name. It's why far too many people wrongly think about radical Islamic terrorists as simply the heirs to the long line of freedom-hating enemies of the West. It's why radical jihadists continue to win and advance, leaving America's leaders without an effective strategy and wondering what to do.

> And let there be no doubt, we are at war. They are at war with us.

Without realizing what truly makes America exceptional and why radical Islamists and many other Muslims hate us, we will continue to lose this war. And let there be no doubt, we are at war. They are at war with us now and will continue to be long into the future, until we are destroyed. The only thing we accomplish by denying this reality is our own demise.

What makes America great is our liberty, our freedom, our rule of law, our diversity, and our Constitution. In other words, our values. Radical Islamists hate and seek to destroy these things because they have different values. Our cultural identities and philosophical views are diametrically opposed. The forces and goals that drive our decision making in America are fundamentally incompatible with those of the Muslim world. It is almost as if we are attempting to solve a mathematical equation and the symbols we use represent different values to each of us.

There are about 1.6 billion Muslims in the world.[1] Most Muslims are peaceful. Yet all Muslims follow some form of Islam, whether radical or peaceful. Islam was born in the Middle East about fourteen hundred years ago in a tribal society. It expanded from there through holy wars in the name of Islam. Under the leadership of the first four caliphs, Islam spread and conquered nearly all of the Middle East.[2] In the next few centuries, Muslims conquered historically Christian lands, such as Spain, Portugal, Egypt, Turkey, and North Africa, as well as other lands such as Persia and the Indian subcontinent. Muslim conquerors forcibly converted the inhabitants of those lands, instituted Sharia, and created some of the well-known Islamic Caliphates.[3] The Ottoman Empire was the last Caliphate, which was abolished after World War I.[4]

> It is almost as if we are attempting to solve a mathematical equation and the symbols we use represent different values to each of us.

Not all Muslims today live in the Middle East, but the Middle East represents much of Islam and the Islamic mentality. When Islam expanded outside the Middle East, it changed other societies to its own mind-set. The Islamic mind is focused on tribal, intergenerational issues. It is bent on pursuing goals that may take many lifetimes to fulfill. It does not care if it destroys its own self-interests—economic, emotional, and social—in the process of seeking retribution or defending its religion and honor. It sees no separation of church, state, and individual. All are under the auspices of Sharia—the law of Allah and Muhammad.

So how does the Muslim mind fundamentally differ from the Western mind? The answer is multifaceted. First, as mentioned, the West and the Islamic world espouse opposing worldviews. The Muslim mind is primarily influenced by Islam, and the Western mind by liberty, freedom, and diversity stemming from Judeo-Christian principles such as the *imago Dei*, which gives inherent value to all human life. Second, the Islamic world and the West operate from two different cultural foundations: the shame culture versus the guilt culture. Third and finally, the Islamic world is intergenerational and community-oriented, whereas the West is much more concerned with individual liberty. Unless we understand these fundamental differences and acknowledge that they represent opposing, contrary views, we will not be able to resolve the conflicts we face today.

Do Muslims and Christians Worship the Same God?

First, we must examine the basic difference of religious worldviews between the Islamic world and the historically Judeo-Christian West. Islam claims it is the religion all prophets before Muhammad preached. According to Muslims, Abraham, Ishmael, Isaac, Jacob, Moses, and even Jesus all preached about the same God that Muhammad proclaimed.[5] The Islamic scriptures state that God sent His message at different times and through different prophets to warn His creation.[6] Muhammad, who was, according to Islam, the last of all prophets, proclaimed the same message of submission to the same God, Allah.[7] As such, Muslims around the world believe that Jews, Christians, and Muslims worship the same God.

The Muslim belief that Islam's Allah and the Judeo-Christian God are one and the same stems first and foremost from the Quran itself, which commands Muslims to "dispute . . . not with the People of the Book [Jews and Christians]. . . . But say, 'We believe in the Revelation which has come down to us and in that which came down to you; *Our God and your God is One*; and it is to Him we bow (in Islam).' "[8] True to this command, Muslims and even some non-Muslims repeat the idea that God and Allah are one.[9]

But Nabeel Qureshi, a Christian convert from and scholar on Islam, maintains that acceptance of this idea dangerously "subverts Christian orthodoxy in favor of Islamic assertions."[10] Qureshi affirms that beyond the most basic contention that there is one Creator God to whom believers owe their worship, the God of the Muslims and the God of the Bible bear no resemblance even in the most fundamental sense, which becomes clear after even a cursory examination of Muslim and Christian doctrines.[11] How the Muslims' view of Allah and his teachings differs from the God of the Bible may be the most important factor in understanding the Islamic world.

Foundational to Christian theology is the concept of the Trinity and, consequently, the triune nature of the Godhead.[12] The very nature of the God of the Bible is tied to this concept. Muslims, however, consider the concept of the Trinity to be heretical nonsense.[13] As Qureshi explains, the Quran explicitly rejects the doctrine of the Trinity.[14] Verse 73 of *Surah Al-Ma'idah*[15] says, "They do blaspheme who say: Allah is one of three in a Trinity:

> The God of the Muslims and the God of the Bible bear no resemblance even in the most fundamental sense.

for there is no god except One God."[16] Further, while the Christian scriptures teach the divinity of Jesus, the second person of the Godhead,[17] the Quran flatly denies it and condemns to hell all those who worship Jesus as God: "They do blaspheme who say: 'Allah is Christ the son of Mary.' . . . Whoever joins other gods with Allah—Allah will forbid him the Garden, and the Fire will be his abode."[18]

Christianity teaches that God is our heavenly Father,[19] that Jesus is His "only begotten Son,"[20] and that Jesus and the Father are one.[21] Again, the Quran flatly denies each of these ideas, command-ing Muslims to "[s]ay: 'He is Allah, the One and Only; Allah, the Eternal, the Absolute; *He begetteth not, nor is he begotten;* and there is none like unto Him.'"[22] This is the Islamic doctrine of *tawheed* (the oneness of Allah), which teaches that it is blasphemous and heretical to connect anyone with Allah.[23] Thus, the most basic characteristics of the Christian God and Allah are set in irresolvable conflict, such that they cannot possibly be considered the same being—or even similar.[24] Qureshi concludes that Allah of Islam and the God of the Bible are "fundamentally incompatible. According to Islam, wor-shipping the Christian God is not just wrong; it sends you to hell."[25]

Why is it necessary to talk about the differences between the Christian God and Allah, and why does it matter that they are not one and the same? It is because the Islamic view of God, to a large degree, drives the Islamic world's thoughts and behavior. At the most fundamental level, a culture is influenced and shaped by the way it views God, and so the vast differences between the Christian God and Allah cannot be ignored if we are to truly understand the Muslim world.

Opposing Personalities

The personalities and nature of the Christian God and of Allah are also opposed to each other. The God of the Bible is a God of uncon-ditional love and mercy[26] who created man in His image,[27] sent His Son to become a man and to die as a substitutionary sacrifice for all mankind,[28] and who desires to have a personal relationship with every individual through the person of His Son, Jesus.[29] These at-tributes of God create a profound connection between the Creator and His creation.

On the other hand, Allah is distant, impersonal, and discon-nected from mankind. He is not a god of love and justice but is rather warlike and vindictive. This is demonstrated by *Surah Al-Ma'idah*, verse 18, of the Quran: "[Both] the Jews and the Christians say: 'We are sons of Allah, and His beloved.' Say: 'Why then doth He punish you for your sins?' Nay, ye are but men—Of the men He created: He forgiveth whom He pleaseth, and He punisheth whom He pleaseth."[30] In other words, his love is random and conditional.

Qureshi emphasizes that unconditional love and mercy come from the Christian God's triune nature.[31] God created the universe because of His love.[32] Qureshi highlights the fact that the Bible teaches that God is our heavenly Father while the Quran denies this.[33] According to Qureshi, the entire message of the gospel is predicated on the person of God and who He is.[34]

The fact that Muslims do not believe man is created in the image of Allah,[35] combined with the doctrine of *tawheed*, prevents any connection between Allah and man. Allah's lack of unconditional love and mercy is expressed in the Muslim mind-set as well, especially in the way Islam views and treats non-Muslims.

The impersonal and distant nature of Allah engenders a ritualistic and formalistic religion in which the individual can have no hope of personal salvation through faith alone.[36] Instead, a Muslim must earn salvation through his works.[37] Even a devout Muslim who diligently performs good works throughout his life has no true assurance that he will enter paradise in the afterlife. Continually working toward the goal of being "good enough" is thus extremely important in Islam.[38] Unfortunately, according to the Quran, jihad is among the good works that earn Allah's favor.[39] In fact, martyrdom for Allah, dying in the way of Islam, is the *only* way to ensure acceptance into heaven.[40] This explains why suicide bombing is attractive to so many radical Muslims.

How Differing Cultural Foundations Lead to Jihad

The second vital factor we must examine in order to truly understand the Islamic world is how Islamic culture is vastly different from Western culture. Inherited from its Middle Eastern tribal roots, Islamic culture is a "shame culture."[41] Psychiatrist Patricia A. Santy explains that shame cultures are essentially collectivist by nature, and individual behavior in such a culture is shaped by the external opinion of others rather than internal values.[42] Under such a mind-set, whether a person is *actually* guilty of wrongdoing is less important than whether a person *appears* to be guilty of wrongdoing. The individual is focused on honor and shame generated by his reputation in the community rather than on personal feelings of guilt generated by violating internalized values.[43]

In a shame culture, if an individual knows he is guilty of wrongdoing but that fact is hidden from his community, his behavior is not affected because the external motivator of shame is not present.[44] This stands in contrast to the more individualistic mind-set of the West, which has been termed a "guilt culture," placing much greater emphasis on objective values such as truth, justice, and individual rights.[45] In a guilt culture, one who knows he is guilty is expected to feel guilty and behave accordingly, even if he is the only one who knows it, because guilt is an internal motivator.[46] Thus a shame culture, by its nature, perpetuates certain behaviors that a guilt culture generally does not. In a shame culture, individuals are free to engage in wrongdoing as long as no one knows they have done so. They are encouraged to take any course of action necessary to avoid public shame, even if it requires secret wrongdoing, because the extrinsic value of honor is more important than intrinsic values of truth, justice, and whether one is actually guilty.[47]

Furthermore, in the case of Islamic Middle Eastern honor and shame culture, acts that Westerners view as reprehensible, such as terrorism, are portrayed as being right, or even praiseworthy.[48] In fact, with regard to fighting nonbelievers, the Quran even instructs Muslims to ignore the promptings of their own consciences, because verse 216 of *Surah Al-Baqarah* (chapter 2) says, "It is possible that ye dislike a thing which is good for you, and that ye love a thing which is bad for you. But Allah knoweth, and ye know not."[49] Thus a radical Muslim can, in the name of Islam, commit atrocities such as mass murder, honor killings, or raping women and young children and feel no shame, because his religion and culture often condone and even encourage those atrocities.[50] He receives no shame but rather great honor for committing them. The huge emphasis placed on cultural honor instead of objective values of right and wrong, therefore, allows the radical Muslim freedom to do virtually anything as long as his community approves of it, which makes Islam's jihadist ideology all the more dangerous.[51]

A High-Profile Case

At the American Center for Law and Justice (ACLJ), we have worked with our international affiliate in Pakistan to combat the egregious international crimes that spring from this and other bigoted and intolerant cultures. One of our more high-profile cases revolves around Parwasha, an eight-year-old Christian girl in Pakistan whom Muslim men attacked in the public streets. Why? Because of the honor and shame culture. Here's what happened.

Parwasha's maternal uncle, Iftikhar Masih, was visiting his Muslim girlfriend, Samina, late one night at her home. Interreligious romantic relationships are not accepted in Pakistan, largely due to the Muslim faith and the surrounding culture impacted by being predominantly Muslim. Therefore the girlfriend's Muslim family was furious. Parwasha's uncle admitted to the relationship and explained that he was invited over. But this did nothing to assuage the dishonor felt by Samina's family, who called the village elders' council. The family lied, telling the council that Iftikhar had robbed their house the night before and stolen a lot of money. Iftikhar told the council the true story. But the Muslim family decided that their honor had been besmirched. In their minds, the only way to correct this would be by humiliating a woman in the Christian family.

So when young Parwasha was walking home from school the next day, they kidnapped her, stripped her naked, beat her, and left her in the streets. When Parwasha's family sought help from the village elders (who were Muslim), they didn't respond. When Parwasha's grandfather went to the police station to file charges, he discovered that the Muslim family had already filed trumped-up charges against his family, charging them with assaulting and shaming Samina. The local police arrested members of Parwasha's family and detained them until the village elders' council could work everything out between the Muslim and Christian families. The council determined that the Christian family would have to sell its property and leave the area within thirty days. This is a common punishment doled out to non-Muslim families who are targeted by Muslims angry at them for any given reason.[52]

Our legal team in Pakistan investigated. We helped the family submit a petition to file criminal charges before the court. Our work helped lead to a settlement so that this Christian family was not targeted with false charges simply because they were Christian. They got to keep their home. This was not perfect justice because Parwasha's attackers will not face punishment for their actions, but our work brought about as much justice as can be expected in a society where the playing field between Muslims and non-Muslims is far from even.[53]

Sadly, this illustrates what America is up against. When a person raised in a shame culture believes he has been insulted, the restoration of his honor becomes his primary goal; and if he's radical, he will pursue any means necessary to accomplish that.[54] Often even a mild insult must be avenged by the death of the alleged insulter.[55] On a societal scale, this can lead to radical and violent fanaticism.[56] No matter how heinous the act, it is justified if purposed to restore honor and dispel shame.[57]

We have faced enemies before whose societies were built upon shame. One non-Muslim example of a shame culture that opposed America militarily was Japan during World War II.[58] The honor-and-shame culture drove Japanese soldiers to use kamikaze suicide tactics and a custom of committing suicide rather than surrendering.[59]

The Added Shame of Non-Muslim Occupiers

One of the greatest perceived insults to Muslims around the world is the presence of non-Muslim powers in Muslim lands.[60] They refer to the non-Muslim powers as "occupiers" and view them as the ultimate shame that allegedly inspires many radical Islamists in their fanaticism. Perhaps the most infamous Muslim jihadist himself, Osama bin Laden, claimed the primary purpose of his fight was to force America to leave his homeland of Saudi Arabia and for the Jews to leave Palestine.[61] The Western mind-set simply does not understand the intensity of this strong commitment and solidarity toward what Muslims see as the defilement of Muslim lands.

For example, if an enemy were to invade Great Britain, America would come to Great Britain's defense, but we would do so based on political reasons and purposes: we are NATO allies, and we have strong economic, political, and cultural ties to Great Britain. In contrast, when so-called infidels "invade" and "defile" the lands of Islam, Muslims around the world view it as a personal affront and shame upon the name of Islam, for the land that has been conquered for Islam is held in *waqf* (Islamic trust) for Muslims; and the only sovereign authority that can legitimately rule over that land is Allah's law, Sharia.[62] Article 11 of the Hamas Covenant states:

> Palestine is an Islamic Waqf land consecrated for Moslem generations until Judgment Day. . . . The same goes for any land the Moslems have conquered by force, because

during the times of (Islamic) conquests, the Moslems con-
secrated these lands to Moslem generations till the Day of
Judgment. . . . Any procedure in contradiction to Islamic
Sharia . . . is null and void.[63]

All Muslims are considered brothers; thus the fight is intensely
personal. This is why Muslims of all nations are enraged over Palestine. They see Israel as an invader. The Quran refers to Muhammad's journey to "the Farthest Mosque," which Muslims believe is
referring to the Al-Aqsa Mosque in Jerusalem, and states that Allah
blessed its "precincts"; Muslims have interpreted this to mean that
Allah set apart Palestine as holy.[64] As long as Israel and other Western powers remain in Palestine and the Middle East, they cause a
continual shame on the entire Muslim world.[65]

Avoiding Shame

One way to avoid shame is by asserting superiority over those viewed
as weaker.[66] This is demonstrated within the Muslim culture in its
treatment of women,[67] but it is also externally displayed through
Islamic supremacy—the belief that Muslims are superior to non-
Muslims.[68] Islam teaches that the blood of infidels is not equal to
the blood of Muslims[69] and commands them to treat non-Muslims
harshly and fellow Muslims mercifully.[70] This basic ideology of superiority is at the core of the historic and modern Islamic quest to
conquer, subjugate, and establish dominance over the non-Muslim
world.[71]

Furthermore, Western guilt cultures are natural targets of subjugation because they are viewed as weak.[72] Unlike shame culture,
guilt culture encourages individuals to harbor internal feelings of
guilt for their own wrongdoing and to seek restoration by apologiz-
ing for error.[73] From the viewpoint of a shame culture, however,
admitting error is a sign of weakness because it brings shame upon

oneself.[74] This is vitally important to recognize, especially when one considers the apologies President Obama made to the Muslim world for past policies and the effect such statements have on the radical Middle Eastern mind.[75]

At the 2015 National Prayer Breakfast, President Obama attempted to make absurd moral equivalencies when he said, "And lest we get on our high horse and think this is unique to some other place, remember that during the Crusades and the Inquisition, people committed terrible deeds in the name of Christ. In our home country, slavery and Jim Crow all too often [were] justified in the name of Christ." [76]

Such apologies validate the reasons why many Muslims join terrorist organizations fighting against the United States. Muslim leaders, such as the ayatollahs of Iran and leaders of terrorist organizations, teach young Muslims that Western powers are oppressing Muslims. They teach that the U.S. invasions of Afghanistan and Iraq were motivated by religion, and that they were wars against Islam to usurp Muslim resources and take Muslim lands.

American apologies just add fuel to the fire and confirm the false claims made by Islamic leaders. President Obama's apology in Cairo, Egypt, within months of taking office is the perfect example: "The fear and anger that [9/11] provoked was understandable, but in some cases, it led us to act contrary to our traditions and our ideals. We are taking concrete actions to change course. I have unequivocally prohibited the use of torture by the United States, and I have ordered the prison at Guantanamo Bay closed by early next year." [77]

If we closed Gitmo the way President Obama has wanted to do for years, it would reinforce the jihadist mentality that Americans are weak. Just look at the absurdity of the Obama administration's rationale in closing Gitmo. White House Press Secretary Josh Earnest said that detaining these terrorists in the heartland of America "would be cleanly in line with American values" and "consistent with the way American citizens are treated."[78] The Obama administration hates American values. How else can you explain their wanting to treat enemy combatant terrorists the same as they treat American citizens?

A second psychological tactic to avoid shame is to project blame on others rather than take responsibility for one's own behavior and actions.[79] This explains why many Muslim leaders refuse to acknowledge responsibility for atrocities committed in the name of Islam, such as the 9/11 attacks, but lay the blame on others instead— for example, on Israel, perceived Western occupation, or terrorists allegedly acting contrary to the ways of Islam.[80]

Fighting Across Multiple Generations

The third factor we must examine in order to understand the Islamic world is its long-range, intergenerational focus. Osama bin Laden notoriously believed and often stated that America did not "have the stomach" for a long, drawn-out battle with al-Qaeda.[81] To some extent, that belief was accurate: the Western mind does not want conflict. It wants to be prosperous, to enjoy life, liberty, and the pursuit of happiness. Our goal is to return as quickly as possible to normal. We won't sacrifice personal comfort for a long-term battle that requires sacrifice.

Former attorney general John Ashcroft described the Western mind as "episodic. . . . We expect things to be completed, wrapped up, put the bow on it and say that's done, it's over."[82] We also value freedom, tolerance, and offending as few people as possible.

In contrast, as mentioned, the Islamic world is focused on issues that extend beyond the lives of individuals.[83] This intergenerational focus of Muslim culture, as opposed to the episodic focus of Western culture, makes sense when one considers the differences between shame and guilt societies. Because it is concerned primarily with the extrinsic opinions of others rather than intrinsic values, a shame culture is inherently collectivist: the community as a whole is more important than the individual. In Islam, this is demonstrated by the concept of *ummah*, the strong social bond that obligates every Muslim to contribute to the Islamic community.[84]

The word *ummah* literally means "nation" or "people group."[85] The Islamic concept of *ummah* has distinct religious connotations because citizenship in the Islamic *ummah* requires commitment to Islam over the purely political Western concept of a nation-state. Thus for Muslims the *ummah* represents a dedication to and common identity found in the Islamic faith and encompasses all Muslims throughout the entire world, regardless of what nation they live in or where they come from.

The latest research into how ISIS recruits, indoctrinates, and uses children perfectly exemplifies this multigenerational mindset. Learning from precedents set by Saddam Hussein's Lion Cubs and the Hitler Youth, ISIS is abducting children while also working to turn female members and even some sex slaves into wives and mothers of future soldiers.[86] "Mothers are given books by ISIS instructing them on how to raise their offspring for 'jihad.' This includes telling bedtime stories about martyrdom, exposing children to graphic content through jihadist websites, and encouraging them to improve their child's military skills and fitness."[87] They tell tales of Muhammad's cousin, grandsons, and other fabled Islamic warriors who fought as children.[88] This reveals not only radical Islam's long-term strategy, but also an understanding of the free world's weakness. After all, as Maajid Nawaz, a counter-extremist leader, points out, "What world leader could possibly authorize an airstrike on a training camp full of children?"[89]

Similar to Muslims, Christians find common identity in their faith and believe in citizenship in the heavenly kingdom of God that transcends earthly citizenship. But there are vital differences between the universal Islamic *ummah* and the Christian kingdom of God. The first is the fact that the Christian kingdom is, in this present age, entirely spiritual. Christ did not come to set up an earthly kingdom, but a heavenly one.[90] In contrast, the Islamic *ummah* is a physical community of believers who follow a religion that is an amalgamation of religion, state, and ancient Middle Eastern culture.[91] There is no separation between temporal and spiritual dominions.[92]

Christians look forward to a day when Christ will return to rule and set up His heavenly kingdom.[93] Muslims, on the other hand, believe that Allah can rule through a human political system based on Islamic law and governed by religious leaders.[94] Thus, while Christians seek to live peacefully in this world until Christ comes,[95] remaining subject to the governing authorities of this world until that time,[96] Muslims have no reason to wait. Many Muslims therefore reject the separation of Islamic nation-states and desire to bring about a perfect unified Islamic society now, wherein all Muslims around the world will be united under a single Islamic religious and political order—the Caliphate.[97]

This is the goal not only of ISIS, Iranian leaders, and Islamic terrorist organizations, but of many Muslims who believe in living under one Islamic authority, Sharia. So the intergenerational focus naturally extends to the radical Islamist. Former attorney general Ashcroft best described this:

> The terrorist culture is largely an intergenerational culture rather than an episodic culture. And you see this in the instruction of the very innocent small children of the terrorist community being told how to hate, how to use weapons of destruction, how to disrupt rational, freedom-loving cultures around the world. And the mentality isn't that we'll get this done [but] the mentality is if we don't do this, our children [will] do it. If they don't do it, the grandchildren will, [or] the great-grandchildren . . . it's intergenerational.[98]

In summary, because the collective religious and social identity of Islam is more important than individual identity, Muslims focus on the big picture that extends through many generations and the Islamic community as a collective whole.[99] In contrast, Western culture is concerned with intrinsic values and is much more individualistic.[100] It is primarily focused on personal freedom and achieving happiness for one's own life, rather than the collective advancement of the societal and religious goals over many generations.[101] This fundamental difference in thinking creates a distortion when Americans project Western motivations, values, and beliefs onto Islamic behavior. Unless we recognize the fundamental differences between these irreconcilable worldviews, we will proceed at our own risk and with very little chance of ultimate success.

The actual motivations, values, and beliefs that radical Islamic terrorists take out of Islam cause death and destruction for communities and civilizations around the world. When Sharia is put into action, we all face peril.

4

Sharia Law and the Muslim World

The debates and battles (both philosophical and physical) within the Muslim world are matters of life and death, not only for the Muslim communities themselves vying for power and influence, but also for the Americans facing terrorism as a result of these battles. Is Islam a faith that is inclusive and tolerant, or does it require fundamentalist purity? And when radical Muslims carry out violent terrorist attacks in the name of Islam, the question arises: does Islam really teach violence, or is it actually a religion of peace? At the center of these debates is Sharia law.

Islam means "submission."[1] The faith teaches that Muslims must submit to the will of Allah[2] and prepare themselves for the final judgment in order to be able to enter paradise.[3] Muslims believe that Allah revealed his will through *Sharia*, which literally means "path" but is generally translated as "Islamic law."[4] Unlike the traditional Western legal system, which is limited to basic civil and criminal elements, Sharia covers everything from religious rituals and private hygiene to principles of conducting business, criminal punishments, and more. Sharia prescribes, for example, how many times a

Muslim must pray, how husbands should treat their wives, and what punishments are to be given for different crimes. It mandates flogging for consuming alcohol,[5] stoning adulterers to death,[6] cutting off a thief's limbs,[7] and executing apostates and blasphemers.[8]

Many Muslims around the world do not adhere to the jihadist ideology of terrorists. Most Muslims are moderate, peaceful people who, while following their religious traditions and rituals—attending mosques for worship, fasting, witnessing to others—reasonably coexist with followers of other religions. They do not impose their beliefs on others. They have non-Muslim friends, neighbors, and coworkers with whom they socialize on a daily basis. To these Muslims, Islam is a religion of peace.

A small but increasingly significant segment of Muslims (some estimate its size as between 10 and 20 percent),[9] however, believe in the supremacy of Islam and Sharia law over any other religion or law and feel obligated to force such beliefs on everybody. This group engages in social, political, legal, as well as violent means to impose Sharia and its way of life on others. A Pew Research Center survey of Muslims in thirty-nine countries revealed that the majority of Muslims in those countries[10] wanted to impose Sharia law as the official law of the land.[11] Strong Muslim minorities in the countries surveyed (except Egypt, where the number was a majority) wanted Sharia to apply to all citizens, not just Muslims.[12] Using as its definition for "politically radical Muslims" those who believed the terrorist attacks of September 11, 2001, were "completely justified" and who had an "unfavorable" or "very unfavorable" opinion of the United States, a Gallup study deemed the percentage of "politically radical" Muslims to be 7 percent.[13]

Both moderate and radical Muslims claim that their respective interpretation of Islam is correct. In fact, both claim that their respective version of Islam is the true Islam as the Prophet Muhammad proclaimed. To make sense of how different groups interpret and apply their beliefs, we need to understand the basics of Sharia.

Sharia Law

Sharia is a comprehensive system of laws that governs all facets of a Muslim's life, including the religious, social, and political aspects.[14] Because there is no separation between religion and state affairs in Islam, Allah ordains the system of government as well as social and personal life to "promote his faith and to maintain and extend his law."[15]

Sharia law does not come from a single source. Several sources make up the overall body of Sharia. The two primary sources are the Quran and hadiths. The word *Quran* literally means "to read" or "to recite."[16] According to Islamic tradition, Allah revealed the Quran to Muhammad through the angel Gabriel. All Muslims are expected to read and study the Quran, as it is considered the "most important source of Islamic law, being the ultimate word of the Divine."[17] Thus the Quran is the supreme authority of Islamic law and cannot be overruled by another source.

Hadiths, second only to the Quran, are compilations of Muhammad's sayings and actions (*sunna*) as recollected by and transmitted through his companions.[18] The literal translation of the word *sunna* is "well-known path."[19] Sunna are Muhammad's examples, utterances, and practices,[20] collectively his way of life. Unsurprisingly, Muslim men and women seek to model their actions and lifestyle after that of Muhammad by looking at the sunna in the hadiths.

Hadiths are of varying authority, depending on their reliability,[21] which is determined by the chain of transmission.[22] Sunni Muslims regard two compilations of hadiths, Bukhari and Muslim, as authoritative.[23] To Shiites, however, hadiths that Sunnis transmitted are not authoritative.[24] Shiites also believe that, in addition to Muhammad's hadiths, opinions of the imams are also sources of law.[25]

There are four different Sunni schools of Islamic jurisprudence (*fiqh*) that further contribute to Sharia, including Hanafi, Maliki,

Shafi'i, and Hanbali.[26] A fifth Shiite school of thought is the Jafari,[27] practiced primarily in Iran. While these schools of thought are identical in the majority of their legal conclusions, they differ in certain aspects of law.[28]

Although the Quran and the hadiths contain an extensive body of law, they do not address every legal issue that may arise in the Muslim world. In situations not addressed by the Quran or the hadiths, Muslims rely on secondary sources of Islamic law, *ijma* (consensus), *qiyas* (analytical reasoning), and *ijtihad* (individual reasoning). Because of the varied sources of Sharia and the religious differences between Sunni and Shiite Muslims, Islamic law varies across countries.

The few Sharia principles discussed in this chapter are by no means a comprehensive study of Sharia law. They only scratch the surface. These principles are the ones that are of greatest concern to a Western reader, primarily due to their incompatibility with Western norms and legal traditions. Before looking at the specifics of Sharia law, we will examine how Sharia law operates in a non-Islamic land. With the growing Muslim population in the West, some Sharia issues have come before Western courts. The prime example is Great Britain.

How Sharia Law Has Crept into Europe

Two types of Sharia institutions have been functioning in the United Kingdom.[29] The first type, called Sharia Councils, began in 1982.[30] These are religious bodies legally classified as mediators.[31] British law allows parties to voluntarily mediate their private, civil disputes.[32] The purpose of mediation is usually reconciliation or reaching an outcome that is mutually agreed upon.

The second type of Sharia institution in the United Kingdom is the Muslim Arbitration Tribunal (MAT). MATs were established to arbitrate personal, civil disputes under the United Kingdom's

Arbitration Act of 1996.[33] Arbitration decisions are binding on the parties, and courts are not expected to review the rulings unless such decisions are manifestly contrary to law or public policy.

English law does not require arbitration or mediation by the MATs or the Sharia Councils, respectively. A person is free to ignore them and go about his or her business or submit disagreements via traditional English legal institutions. But if a person seeks an Islamic *religious* divorce, then he or she must appear before a MAT or Sharia Council. Religious divorces granted by MATs or Sharia Councils are not recognized as valid by the British courts. Hence Muslims, like all others seeking divorces, must obtain a civil divorce from British courts in order to be officially divorced under English law.[34]

Technically both MATs and Sharia Councils are Alternative Dispute Resolution (ADR) systems, before which the parties *voluntarily* appear to resolve their disputes. But there are increasing numbers of reports that Muslim men and women are pressured by their families and the Muslim community to resolve family disputes, such as divorce, inheritance, child custody, and spousal abuse, before a Sharia Council or a MAT. Because many Muslim women have immigrated to the United Kingdom from Islamic countries where they may not have received formal education, they are usually not aware of their legal rights—that they are not legally bound to appear before a MAT or a Sharia Council. Community pressure is not limited to women. According to a United Kingdom–based group that studies Sharia Councils and MATs, one father who went to English courts for a custody decision had a Sharia Council issue a Worldwide Expulsion and Boycott Order against him to shun him from the community.[35]

Neither MATs nor Sharia Councils are legally empowered to deal with criminal cases such as domestic violence.[36] Yet in practice, some MATs and Sharia Councils deal with these issues in total disregard of British law. For instance, Sharia Councils advise battered women to reconcile with their abusive husbands instead of going to the police and pressing criminal charges. The council tells the women that speaking to police should be the last resort.[37] As a result, some women drop pending criminal complaints against their abusive husbands in British courts.[38]

A female BBC undercover reporter went to a Sharia Council with a story of abuse. She was advised not to tell the police because she would end up in a shelter, but instead she should ask her husband whether it was her fault—was it because of her cooking or because she saw her friends?—so she could correct herself.[39]

Another woman, not a reporter, who already had obtained custody of her children with restrictions on her ex-husband's visitation and a civil divorce from the English courts, went to a Sharia Council for an Islamic divorce and was told that in order to get one, she would have to give custody of her children to her husband.[40] She said: "I could not bear the thought of such a violent person having my children. . . . What was even more shocking was when I explained this to them . . . why he should not have that access to the children; their reaction was, well, you cannot go against what Islam says."[41] Only after she threatened to go to the police did the council relent and give her a religious divorce without conditions on her children's custody.[42]

Examples like these reveal that this issue extends beyond debates about religious viewpoints and legal systems; this is fundamentally an issue of human rights and protecting women and children from abusive, predatory men.

Disregard of British law is not limited to Sharia Councils in divorce and custody issues. In an ITV documentary, an undercover reporter called fifty-six mosques and asked if they would perform a marriage involving a fourteen-year-old girl. Eighteen of them said they would,[43] even though United Kingdom law does not permit marriage until age sixteen.[44]

Evidence suggests that Sharia Councils also cover up illegal marriages.[45] A girl who was married at the age of thirteen was informed by three different imams that she was lawfully married under Sharia. The imams advised her to seek counseling.[46]

Noting the abuse of law by Sharia Councils and family pressure on Muslim men and women to choose religious arbitration or mediation over the United Kingdom's civil law, Jack Straw, Lord Chancellor and Secretary of State for Justice,[47] stated, "Arbitration is not a system of dispute resolution that may be used in family cases."[48]

The British have begun to respond by proposing changes to the Arbitration and Family Law Acts of 1996 and others as well as establishing a parliamentary inquiry[49] to help determine the solution to this obvious problem.

In the United States, matters have not yet progressed this far, but we must remain vigilant. Some Muslims, such as Imam Rauf, who tried to erect the Ground Zero Mosque, argue that Sharia law is compatible with the U.S. Constitution.[50] Make no mistake, he is not saying the Constitution and Sharia are similar; rather he wants to amend the Constitution, to fundamentally alter our government from one that allows freedom to flourish to one that squelches liberty in the name of Sharia. We cannot allow this.

Andrew McCarthy, former assistant U.S. attorney for the Southern District of New York, says,

> What I think the imam means about this is that there are mechanisms within the Constitution [such as amendments] that can be exploited to completely change the Constitutional system. . . . If laws get enacted, or if litigation is brought in courts, the Sharia agenda can be advanced. So he sees in our Constitution the sort of loopholes and mechanisms that he can use to advance Sharia, in that sense it's Sharia-compliant.[51]

The practice of advancing jihad by implementing Sharia is perhaps one of the most strategically coordinated and far-reaching politico-religious agendas in the world today, and Americans must recognize it in order to protect America from such laws. This chapter examines some fundamental principles of Sharia and then considers how American legal principles differ in significant ways.

Freedom of Religion and Speech

The rights to freedoms of religion and speech that are fundamental to the American and other Western legal traditions are not protected by Sharia. Instead, under Sharia, a Muslim is not allowed to leave Islam or convert to any other religion.[52] *Riddah* (apostasy) includes acting irreverently toward Allah, denying his existence, leaving Islam, or denying any part of the Quran.[53] Some schools of Islamic thought allow repentance while others believe that an apostate (*murtad*) should not be given the opportunity to repent and return to Islam; instead, an apostate should be killed immediately, especially if the offender apostasies by blaspheming against Muhammad.[54] "The punishment of those who wage war against Allah and his messenger, and strive with might and main for mischief through the land is: execution, or crucifixion, or cutting off of hands and feet from opposite sides, or exile from the land."[55] Fourteenth-century Muslim scholar Al-Misri of the Shafi'i school of thought states:

> Among the things that entail apostasy from Islam . . . are: to speak words that imply unbelief such as "Allah is the third of three," or "I am Allah"; to revile Allah or His messenger; to be sarcastic about Allah's name; to deny any verse of the Koran or anything which by scholarly consensus belongs to it, or to add a verse that does not belong to it; to mockingly

say, "I don't know what faith is"; to describe a Muslim or someone who wants to become a Muslim in terms of *unbelief*; to revile the religion of Islam; to be sarcastic about any ruling of the Sacred Law; or to deny that Allah intended the Prophet's message . . . to be the religion followed by the entire world.[56]

According to a hadith, Muhammad said, "Allah has accepted my invocation to forgive what whispers in the hearts of my followers, unless they put it to action or utter it."[57]

Many countries that follow Sharia punish apostasy with the death penalty. For example, in Saudi Arabia, courts are permitted to give apostates the death penalty.[58] Iran also allows apostasy to be punished by death. In fact, the Islamic Penal Code of Iran, which deals with criminal offenses, states, "Anyone who insults the sacred values of Islam or any of the Great Prophets . . . shall be executed; otherwise, they shall be sentenced to one to five years' imprisonment."[59] While it is not surprising that many countries that follow Sharia punish apostasy with the death penalty, surprisingly, a survey found that "a significant portion of British Muslims think that [killing apostates] is not merely right, but a religious obligation."[60]

Some Islamic nations—including Saudi Arabia, Afghanistan, Pakistan, and Iran—have strict blasphemy laws that prescribe the death penalty upon conviction.[61] Other countries, such as Egypt, Jordan, and Kuwait, call for imprisoning such offenders.[62] Of the countries mentioned, Pakistan has the strictest blasphemy laws. And although Pakistan is not governed entirely by Sharia principles, it is increasingly intolerant of blasphemy, including mere "defamation" of Islam. For example, Pakistan's Penal Code institutes strict criminal liability for blasphemy of Islamic religious figures,[63] desecration of the Quran,[64] and anything that may be interpreted as blasphemous against Muhammad.[65] Additionally, Pakistan's Federal Shariat Court, which is empowered to "examine and decide the question whether or not any law or provision of law is repugnant to the injunctions of Islam, as laid down in the Holy Quran and Sunnah of the Holy Prophet," as well as to "enhance the sentence" of any criminal punishment,[66] has made blasphemy of Muhammad an offense mandating the death penalty.[67]

Similarly, the Iranian Penal Code mandates execution for anyone whose "insults [to] the Islamic sanctities" rise to the level of "speaking disparagingly of Prophet Muhammad."[68] The Iranian Press Code—which governs media in Iran—also requires that a person whose "insults [to] Islam and its sanctities through the press" amount to apostasy must be "sentenced as an apostate."[69]

On the international level, the Organisation of Islamic Cooperation (OIC), a group of fifty-six Muslim countries, has repeatedly refused to guarantee freedom of speech, particularly religious speech, to their citizens, with their very charter declaring the purpose of "combat[ing] defamation of Islam" to be among the OIC's primary objectives.[70] OIC member states have effectively disregarded religious free speech rights altogether because the OIC charter limits speech to that which is "in conformity with Islamic values,"[71] meaning that criticism of Islam is not protected speech. This limitation on the freedom of speech is also evidenced by some OIC member states' reservations to the International Covenant on Civil and Political Rights' (ICCPR) free speech provisions.[72] Disturbingly, many OIC countries also make reservations to provisions related to women's rights and freedom of religion, qualifying their support with adherence to Sharia law.[73] In addition, OIC member states adopted their own version of international human rights standards through the Cairo Declaration.[74] This declaration limited free speech rights only to speech that is not contrary to Sharia principles.[75]

In addition to domestically focused efforts to limit freedom of speech and expression, Muslim countries have moved their focus outward, repeatedly presenting resolutions to the United Nations

Human Rights Council condemning "defamation of religions" worldwide.[76] Because these resolutions' purpose is to employ an international mechanism to prevent all people from speaking out against Islam,[77] many Western nations, including the United States, oppose them.

Due to growing fears that foreign judgments in blasphemy cases will be brought to the United States for enforcement, the U.S. Congress passed a bill in 2010 expressly designed to disregard any foreign defamation judgment that threatens to restrict Americans' freedom of speech. The Securing the Protection of Our Enduring and Established Constitutional Heritage Act (the SPEECH Act) declares that the United States will recognize foreign defamation judgments only to the extent that "the defamation law applied in the foreign court's adjudication provided at least as much protection for freedom of speech and press in that case as would be provided by the First Amendment to the Constitution of the United States."[78] In other words, any judgment issued by a foreign court finding defamation must be compliant with the United States' broad protections for free speech under our First Amendment.

The SPEECH Act is just one step toward prohibiting the application of foreign judgments and Sharia principles in the United States. In an effort to prevent U.S. courts from indirectly enforcing Sharia in the United States, thus infringing on freedom of speech, freedom of religion, women's rights, and so much more,[79] many states have passed laws that affirm our public policies of due process and equality.

Marriage

Sharia issues that have already been presented in the U.S. judicial system involve marriage, divorce, child custody, and other family law issues. Under Sharia, marriage is a contract between a man and a woman.[80] There is some debate among Islamic scholars as to whether the contract is between the bridegroom and the bride or between the bridegroom and the bride's legal guardian (*wali*).[81] In Islam, every woman has a *wali* throughout her life, and he is generally the woman's closest male relative,[82] for example, her father, husband, brother, or uncle.

Muslims are supposed to marry people within the faith. Muslim women are prohibited from marrying outside the Islamic faith.[83] Muslim men, however, are not so limited. While men are strongly encouraged to marry Muslim women, they are not forbidden to marry Jewish or Christian women.[84] Further, they are allowed to have as many as four wives.[85]

There is no concept of marital rape in Sharia, thereby allowing a husband to force his wife to have sexual intercourse.[86] It is "obligatory for a woman to let her husband have sex with her immediately when: (a) he asks her; (b) at home . . . (c) and she can physically endure it."[87]

Additionally, *muta* is the concept of a temporary, contractual marriage in which the man pays the woman for the right to have sexual relations with her for the length of the contract.[88] The idea of *muta* originated with Muhammad, who allowed *muta* marriages for Muslim men during wartime while they were away from their homes, to avoid their engaging in unlawful sex. It is used today primarily by Shiite Muslims.[89]

The Sharia name for a marriage contract is *nikah*,[90] and the marital gift promised from the husband to the wife is called *mahr*.[91] *Mahr* usually includes a promise by the husband to pay an agreed-upon sum of money to the wife if the husband divorces her. But if the wife is at fault for the divorce, the husband is not obligated to pay the *mahr*.[92]

The issue of *mahr* arises in United States case law from time to time. For example, in *In re Marriage of Obaidi*,[93] a Washington State trial court heard evidence on Islamic law to determine the meaning of the *mahr*[94] agreement. The Court of Appeals held that the trial court erred by considering Islamic law.[95] It should have applied the "'neutral principles of law' approach that allows religiously motivated agreements to be enforced based on neutral principles of law, not religious doctrine."[96] On this basis, applying Washington State contract law, the *mahr* was held invalid because there had been no meeting of the minds and so no agreement existed between the husband and the wife about its terms.

Other courts following the "neutral principles of law" approach have enforced *mahr* agreements. In *Akileh v. Elchahal*,[97] the *mahr* agreement was enforced because it complied with Florida's requirements of consideration and meeting of the minds for a premarital agreement to be valid.[98] In *Rahman v. Hossain*,[99] a New Jersey court enforced a *mahr* agreement after determining what the custom of *mahr* meant under Islamic law. An expert testified that "the payment and retention of the [*mahr*] is contingent upon neither party having fault that leads to the termination of the marriage."[100] There, the wife-defendant had failed to appear and contest the divorce or challenge the *mahr* agreement after being given proper notice.[101] The court enforced the agreement.[102]

Because Islam gives elevated status to men, once a marriage contract is entered into, the husband has certain rights over his wife. For example, the husband can forbid his wife to leave their home and, if she does not obey him, he may physically beat her.[103] Verse 34 of *Surah al-Nisa* of the Quran states: "(Husbands) are the protectors and maintainers of their (wives). . . . Therefore the righteous women are devoutly obedient. . . . As to those women on whose part ye fear disloyalty and ill-conduct, admonish them (first), (next) refuse to share their beds, (and last) beat them (lightly)."[104]

This law also appears in a hadith. Muhammad told Muslim men: "[I]t is your right upon [your wives] that they do not allow any man whom you dislike to sit on your mattress; and if they do so, beat them, but not violently."[105] He further explained that men should beat their wives only if the wife is guilty of "immoral conduct," but the beating should be light.[106]

Some Islamic schools of jurisprudence believe that men, if they beat their wives at all, should do so "with a toothbrush, or some such thing."[107] Sunni schools of thought believe that beating is a proper punishment and offer the following procedure for beating one's wife.[108] First, the husband must see "signs of rebelliousness" in his wife.[109] He can make this determination using her words (for example, she is cold or rude) or acts (for example, she refuses to go to bed with him).[110] After seeing these signs, the man must give her a warning. If his wife continues to act the same way, she "commits rebelliousness," and the man may physically strike her.[111] Some Islamic authorities suggest that a husband should strike his wife so as not to break any bones or cause her to bleed.[112]

Cases of spousal abuse in the Muslim community have come before U.S. courts. *S.D. v. M.J.R.* is a New Jersey case in which the wife had petitioned for a protective order and was denied.[113] The wife alleged that her husband forced her to have sex on several occasions.[114] He had also beaten her.[115] The trial court denied a protective order, finding that the husband lacked the criminal intent of sexual assault because he believed he had a right to engage in sex with his wife whenever he wanted.[116] The wife appealed.[117] The New Jersey Appeals Court reversed the trial court's ruling and granted a protective order,[118] maintaining that criminal intent laws were applicable regardless of religious belief.[119] The court did not allow the husband's beliefs to be considered as a proper defense when those beliefs allowed a husband to compel his wife to have sex with him whenever he demanded and permitted a disobedient wife to be beaten.

Divorce

Unsurprisingly, Sharia divorce is significantly easier for Muslim men than it is for Muslim women. There are five ways to terminate a marriage under Sharia: repudiation, separation, oath of abstention, unchastity, or apostasy.[120] Repudiation is an option available to a husband wherein he disavows the marriage.[121] This is known as *talaq*.[122] Under *talaq*, the husband articulates to his wife his desire for a divorce three times.[123] A court then must finalize it.[124] An oath of abstention occurs where a husband abstains from having sex with his wife for a period of four months, after which time the marriage is over.[125] A marriage may also end through separation, when one of the parties petitions a court for divorce on grounds of lunacy, chronic disease, or impotence.[126] The final two grounds for divorce are unchastity (adultery) and apostasy. Under Sharia, marriages are automatically void if one of the spouses denounces Islam.[127] A wife's grounds for divorce are limited only to separation, unchastity, and apostasy.[128]

The concept of *talaq* has appeared in U.S. courts in conflicts of law and comity issues. U.S. legal rules on conflicts of law decide what law a judge should use in a given case when there are multiple laws that could apply in that situation. *Comity* refers to when a U.S. court enforces another court's judgment from a different state or country.[129]

In *Chaudry v. Chaudry*,[130] a *talaq* (divorce) decree was enforced.[131] The *Chaudry* court found that, because the wife and children residing in Pakistan had appeared before the Pakistani courts, which entered a divorce decree, comity required recognition of the divorce.[132] Other courts have also recognized a *talaq* divorce.[133] But several other courts[134] have found *talaq* divorce unenforceable on due-process grounds. In *Aleem v. Aleem*, the court noted that "[t]alaq lacks any significant 'due process' for the wife, and its use moreover, directly deprives the wife of the 'due process' she is entitled to when she initiates divorce litigation in this State. The lack and deprivation of due process is itself contrary to this State's public policy." [135] The *Aleem* court refused to recognize and enforce the *talaq* divorce.

Child Custody

Under Sharia, as a general matter, fathers have a duty of "maintenance" for their children. [136] What does "maintenance" for children include? It encompasses food, shelter, education, and love for the child. [137] The mother has a duty to care for the child. Specifically, in regard to child custody, it's presumed that a boy should be with his mother until he is between seven and nine years old, depending on the Islamic school of jurisprudence being applied, [138] and a girl until she is of age. [139] A girl is considered of age when she has her first menstrual period. [140] Although this presumption exists, there are several grounds by which the mother could lose her right to the child. [141] These grounds include apostasy, the mother's marriage to a man who is one of the child's close relatives, child abuse, and when the mother kidnaps the child from the father. [142] After a child reaches the age of discretion, or comes of age, the child's wishes are also considered in determining custody.

All American states apply some version of the Uniform Child Custody Jurisdiction Enforcement Act (the UCCJEA). [143] The UCCJEA is a jurisdictional statute and does not address *how* a court should determine custody but only *how and when* a court will enforce the order of a different court from another state or nation. A court will enforce a different court's order only if the other court's child custody laws are in accord with "fundamental principles of human rights." [144] Further, the court must have a basis for jurisdiction over the case, such as the child's residence or recent prior presence.

In determining custody, all states apply some version of the "best interests of the child" standard, and all states require notice and an opportunity for both parents to be heard. In the case of *In re Marriage of Malak*, California courts enforced a court order from Lebanese courts but refused to enforce a court order from the United Arab Emirates (UAE).[145] The parties were a husband and wife who were Lebanese citizens but had resided in the UAE. The wife left the UAE and went to California with the children. Both the Lebanese and UAE courts awarded custody to the father. But while the wife had no opportunity to be heard in the UAE courts, she had an opportunity to be heard in the Lebanese courts but had not appeared.[146] The California court found the opportunity to be heard in Lebanon critical and enforced the Lebanese order. She had had at least forty-five days' notice of the Lebanese hearing.[147] Further, the court found that the Lebanese court had considered the best interests of the children, while the wife had failed to prove that custody invariably went to the father in Lebanese courts.[148] Although this case is now three decades old, Malak provides an example for U.S. courts as they consider complicated family legal issues, specifically in cases in which Muslim courts have previously ruled.

In 2012, a New York circuit court upheld and enforced a UAE court order from Abu Dhabi in the case of *S.B. v. W.A.*[149] because it recognized that the Federal UAE Supreme Court[150] had indeed determined that the best interest of the child was considered and applied, regardless of Sharia law.[151]

In 2010, a Massachusetts court refused to enforce a Lebanese court order in *Charara v. Yatim*.[152] The parents had entered into a custody agreement while in Lebanon (where they were from) that gave custody to the father.[153] A Lebanese court made an order to that effect.[154] Because the Lebanese court had a presumption that paternal custody was in the best interest of the child and would not inquire into the mother's fitness, the Massachusetts court refused to honor the Lebanese decree, set aside the agreement on grounds of duress, and ordered custody to the mother.[155]

These differing results demonstrate how complicated many of these cases can be. They also reveal the need for practicing attorneys to prove, first, how the origin country came to its decision, and second, the extent to which said ruling is compliant with U.S. law.

Criminal Law

It seems as though there's a new atrocity in the news every week and, tragically, sometimes every day: jihadists executing dozens of people by throwing them off buildings, stoning them to death, or crucifying them. Where do these extreme punishments come from? How do terrorists come up with these medieval methods of murder? The answer is simple: Sharia law.

Sharia does not recognize the American legal distinction between criminal law and civil law.[156] Sharia covers both under Islamic penal law.[157] Crimes are generally classified as "claims of Allah" and "claims of man."[158] "Claims of Allah," or *hadd* offenses, include crimes against the Islamic religion, and their punishments are prescribed in the Quran or by the sunna.[159] These offenses include unlawful sexual intercourse (rape, adultery, fornication, homosexual acts), false accusation of unlawful sexual intercourse, consuming alcohol, theft, highway robbery, and apostasy.[160] The punishments for these offenses include imprisonment, lashes, death by stoning, crucifixion, and cutting off limbs.[161]

"Claims of man" are private claims, such as murder, manslaughter, bodily injury not resulting in death, property damage, and perjury.[162] These crimes are punished with *tazir* (discretionary) punishments prescribed by the *qadi* (Islamic judge) or the victim or his next of kin.[163] The victim or his family may seek either *qisas* (legal retaliation, equal punishment) or *diya* (blood money).[164]

American criminal law has several purposes, including deterrence of crimes, retribution for society, and rehabilitation of the criminal so he or she won't commit the crimes again and can become a responsible member of society. Because religious and state affairs are one and the same in Islam, and because every action is performed (or omitted) to promote Islam, fulfill Allah's will, and preserve *ummah*, individual rehabilitation is not a primary purpose of Islamic penal law.[165] Instead, punitive motives, such as deterrence and retribution, are given more importance.[166] As such, Sharia penal rules are intended to provide an eye-for-an-eye type of justice.

The equality in punishment, however, does not mean that Islam treats all human beings the same. Non-Muslims are not equal to Muslims,[167] and women are not equal to men.[168] Verse 178 of *Surah Al-Baqarah* reads: "O ye who believe? The law of equality is prescribed to you in cases of murder: The free for the free, the slave for the slave, the woman for the woman." This means, under Sharia, a Muslim may not be sentenced to death for killing a non-Muslim.[169] Therefore in practice, an-eye-for-an-eye justice varies depending on the category of person being tried.

The rule on equality or proportionality in punishment is available only in private claims, such as murder, personal injury, or property damage. For *hadd* offenses (offenses against Allah), the Quran and the hadiths prescribe strict penalties. Because Allah explicitly ordained these penalties, man may not change them. An Islamic state strictly ruled by Sharia has no room for amendment to these punishments.

Because of the severe mandatory penalties, Sharia requires strict evidentiary proof for *hadd* crimes. The rules of evidentiary proof, however, reveal a serious problem regarding equality of men and women. Two male witnesses are required to prove an offense.[170] If two men are not available, testimony of one man and two women is required because a woman's testimony is valued as half that of a man's.[171] According to a hadith, Muhammad said the reason for this rule is deficiency of a woman's mind.[172]

Especially disturbing are rape laws under Sharia law, in which female victims can actually be charged with a serious crime simply for bringing up rape allegations.

Zina is the Arabic word used to describe unlawful sexual intercourse.[173] It includes "all extramarital sexual intercourse between a man and a woman,"[174] such as rape, fornication, and adultery.[175] Adultery and fornication are punished with stoning and flogging, respectively.[176] In order to prove *zina*, Sharia requires testimony of four male eyewitnesses.[177] While this requirement may serve as a safeguard against false allegations of adultery and fornication, it is problematic in cases of rape. If a woman is unable to prove she was raped by presenting the testimony of four witnesses, it is very likely she will be prosecuted for adultery or fornication.[178] This happens because when a woman claims she was raped (thereby admitting that sexual intercourse has occurred) and is unable to produce four male eyewitnesses to corroborate her claim, she is unable to prove lack of consent to the unlawful act of sexual intercourse that she has admitted took place.

There are a few cases in the United States where criminal defendants or others have attempted to use Islamic belief as a defense of crimes or assertion of privilege. In the case of *People v. Jones*,[179] the defendant beat his wife to death. At trial, he argued that his Islamic religious belief permitting him to "discipline" his wife negated any criminal intent he had to commit murder or great bodily harm and so he was guilty, at most, of involuntary manslaughter.[180] The trial court disagreed, found him guilty, and sentenced him to life in prison.[181] The appellate court affirmed the life sentence.[182]

In *E. Band of Cherokee Indians v. Sequoyah*,[183] the victim of domestic violence attempted to stop the prosecutor from using pictures of her taken by a victims' advocate agency as evidence to prosecute her husband.[184] She asserted a free-exercise claim that Islam did not permit her to be seen unclothed by anyone other than her husband, that the pictures would show her unclothed, and that this violated her religious beliefs.[185] The trial court denied her motion because she had not objected to the pictures being taken in the first place.[186]

Oddly, neither case referenced *Reynolds v. United States.*[187] In *Reynolds,* the Supreme Court of the United States held that though the government could not interfere with religious *belief,* it could interfere with *practices* that were harmful to society.[188] The Court stated:

> Suppose one believed that human sacrifices were a necessary part of religious worship, would it be seriously contended that the civil government under which he lived could not interfere to prevent a sacrifice? Or if a wife religiously believed it was her duty to burn herself upon the funeral pile of her dead husband, would it be beyond the power of the civil government to prevent her carrying her belief into practice?[189]

Religious beliefs are not held superior to the duly enacted laws of the land.[190] The ability to regulate action based on religion, however, is limited.[191]

Honor Killings

More common than these cases—where a religious defense or privilege is asserted—are cases with behavior prevalent in some Islamic cultures that violates U.S. criminal law but in which Sharia is *not* raised as a defense. This includes the practice of honor killings in Muslim communities. Every year many women are killed in Muslim countries in the name of preserving the family's honor.[192] Their "offenses" include dating without the family's approval, marrying a non-Muslim, or having an extramarital affair.[193]

The practice of honor killing is not limited to predominantly Islamic countries. It has traveled from the honor-based Islamic cultures to Western countries, including America, with Muslim immigration. There are examples of honor killings right here in the United States. The existence of these murders is undeniable; we just do not know to what degree they actually occur. All we know is that honor killings happen, and statistics on them are "non-existent." [194]

One clear case involved Faleh Almaleki of Phoenix, Arizona, who was convicted of killing his daughter for refusing an arranged marriage with an Iraqi male. [195] Rahim Alfelawi was prosecuted in Michigan for murdering his daughter for living an American lifestyle. [196] The prosecutor insisted to the press that it was not an honor killing and that he did not want the case used "to promote a continued Arab bias." [197]

The idea and principle of religious tolerance, based on the Christian virtue of charity and its "neutral principles of law" approach to religious law, is so inimical to Sharia because religious tolerance prohibits discrimination in favor of Islam.

Islam traditionally eschews missionary work of conversion by persuasion and ultimately resorts to the sword. It does not hesitate to destroy the symbols of other religions, like Buddhist statues in Afghanistan [198] or Catholic monasteries in Iraq, [199] regardless of historical importance or present-day practice. The killing and harassment of religious minorities in Muslim lands are well documented. Moderate Muslims claim that Islam is a religion of peace. Yet historically Islam has never spread into a nation peacefully, but only by the sword. [200] This religious conversion by the sword is called *jihad*. As Andrew McCarthy points out,

> We still don't get what jihad is. Jihad, whether it is done through violence, or whether it is done by stealthier measures, is always and everywhere about Sharia. It is about the implementation of Sharia, the spread of Sharia, and the defense of Sharia. Sharia is the Islamic legal and political framework. We would like to think of Islam as just another

religion, just a set of religious principles that's separate from our secular or societal life. It's anything but. It is a full service, comprehensive, political, social, and economic system—a military system—that happens to have some spiritual elements. But its ambitions are actually authoritarian in the sense that you have a central Islamic state that controls everything, and it's totalitarian in the sense that it really does want to control everything, every aspect.

Jihad leads to implementation of Sharia law in all lands for all people. That's what makes Sharia so dangerous. The two are inextricably intertwined. You can't combat one of these without combatting both of them.

5

Islam

A Religion of Peace?

As the Western world continues to confront radical Islam, a debate is taking place in university lecture halls, on social media, in the halls of power, and on the news. This debate centers on one question: is Islam a peaceful religion? After 9/11, President George W. Bush referred to Islam as "a religion of peace."[1] President Obama has reiterated time and time again that Islam teaches peace.[2] The debate about the definition of "true Islam" is interesting. But this debate undergirds the West's understanding of terrorism, Islam superiority, the pursuit of Sharia, and the emergence of the unholy alliance. Some point to passages in the Quran about peace, while others point to passages that seem to encourage violence and have spurred terrorists to kill anyone who disagrees with them and destroy entire civilizations—churches, art museums, architecture, and more.

It is true that the Quran contains multiple verses that command peace—as well as violence. The majority of Muslims do not engage in violent, forcible imposition of Sharia on others, justifying their position based on verses in the Quran that teach peace and kindness. However, significant parts of Islam's history are characterized by wars of Islamic conquest and forcible imposition of Islam over nonbelievers on the basis of Quranic teaching of jihad to establish Sharia law. Today ISIS and other radical Islamic terrorists point to sections of the Quran and Islamic history not only to justify their jihad and terror but also to insist that Allah and Muhammad require it of them. It's this history that we must reckon with in order to truly understand the enemy we face and how to defeat it.

The Quranic Revelation

The Quran is the primary source of Islamic teachings and much of Sharia law. Muslims believe that Allah[3] revealed the Quran to Muhammad through the archangel Gabriel (Jibreel) over a period of twenty-two years.[4] The Quran contains 6,236 *ayahs* (verses) and 114 *surahs* (chapters), eighty-six of which were revealed while Muhammad lived in Mecca, starting from AD 610, when Muhammad was about forty years old.[5] The remaining twenty-eight *surahs* were revealed after Muhammad had migrated (*hijra*) to Medina in AD 622 (the beginning of the Islamic calendar).[6]

The Quran contains many of the Islamic laws that control a Muslim's life. It designates everything from times of prayers and how to fast to family law and punishments for different crimes. Not only does the Quran contain Allah's specific commandments, it also contains stories from the Bible, both the Old and the New Testaments. It talks extensively about the Hebrew prophets and claims that the God of Abraham, Isaac, and Jacob is the same God as the Allah of Muhammad and Islam.[7] As I discussed in chapter 2, the triune God of Christian theology is wholly incompatible with the Islamic theology of Allah. Regardless, Islam also teaches that prophethood and revelation ended with Muhammad, who is said to be the last and the seal of prophets.[8]

Muhammad is thus believed to have been given the same message that Allah gave to the Hebrew prophets. The Quran teaches that Allah revealed his word to Moses (and then to David), whose followers, Muslims believe, disobeyed and corrupted the law.[9] Allah then revealed his word to Jesus, whose followers also disobeyed and corrupted the Word.[10] Finally Allah sent his last prophet, Muhammad. Interestingly, all of the Islamic prophets in the Quran, except Muhammad, were Hebrews who came from the lineage of Isaac. Only Muhammad is claimed to have descended from Ishmael.

Muhammad was born circa AD 570 in Mecca during a time when many Arabs worshipped a multitude of idols displayed in the Kaaba.[11] He would frequently visit the Cave of Hira to meditate;[12] and during a meditation in AD 610, the archangel Gabriel is said to have visited Muhammad with the first revelation.[13] Muhammad was frightened by this experience and went back to his wife, Khadija, and told her to cover him.[14] Khadija was Muhammad's first wife—a rich merchant widow who had also been Muhammad's former employer.[15] Muhammad married Khadija when he was twenty-five years old, after one of his business trips had made a great profit for her.[16] Impressed by Muhammad, Khadija sent a marriage proposal.[17] Muhammad's relationship with Khadija is important because she was influential in confirming Muhammad's prophethood and was one of Muhammad's first followers and adherents of Islam.[18]

Muslims believe that Khadija relayed Muhammad's encounter with Gabriel to her Christian cousin, Waraqah ibn Nawfal, a learned man in the Torah and the Gospels.[19] Waraqah told Khadija that Muhammad was a prophet.[20] Reluctantly Muhammad started preaching the idea of one God.[21] Yet the Meccans who worshipped many idols at the time were not ready to accept the new religion and the self-proclaimed prophet. Muhammad's earliest followers were his close companions and a few relatives, including his wife and cousin Ali (who later became Muhammad's son-in-law).[22]

Ali, the first caliph from Muhammad's family,[23] was the fourth Sunni caliph and the first imam of the Shiites.[24] Ali's successorship to Muhammad is the cause of the ongoing fight between Sunnis, who believe any devout Muslim could succeed Muhammad, and Shiites, who believe only someone from the Ahl al-Bayt (family of the prophet) could be Muhammad's successor.[25] This division between Sunnis and Shiites is vital to understanding centuries of war between Muslims and the ever-shifting instability of the Middle East today.

Quranic Revelation in Mecca

Muslims believe that for the next thirteen years (610–622), Muhammad continued to receive divine revelation and preached the divinely inspired message. During those years, the revelation he received contained verses that taught peace, love, kindness, and forgiveness, that is, jihad or struggle against one's inner self.[26] These chapters are called the Meccan Surahs.[27] Interestingly, much of the Quran that was revealed in Mecca contains chapters that tell the story of Hebrew prophets, such as Abraham, Jacob, Moses, Aaron, Elijah, Zechariah, and Jesus (considered a prophet in Islam), and the message of peace that was given to them. Overall the Quran reveres all of these prophets and even calls the Jews a special people chosen by Allah, speaking of "grant[ing] to the children of Israel the Book, the power of command and prophethood."[28]

The most revered prophet named in the Quran is not Muhammad; it is Jesus, whom the Quran calls *Ruhullah* (the Spirit of Allah).[29] But the Jesus found in the Quran is a prophet who performed miracles with the power given by Allah. The Quran claims that Jesus never died on the cross.[30] Instead, according to the Quran, the man who died on the cross was an impostor and the actual Jesus was taken to heaven alive.[31] Shiite Muslims believe that Jesus will come back as a Muslim to rule with the Mahdi, the twelfth and hidden imam of the Shiites.[32]

During Muhammad's ministry in Mecca, while teaching the message of peace and forgiving one's enemies, he gained only a handful of followers, primarily his family.[33] Mecca had always been the site of pilgrimage for many Arabs and was an economic hub as well.[34] Muslims believe Abraham built the Kaaba,[35] which, at the time of Muhammad, hosted hundreds of idols of Arab deities to which many paid homage every year.[36] The Muslim god Allah (derived from *al-Ilah*) was also one of the pagan deities worshipped by Meccans. Fearing that Muhammad's idea of one God might jeopardize their lucrative business, the people of Mecca persecuted Muhammad,[37] though he was born into the tribe of Quraysh, the custodians of the Kaaba.[38] Fleeing persecution, Muhammad migrated to Medina, where he received protection by Jewish and Christian leaders and freely preached his message.[39]

Quranic Revelation in Medina

In Medina, Muhammad's message was well received, and he gained more followers.[40] As the Muslim *ummah* grew in size, Muhammad gained power and influence. He began receiving revelation that taught outward struggle, or jihad with the sword, against his enemies. In Medina, he began preaching about punishing one's enemies and fighting against nonbelievers to establish the right religion, Islam. In fact, the vast majority of Islamic law was revealed in Medina.[41] The revelations that Muhammad received in Medina are called the Medinan *surahs* (chapters).[42] At Medina, Muhammad became a prophet, a political leader, and the commander in chief of the army of the Muslim *ummah*.

Interestingly, the term *jihad*—which literally means "struggle," carrying the dual meaning of peaceful, spiritual struggle in addition to the better-known physical, outward fight—does not appear frequently in the Quran. Only a few verses mention jihad in the context of physical fighting, and thus moderate Muslims argue that jihad is not primarily about physically fighting.[43]

The term the Quran uses in most of the verses that command fighting against nonbelievers is *qatl* (kill).[44] Abdullah Yusuf Ali and

Muhammad Asad (two of the most revered translators of and commentators on the Quran) translate that word as "fight." For instance, verse 216 of *Surah al-Baqarah* (revealed in Medina) reads, "Fighting [*qital*] is prescribed upon you, and ye dislike it. But it is possible that ye dislike a thing which is good for you, and that ye love a thing which is bad for you."[45] Verse 89 of *Surah an-Nisa* (another Medinan chapter) reads, "So take not friends from their [unbelievers'] ranks until they flee in the way of Allah (from what is forbidden). But if they turn renegades, seize them and slay [*qatel*] them wherever ye find them; and (in any case) take no friends or helpers from their ranks." Verse 60 of *Surah al-Anfal* commands: "Against them [unbelievers] make ready your strength to the utmost of your power, including steeds of war, to strike terror into the hearts of the enemies of Allah and your enemies. Whatever ye shall spend in the cause of Allah, shall be repaid unto you, and ye shall not be treated unjustly."[46]

The importance of fighting for the cause of Allah is evidenced from the revelation Muhammad received in Medina. These verses grant a higher status to the mujahideen (the ones who perform jihad) and to those who die and become martyrs (*shaheed*) fighting the unbelievers than to ordinary Muslims. According to verse 95 of *Surah al-Nisa*, "Not equal are those believers who sit (at home) and receive no hurt, and those who strive [jihad] and fight in the cause of Allah with their goods and their persons. Allah hath granted a grade higher to those who strive and fight with their goods and persons than those who sit (at home)."[47]

The same verse continues, "But those who strive [mujahideen] and fight hath he distinguished above those who sit (at home) by a special reward."[48] Verse 154 of *Surah al-Baqarah* reads, "And say not of those who are slain in the way of Allah: 'They are dead.' Nay, they are living, though ye perceive (it) not."[49]

These verses show that martyrdom (*shahada*) is the highest status one can achieve in Islam.

The term *shahada* has an interesting dual meaning in Islam.[50] It is used for the Islamic profession of faith (there is no god but Allah and Muhammad is his prophet) as well as for martyrdom. A *shaheed* (martyr) is one who witnesses to another about the Islamic faith as well as one who dies fighting for Islam. Because there is no concept of substitutionary atonement in Islam,[51] a Muslim has to earn his way to paradise (heaven). Even then, a Muslim can never be sure if Allah will grant him access. A *shaheed*, however, goes directly to paradise. It is therefore no surprise that thousands of young Muslims join groups like ISIS and al-Qaeda to carry out suicide bombings to achieve *shahada*.

Jihad or Coexistence?

Because the Quran contains verses that teach both peace and violence, how can one know whether the moderates' version of Islam or the radicals' version of Islam is true? In one sense, it does not matter which version is the "true Islam." Even if the moderates and/or reformers within Islam are correct that the extremists misrepresent Islam, the threat of radical Islam and terrorism still remains. The attacks on our towns and cities and the millions being slaughtered and enslaved around the world are no less real if the radical version of Islam driving these historically evil practices is not the "true Islam." Even if 10 percent of Muslims wrongly believe in violent jihad against non-Muslims, what Islam actually teaches does not matter, since the radicals are acting on their understanding of what Islam requires.

Yet there is a theological and more troublesome issue to realize about the "true Islam" debate. To determine whether the moderates' or the radicals' Islam is true Islam, one must understand the doctrines of progressive revelation and *naskh* (abrogation).[52]

Muslims believe that the Quran is the last in the chain of progressive revelation. Allah revealed his word to different generations through different prophets. First, he sent his revelation to Moses in the form of Torah, then to David in the form of Psalms, then to Jesus in the form of the Gospels, and finally to Muhammad in the form of the Quran. Many Muslims believe that all four revealed books come from the *Umm al-Kitab* (Mother of the Book) or the Preserved Tablet that is in heaven.[53] This is why the Quran calls Jews and Christians "People of the Book."[54]

Muslims claim that Jews and Christians have corrupted the first three revelations (the Torah, the Psalms, and the Gospels); and because the Quran is the final word of Allah given to the last prophet, Allah has promised to protect the Quran from corruption.[55] Furthermore, because the Quran is the final divine law, Muslims believe it is timeless and is to be applied everywhere by every generation.[56]

Concerning the Quranic revelation, *progressive revelation* means that the archangel Gabriel transmitted the Quran to Muhammad in separate stages.[57] As such, even though the Quran as it is available today was not compiled in a chronological order, the *surahs* (chapters) and *ayahs* (verses) can be chronologically divided into two parts, the Meccan Verses (the early verses) and the Medinan Verses (the later verses). According to the doctrine of abrogation, a subsequent revelation supersedes a prior, *contrary* revelation.[58] Abrogation is "the 'lifting (*raf'*) of a legal rule through a legal evidence of a later date.' The abrogating text or evidence is called *nasikh*, while the repealed rule is called *mansukh*."[59]

The abrogation doctrine, when applied to the dispute between the moderates and the radicals, indicates that the Medinan Verses that prescribe violent jihad and fighting with nonbelievers abrogate contrary Meccan Verses that prescribe forgiving and making peace with them. The newer revelations command spreading the word of Allah through the sword. The first four caliphs after Muhammad's death, in fact, did just that—they brought the entire Arabian Peninsula under the rule of the Caliphate that enforced Allah's law.[60]

Because most Islamic jurists accept the doctrine of *naskh*,[61] moderate Muslims apparently do not have a firm textual and historical ground on which to base their view that Islam is a peaceful religion.

Those Muslims who claim that Islam is a religion of peace argue that the extremists take out of context the verses that prescribe violent jihad. Indeed, such arguments are also often made when interpreting the Bible or other texts. But the contextual argument can be more aptly applied to the Bible because the Bible is also a historical document, in that it contains many passages that are not taken as universal, timeless commands. Those passages simply explain the history of the Jewish people or apply solely to the Jewish people as God's covenant people. Thus, context is important.

The Quran, however, is considered universal and timeless by Muslims. As mentioned, it was revealed to Muhammad in separate stages, and each verse was transmitted at a specific time when it made sense: "The verses were appropriate for [either] informing some feature of the life of the Prophet, or of the community (*ummah*) that the Prophet led. Muslims say a particular verse was revealed at a specific moment because the meaning of that verse would be clear in that moment, in the context of that moment."[62]

Yet the message of the Quran is purportedly timeless because it is believed to reflect the will of Allah, which "applies to all times and circumstances."[63] Therefore, while a particular Quranic verse may have helped resolve a specific problem in Muhammad's time (historical context), it equally resolves a similar issue anytime due to the Quran's timelessness.[64] For instance, consider verses 38 and 39 of *Surah al-Anfal*:

> Say to the unbelievers, if (now) they desist (from unbelief), their past would be forgiven them; but if they persist, the punishment of those before them is already (a matter of warning for them). And fight them on until there is no more

tumult or oppression, and there prevails justice and faith in Allah altogether and everywhere, but if they cease, verily Allah doth see all that they do.[65]

These verses were most likely revealed before the Battle of Badr, which Muhammad and his followers fought against the nonbelievers of Mecca.[66] Yet due to the nature of the Quran, it also provides guidance for all Muslims concerning how to act in the face of unbelief at any time. This raises a series of questions. How should the Muslim *ummah* act today when it faces people who do not believe in Allah or his prophet? What is the meaning of *tumult* or *oppression* in the mind of a Muslim? What is *unbelief*? What is the *right religion*? How do Muslims define *terrorism*? Are Muslims commanded to be in a constant state of war until "there prevails justice and faith in Allah" as prescribed by the verse quoted above, or can non-Muslims coexist peacefully with Muslims?

Muhammad's Final Marching Orders

To the Western mind, peace is the state of coexisting with neighbors, respecting their rights and beliefs, and requiring others to respect ours. To radical Muslims, peace occurs when all people everywhere are under the authority of Sharia.[67] Once it is established everywhere and all infidels have been converted, killed, or forced to pay tribute and live by Sharia, then "peace" will be established. In verse 29 of *Surah al-Tawbah*, Allah commanded: "Fight those who believe not in Allah nor the last day, nor hold that forbidden which hath been forbidden by Allah and his messenger, nor acknowledge the religion of truth [Islam], from among the People of the Book, until they pay the jizyah with willing submission, and feel themselves subdued."[68]

Note another verse in *Surah al-Ma'idah* (5:33): "The punishment of those who wage war against Allah and his messenger, and strive with might and main for mischief through the land is: execution, or crucifixion, or the cutting off of hands and feet from opposite sides, or exile from the land."[69] The next verse says, "Except those who repent before they fall into your power: In that case, know that Allah is oft-forgiving, most merciful."[70]

These verses show that unbelief in Allah and his prophet is a cause for war. Nabeel Qureshi, a scholar on Islam, explains that chapter 9, *Surah al-Tawbah*, is one of the last chapters of the Quran that was revealed to Muhammad,[71] and asserts that it constitutes Muhammad's marching orders to all Muslims: bring nonbelievers into the fold of Islam.[72]

Islam divides the world into two parts: *dar al-Islam* (house of Islam), places where Sharia is the highest authority, and *dar al-harb* (house of war), places where Sharia is not the highest authority and must be brought within the fold of Islam.[73] The distinction between *dar al-Islam* and *dar al-harb* proves that the Muslim *ummah* (community) is not limited by national boundaries or identities. Rather it is unified by Islam. That is why Muslim individuals from around the world leave their home countries to join ISIS and other terrorist groups to participate in jihad against the infidels. From the radical Muslim's perspective, the jihad to transform *dar al-harb* into *dar al-Islam* does not end until the mission is fully accomplished.

Although most Islamic jurists agree that only the head of state or the caliph (head of the Islamic *ummah*) has the authority to wage a holy war (jihad),[74] radical Muslims argue that when the head of the state fails to faithfully perform his duties (one of which is to proclaim Sharia everywhere), it becomes incumbent on individual Muslims (members of the *ummah*) to carry out Allah's commands.[75] Only Allah is the legislator, and the prophet and his successors are vicegerents who enforce his law. Hence, peace occurs only when everything is either subject to Allah's law or, for temporary periods, when Muslims regroup and prepare for the next campaign. Until then, a constant state of war between the *ummah* and nonbelievers exists. Israeli author and scholar of Arabic literature Mordechai Kedar said:

> Peace in their mind is not between Muslims and infidels. Peace is when infidels live under the umbrella of Islam. The conquest brings peace in their minds. Theoretically there cannot be [peace] between Islamic State, the Caliphate state, and other infidel states. Eternal war should be between them. Peace can reign only when everybody comes under the umbrella of Islam.[76]

Accordingly, the people who live in *dar al-harb* and do not accept Sharia are not considered innocent and can be killed or subdued. The Western mind views suicide bombing as an act of terrorism designed to kill innocent people. To the radical Muslim mind, however, Western victims of suicide bombings are not innocent because they have not surrendered to Sharia and Muslim rule. They are still part of the house of war (*dar al-harb*). As a result, they have not acquired protected status under Islam, and accordingly, they are morally complicit in their own destruction. So the distinction between combatant and noncombatant status, as defined by international law, has no meaning to the Islamic radical's mind.

Referring to Hamas's indiscriminate rocket attacks on Israeli civilians, Moshe Ya'alon, former chief of staff of the Israel Defense Forces (IDF), aptly noted: "[O]ur enemies today actually do not distinguish between civilians and combatants. They target deliberately our civilians, and they use their own civilians as human shields."[77] An Israeli soldier said, "We try to learn on a daily basis, what kind of movement is [civilian] movement, what kind of movement doesn't serve any cause except Hizballah. . . . They live among the citizens. Among the citizens you can see a Hizballah house, regular people house . . . it becomes a little war zone inside the village."[78]

It is important to note that most Muslims have adopted the

Western definition of peace. They have chosen to interpret the Quran to allow them to coexist with those who do not share their beliefs. Reformers within Islam like Dr. Zuhdi Jasser talk about the need for peace-loving Muslims to lead the fight against what he calls Islamism, or politicized Islam.[79] Such Muslims attempt to separate religion and politics and propagate a theology that is compatible with other cultures and religions. Nonetheless, a significant minority of Muslims continue to believe and teach that they must wage jihad to obey Allah's commands. It is that group of Muslims that causes moderate Muslims to remain quiet for fear of violence against them. Thus, Islam becomes justifiably defined as a warlike religion to many outside observers.

These theological differences have life-or-death implications. While it may be tempting to view the debate as solely academic, we know all too well what is at stake—our very lives. When radical Islamic terrorists interpret the Quran and the Islamic faith as commanding jihad against anyone and everyone who disagrees with them, women and children are raped, enslaved, and slaughtered. Suicide bombings take innocent lives. Entire governments are thrown into chaos. People groups are wiped off the map[80] and entire civilizations are destroyed.[81] Churches are pillaged.[82] Christians in the cradle of Christianity are endangered.[83]

Further, jihadists are destroying classic art and architecture.[84] They're blowing up tombs in ancient cities and even selling some antiquities on the black market.[85] They razed the tomb of Jonah.[86] Every day the battle continues.

Western civilization is in the crosshairs. The question remains, how will we fight back?

6

The Sunni-Shiite Divide
and the Iranian Revolution

The greatest mistake you can make is to assume all Muslims are the same. They are not simply fundamentalist jihadist extremists or moderates. One difference between moderates and jihadists is patience. They both desire Sharia to be imposed around the world; they simply seek different means to achieve this same end. Moderates are distinct from reformers as well. Reformers recognize the West views Islam as dangerous, that Sharia is politically incompatible and should therefore not be imposed everywhere on everyone. Even with these distinctions, it's important to note that the greatest historical divide within the Muslim community is between Sunnis and Shiites.

Although the Muslim *ummah* is bound by its Islamic identity, it is not absolutely free from internal strife. In fact, from the faith's inception, strife within the Muslim community has resulted in civil wars, the formation of terrorist organizations, and so much more. The *ummah* bond is probably the weakest regarding who is the leader of the Islamic world. The approximately 1.6 billion Muslims in the world[1] are divided primarily into two large groups,

Sunnis and Shiites. Prior to his death in AD 632, Muhammad had not designated a successor to lead the Muslim *ummah*. As a result, Muhammad's death caused a split among his followers concerning who should be Muhammad's rightful successor, which in turn led to the creation of these two sects. Both Sunnis and Shiites consider adherents of the other sect to be heretical. Their rivalry continues to this day and often results in attacks on the members of the opposing sect, including civil wars and battles that rip nations apart and have destabilized the Middle East.

Who Is the Rightful Successor to Muhammad?

It's history that sounds like an epic novel or TV miniseries, but it's all true and it's necessary to understanding the Muslim world today. While many older Americans remember the 1979 Iranian Revolution and many younger Americans have learned about it in school or by watching the Academy Award–winning film *Argo*, modern terror has its roots in the history of Iran and even the Muslim faith altogether.

Soon after Muhammad's death, several of his relatives believed they should succeed Muhammad. On one side was Ali, Muhammad's cousin, whom Muhammad and his first wife, Khadija, had raised after his father's death. Ali was also the husband of Muhammad's daughter, Fatima,[2] making him Muhammad's son-in-law as well. On the other side were Abu Bakr and Umar, two of Muhammad's fathers-in-law, since Muhammad practiced polygamy.[3] After Muhammad's death, a *shura* (consultative) council composed of Muhammad's closest and earliest followers met, and Abu Bakr, Muhammad's wife Aisha's father, was selected to be the first caliph.[4] After Abu Bakr's death, Umar became the second caliph.[5] Upon Umar's death, Uthman (another of Muhammad's sons-in-law) became the third caliph. Due to Uthman's corrupt rule, a group of rebels arose, assassinated Uthman, and pledged allegiance to Ali as the fourth caliph,[6] unleashing a rivalry that has continued for the last fourteen hundred years. Ali, however, decided to choose for himself the title of imam instead of caliph, and his followers are called *Shiat Ali* (followers of Ali). Ali was later assassinated too.[7]

While Sunnis believe Ali was the fourth caliph, *Shiat Ali* or Shiites never accepted the first three caliphs as legitimate successors of Muhammad. They believe that, according to the principle of *nasb* (noble lineage), Ali was supposed to succeed Muhammad all along as he was from the *Ahl al-Bayt* (family of the Prophet). Ali was caliph until AD 661, when he was assassinated in a political dispute. His son Hussein did not succeed him but was killed by Muawiyah, the next caliph. Shiites think Hussein was the rightful caliph and Muawiyah was a usurper, while the Sunnis believe Muawiyah to have been a lawful caliph.

> As such, the fight between Sunnis and Shiites can easily be termed a family feud between Muhammad's blood relatives and his in-laws.

Sunnis believe that Muhammad did not preach hereditary succession, and therefore any Muslim believer could be caliph. Interestingly, although the first three caliphs were not from Ahl al-Bayt, they nonetheless were part of Muhammad's extended family. As such, the fight between Sunnis and Shiites can easily be termed a family feud between Muhammad's blood relatives and his in-laws.

Shiites and Iran: The Ancient Birth of Modern Terror

Shiites make up about 13 percent of the total worldwide Muslim population.[8] While some Shiites live in Lebanon, Iraq, Bahrain, Afghanistan, Kashmir, and Pakistan, Shiite Islam is primarily represented by the Islamic Republic of Iran, the first and largest Shiite country. The tactics of modern-day terrorism used by Muslim terrorist organizations worldwide have their roots in Shiite history and the Islamic Revolution of Iran.

The state we know as Iran has been a kingdom since ancient

times. The first people who inhabited Iran were originally a conglomeration of several ethnicities whose descendants are collectively known as the Medes and the Persians.[9] By 700 BC, the Medes had established an independent kingdom, which in turn became the first Iranian Empire.[10] Around 549 BC, Cyrus the Great united the Medes into the Persian Empire.[11] Alexander the Great conquered the Persian Empire in the 300s BC.[12] After Alexander died, his empire was broken up into smaller empires. Iran became the Parthian Empire and later the Sassanian Empire. The Sassanian Empire, worn down by fighting from without and within, fell in AD 644 to the Arab Muslim armies of the second caliph, Umar.[13]

After centuries of Arab Islamic rule, the Seljuk Turks, and later the Mongols, controlled large portions of Iranian territory.[14] As the Mongols ravaged Iranian lands, Shiism truly began to take hold in Iran through assimilation. Throughout its history, Iran had continuously assimilated foreign cultures, including Greek, Egyptian, and Indian, and blended them into its own culture.[15] This assimilation and tolerance of other cultures came in part from Iran's leading religious belief system at that time, Zoroastrianism, which taught a message of social justice for all.[16] Similarly, assimilation occurred with Islam. Initially, when the Arabs under Caliph Umar conquered Iran, they forced Sunni Islam upon the Persians.[17] Over time, however, Shiism replaced Sunnism.[18]

The dominance of Shiism came about in Iran largely because it reinforced already long-standing Zoroastrian beliefs. Zoroastrianism taught that subjects should submit to virtuous rulers and rise up against those who are wicked. Leaders were from God, and if they did not rule wisely and justly, they did not deserve their subjects' allegiance.[19] Such ideas meshed well with Shiism due to its history.[20] Because Shiism stems from the belief that the rightful heir of Muhammad was Ali, and that the Sunnis usurped that right by killing Ali, Hussein, and the other imams in their lineage, it is the product of a long-standing sense of injustice perpetrated by the Sunnis and, in particular, by Sunni leaders. The Sunni leaders were wicked and hence not virtuous because they resorted to killing Ali, while Shiites consider Ali the most enlightened and virtuous leader ever to have lived, besides Muhammad himself.[21]

According to Zoroastrianism, rulers who murdered a virtuous leader did not deserve to rule, and it was the duty of the people to oppose such injustice.[22] Shiism, then, gained strength over Sunnism because it emphasized preexisting Zoroastrian beliefs about who had the right to rule.

Iranian Shiites spoke out against the corruption and excess of the Seljuk Turks and the brutality of the Mongol hordes. Shiites urged the people to exercise their right—indeed, their duty—to defeat their wicked rulers.[23] The Iranian Shiites believed that neither the Turks, the Mongols, nor the Arab Sunnis should rule Iran. Instead, they should rule.

In the late fifteenth century, the Shiites prevailed and took power when Ismail,[24] a Muslim conqueror, defeated the Mongols and established the Safavid dynasty.[25] The battle cry of his warriors illustrates their strong Shiite beliefs: "We are Hussein's men, and this is our epoch! In devotion we are slaves of the Imam! Our name is Zealot and our title is Martyr!"[26]

Ismail made himself shah, and his first act after taking the throne was to proclaim Shiism the official religion of the empire.[27] Although it would take many years before Shiism truly took hold among the people, the Safavid dynasty was the first step in elevating Shiism over Sunnism in Iran.[28]

Eventually, however, the Safavid dynasty weakened, and invasions from Afghan tribesmen destroyed the kingdom in the 1700s.[29] After decades of power struggles, the Qajar dynasty emerged in the late 1700s.[30] The Qajars were a Turkish tribe originating around the Caspian Sea.[31] Their dynasty lasted until 1925, when Reza Khan was chosen as the new king.[32] The Qajar period was marked by severe poverty and backwardness.[33] The rulers were corrupt, weak, self-interested, and decadent.[34] As a result, foreign states took advantage of the weakness and exploited Iran.[35]

The Qajar rulers sold off legal monopolies in their country to the highest bidder, which was Britain in most cases.[36] These sales were known as "concessions," and they involved everything from industry to railroads to oil.[37] Oil would serve as the catalyst for immense change in Iran's future. Oil was first discovered in Iran in 1908, and the British had previously negotiated for the exclusive right to search for, drill, and export oil found within an extremely large geographical area of Iran.[38] In return, the Qajars received an annual stipend based on net profits.[39] This deal became known as the D'Arcy Concession, and it was massively tilted in favor of the British.[40]

In the ensuing years, the Anglo-Persian Oil Company exported millions of barrels of oil for only a fraction of a price paid to the Qajars.[41] Although initially a private company, the British government eventually bought 51 percent of Anglo-Persian's shares, giving the British government ownership and control over the company's operations.[42] Thus, the British government became closely involved to protect its oil interests. With vast amounts of wealth flowing from Iran to the British Isles, severe discontent arose among Iranians.[43]

As time went on, the Iranian people became outraged with the Qajar rulers, their corruption, and the concessions.[44] The people demanded a parliament and an end to foreign involvement.[45] Spearheading this movement was Reza Khan, a former soldier and officer in the Cossack Brigade.[46] In 1921, he led the successful coup overthrowing the Qajar ruler, Ahmad Shah.[47] The British assisted him because they had grown tired of dealing with the backward, tribal Qajars and desired a more centralized government to increase the efficiency of oil export.[48] This would not be the last time a Western power helped overthrow an Iranian leader in hopes of protecting its own economic and national security interests while appeasing unrest among the Iranian population.

In 1926, Reza Khan named himself shah, founding the Pahlavi dynasty.[49] His reign was extremely heavy-handed and brutal.[50] When a group of several hundred people protested against his decree forbidding women to wear veils and requiring men to wear billed caps that prevented their foreheads from touching the ground during prayer, Reza Khan ordered them to be massacred in the mosque where they had gathered.[51] More than a hundred were killed, and no one dared to protest against him again.[52]

During the 1930s and into World War II, Reza Khan increased his ties to Nazi Germany.[53] He allowed hundreds of German agents to operate in Iran and establish networks, and he entertained Nazi dignitaries inside Iran.[54] The British feared that Nazi Germany would use Iran as a staging ground to attack the Soviet Union.[55] British and Soviet troops entered Iran in August 1941, but Reza Khan refused to work with the Allies.[56] As a result, the Allies forced Reza Khan to abdicate his throne.[57]

His son Mohammad Reza Shah Pahlavi assumed control.[58] Reza Shah instituted many changes at the direction of the British.[59] He changed Iranian political procedures by giving himself sole power to select the prime minister.[60] Immediately after his coronation, the British had him appoint pro-British politician Mohammad Ali Foroughi as prime minister.[61] He also allowed the establishment of supply bases in Iran for the Allies' war effort.[62] Yet it would not be Reza Shah who would dominate the Iranian public eye in the coming decade, but rather the nationalist Mohammad Mosaddegh.

Mosaddegh's worldview was shaped by two defining beliefs: the rule of law and a truly independent Iran free from outside interference.[63] Mosaddegh rose to prominence in the Majlis, the parliamentary system within Iran established in the early 1900s.[64] He was a wealthy landowner who resented the Anglo-Iranian Oil concession.[65] Mosaddegh became a harsh critic of Reza Shah, the British government, and the Anglo-Iranian Oil Company (since renamed from Anglo-Persian), and was an avid proponent of democracy and Iranian self-reliance.[66]

Many people shared Mosaddegh's political beliefs, and they subsequently formed the National Front, a new political party dedicated to nationalism and democracy that chose Mosaddegh as its leader.[67] Years later, after being elected prime minister, Mosaddegh nationalized the Anglo-Iranian Oil Company.[68] As a result, the British hated Mosaddegh and made plans to overthrow him.[69] The United States also took notice of the increasing presence of a communist party called the Tudeh.[70] The United States grew concerned over a future Soviet presence in Iran[71] but could not come to an agreement with Britain over what course of action to take. President Truman wanted the British to compromise with Mosaddegh over Anglo-Iranian Oil, but the British refused to yield any ground and even suggested invading Iran.[72] Truman was absolutely against any sort of invasion, and the disagreement caused the United States and Britain to grow further apart on the matter of Iran.[73]

A Successful Coup Leads to a Western-Friendly Iran

Then, in 1950 and 1952, changes occurred in both British and American leadership and led to immense changes in Iran. Winston Churchill and his Conservative Party took control from the Labour Party, and Dwight D. Eisenhower was elected president.[74] Both men had run on anticommunist platforms, and each saw a growing communist threat in Iran.[75]

In fact, a U.S. oil consultant who investigated the situation in Iran concluded that without British tankers and support, the Iranian government would be unable to continue exporting oil for many years.[76] As the Iranian economy disproportionately relied on the oil export revenues, the loss of oil revenue would be catastrophic.[77] Iran would be destabilized, Mosaddegh would be ousted, and a Soviet-sponsored communist takeover would occur.[78] Eisenhower and his intelligence agents became convinced, then, that Iran was collapsing and a Soviet takeover was imminent.[79] Immediate steps had to be taken to prevent the spread of communism and Soviet power into the Middle East. To remedy the situation, the United States agreed with the British that Mosaddegh needed to be removed, the oil situation stabilized, and control given to the Shah.[80]

Official plans were approved for the British-favored coup, named Operation Ajax.[81] The first attempt, on August 15, 1953, failed,[82] but the second attempt only four days later succeeded.[83] Mosaddegh was sentenced to three years' imprisonment and house arrest for life.[84] In the first failed coup attempt, Reza Shah had fled to Iraq for fear of being implicated in the plot.[85] When news arrived of the successful second coup attempt, he returned to Iran with hundreds of supporters, including many of those who had been critical of the coup.[86] The coup saw the Shah returned to the throne with a tremendous debt owed to the Americans and British for removing Mosaddegh and solidifying his power as monarch.[87]

Relations between Reza Shah and the United States grew in the aftermath of the 1953 coup. The Shah received an initial $6 million from the United States to help stabilize the economy,[88] and a new deal brokered by an international consortium saw oil profits shared fifty-fifty with Iran.[89] Reza Shah denationalized the oil industry, and five American companies purchased control of almost half of the Iranian oil trade.[90] Reza Shah bought billions of dollars' worth of weaponry from the United States, spending $10 billion between 1972 and 1976 alone, drawing the two countries ever closer.[91]

Iran also enjoyed a favorable relationship with Israel. The SAVAK, Iran's secret police agency, and the Israeli Mossad collaborated, and the Shah verbally supported Israel in the 1973 Arab-Israeli War.[92] During this time, Israel also sold weapons to Iran.[93]

Not only did relations between Iran and the West improve, but Iran itself began to modernize. Iran organized its armed forces along Western lines; constructed a new network of modern roads, railways, and airways; and reconstructed parts of major cities.[94] Iran also changed its legal system to a secular system based on Western models,[95] instituted state-sponsored education of Iranians abroad in Western countries, and developed state-sponsored industrial monopolies.[96] Finally, Reza Shah pushed for Western-style clothing, particularly for women.[97] He banned all women from wearing veils in public.[98] Reza Shah called this process of radical change in Iran Western-style modernization.[99] Referring to this time, Dan Meridor, deputy prime minister of Israel, said that "Iran was [once] a free country . . . very advanced, very Western, scientifically very impressive. It was taken over by its regime of fundamentalism and a black night came over Iran."[100]

In the years following the 1953 coup, although he was involved in Westernizing Iran, Reza Shah became more autocratic. He crushed dissent among his people wherever he found it and by whatever means necessary.[101] All political parties against him were disbanded and opposition groups eliminated.[102] As the Shah's human rights violations grew, so did dissent among his people.[103] When Ayatollah Ruhollah Khomeini arrived center stage, Iran was ripe for radical change.[104] What happened next turned a country that was once one of the closest allies of the United States and Israel into the United States' and Israel's greatest enemy. This historical shift was a result of the ayatollahs and their rhetoric of jihadist martyrdom.

How Iran Became the Exporter of Jihad

Ayatollah Khomeini was born in 1902 and claimed to be a descendant from the Prophet Muhammad through the seventh imam.[105] Khomeini's ultimate desire was for Iran to become an Islamic republic.[106] In his view, Iran did not need legislatures, statutes, or elections.[107] In his mind, such things were core components of democracy, a product of Westernism, which Khomeini despised.[108]

The only things Iran needed were the Quran and the Traditions of the Prophet (sunna).[109] It was the religious leaders, not freely elected politicians, who should be leading Iran because Iran needed Islamic, not secular, leadership.[110] When he was once told that he should leave politics to government officials, Khomeini replied that since government was a matter of the "people's business, then of course Islam has something to say."[111]

Khomeini sparked the 1963 Tehran uprising by giving a scathing sermon against the Shah and his connections with the Western world.[112] Shortly after this speech, Khomeini was arrested, but his followers became outraged and took to the streets in violent demonstrations.[113] With other people in Tehran joining in, they fought against the police and military and attacked government buildings all throughout Tehran.[114] The uprising soon spread to the surrounding villages as well.[115]

Reza Shah responded with overwhelming force, deploying tanks and combat troops into the city.[116] The military forces successfully suppressed the uprising, and Reza Shah exiled Khomeini to Turkey.[117] Later Khomeini was sent to Iraq[118] and from Iraq to France.[119] After fourteen years of careful planning and preparation in exile, as the Shah suffered from cancer and departed Iran for medical treatment in the West, Khomeini returned to Iran in 1978 and helped lead the successful overthrow of the Shah in the 1979 Iranian Revolution.[120]

Khomeini held a passionate hatred toward America. He painted the United States as Iran's greatest enemy.[121] Khomeini loathed cinemas because they were places where the West and America spread their secular propaganda and distracted the Iranian people from their religious duties.[122] According to Khomeini, the United States, not the Shah, posed the greatest threat to Iran: "Let the American President know that in the eyes of the Iranian people, he is the most repellant member of the human race."[123]

Soon after the success of the 1979 revolution, Iranians did

not focus on internal, domestic issues, or still rebellious factions within.[124] Instead the Iranian people turned their focus to the United States and stormed the U.S. embassy in November 1979, leading to what is commonly known as the Iranian Hostage Crisis.[125] When President Carter announced the failed U.S. rescue attempt of the hostages, Khomeini used it to further demonize America and its threat to Iran and Islam.[126]

After the revolution succeeded in 1979, people in Tehran chanted the slogan: "Now the Shah is gone, America is next."[127] Using the Shiite history of injustice perpetrated by Sunnis in his rhetoric and actions, Khomeini united the Iranian people under his cause by painting the United States as the "Great Satan"[128] and the ultimate, common enemy for all Iranians.

How Radical Extremists Find Inspiration in Islamic History

The divide between Shiites and Sunnis arises from a significant historic event branded into Shiite memory: the martyrdom of Hussein, the son of Ali and the third Shiite imam, at Karbala, in what is now Iraq.[129] Every year, on the tenth day of the Islamic month of Muharram, Shiite Muslims commemorate this martyrdom through Ashura, a time of remembrance.[130] The Day of Ashura is the climactic final chapter of a ten-day period of grief and mourning.[131] This one event has become a central symbol of the battle between good and evil that has guided Shiite beliefs for centuries.[132]

The story of Ashura occurred in the year AD 680, when a man named Yazid became the sixth caliph to rule the Muslim people.[133] Yazid ordered the arrest of his rival Hussein, who was in Medina at that time, in order to force Hussein to give public allegiance to Yazid as the sole leader of the Muslim *ummah*.[134] Hussein learned of the plot and fled with his family from Medina to Mecca under the cover of night.[135]

While Hussein was in Mecca, he received urgent word begging him to come to Iraq to save the people there from the egregious brutality of Yazid and those under his authority. The messages urged him to lead a rebellion to seize the Caliphate and rule the Muslim *ummah* himself, taking his "rightful" place as Muhammad's successor.[136] The messages assured him that twelve thousand men were waiting in Iraq, ready and willing to stand with him in his fight against Yazid.[137] Persuaded by these calls for help and the pledge of their allegiance, Hussein left Mecca with his family and seventy warriors and headed for Iraq.[138]

Hussein never made it to his destination. Yazid's much larger army of four thousand men, led by a ruthless general named Shimr, surrounded his encampment[139] and besieged it for seven days.[140] The siege ended on the Day of Ashura, when Hussein and all of his warriors were slain one by one.[141] The Shiites tell a detailed and epic tale of those seven days of siege, filled with individual stories of larger-than-life heroism and valor as Hussein's warriors bravely met their fate.[142]

They tell the tale of Hussein's nephew Qasim, who married his fiancée in the midst of the siege but immediately rode out to his death against the oppressors while still shrouded in the white raiment of his wedding.[143] They tell of Hussein's half brother Abbas, who valiantly snuck through enemy lines to fill a goatskin of water to save the children in Hussein's encampment from dying of thirst.[144] As the story goes, he was ambushed on the way back, and Shimr's men had to cut off both of his arms so they could stop him from fighting long enough to slay him.[145]

They tell of Hussein's three-month-old son, who was dying of dehydration when Hussein stepped out before his enemies and lifted the infant in the air, begging the enemy to show mercy to the children.[146] Instead, the baby was pierced by an arrow while Hussein held him aloft.[147] As the Shiite legend goes, Hussein offered the child's blood as a sacrifice to Allah, and the blood supernaturally rose to the heavens instead of falling to the earth.[148]

Hussein's own death was particularly gruesome. The stories say he was shot by an arrow, stabbed thirty-three times, and beheaded. After his death, his corpse was trampled by horses and his head impaled on a pike for delivery to Yazid, all at Shimr's command.[149] Those of Hussein's family who were not slain were taken captive, and the headless corpses of Hussein and his warriors were left to rot where they had fallen until nearby villagers came to bury them there.[150] The mass grave was named Karbala, or "the place of trial and tribulation."[151] It became a symbol of the Shiite anguish at injustice for centuries to come, anchored forever in the graphic imagery of the legendary martyrdom of Hussein ibn Ali.[152]

The tale of the martyrdom of Hussein at Karbala has become the primary rallying cry of Shiism, motivating the deeply felt sense of injustice and outrage at the core of the Shiite identity.[153] The powerful collective memory of Karbala is demonstrated in Iran by the ten days of remembrance that Shiites recognize each year leading up to Ashura.[154] This period is marked by deep sorrow expressed through public grieving, and the quasi-mythical events of Karbala are reenacted extensively in meticulously composed dramatic presentations.[155] The name Hussein is chanted over and over in desperate prayers.[156] On the tenth day, a grand procession is held in which hundreds of thousands of men march together, chanting the name of Hussein and striking themselves repeatedly.[157] Some even use chain flails with blades attached to beat themselves, horrifically injuring their own bodies out of devotion to the memory of Hussein's martyrdom.[158]

Khomeini utilized the deep sense of injustice at the core of Shiite religious devotion to incite the Iranian people to revolt against the Shah in 1979.[159] "Let the blood-stained banners of Ashura be raised wherever possible as a sign of the coming day when the oppressed shall avenge themselves on the oppressors," Khomeini wrote in 1978.[160] Comparing the Shah of Iran to the figures of Sunni oppression that Shiites already despised, Khomeini was able to tap into an already existing animosity and funnel its force toward his own goals.[161] Khomeini redefined Hussein's death "as an act of liberation."[162]

That year, the processions in commemoration of Ashura became not just a ritual of remembrance, but an act of political defiance. The marchers shouted the traditional phrase "Death to Yazid!" and added a new phrase: "Death to the Shah!"[163] Khomeini compared the deaths of those who stood against the Shah to the deaths of Hussein's men at Karbala, invoking the deeply felt sense of injustice and oppression that lies at the root of Shiism, and incited religious rage to fuel his political goals.[164]

Khomeini was able to inspire devout Shiites to literally sacrifice their own lives in the fight against the Shah. Again, in the 1980s, during the Iran-Iraq War, soldiers on the front lines were continually reminded of the events of Karbala through songs and performances, and young Iranian boys were inspired by religious fervor to sacrifice themselves as human minesweepers while wearing headbands bearing a single word: "Karbala."[165] As one historian explains, "The Ayatollah grasped that Karbala was an enormously loaded symbol, a deep well of emotional, social, and political significance, seemingly infinitely adaptable to time and circumstance."[166]

The fact that Khomeini labeled himself an imam bears great significance. The term *imam* has different meanings for Sunnis and Shiites. For Sunnis, an imam is a leader of prayer in a mosque.[167] For Shiites, an imam is a much higher authority who is the "divinely inspired, sinless, infallible, religiopolitical leader of the community."[168] Shiite Muslims consider an imam's word to be very authoritative.[169] Khomeini used the title *imam* and inspired the Iranian people to follow him with his religiously charged words. First, he used this influence against the Shah, leading to the 1979 revolu-tion.[170] Then he used the same influence to foment hatred for and opposition to America.[171]

The new Islamic Republic was also founded on the principle of the *Vilayat-e-Faqib*, "Stewardship of the Jurist."[172] The "jurist" was to be the Supreme Leader of the people.[173] Not just anyone could be leader. He had to be an exceptional individual possessed of piety, administrative abilities, and good character.[174] He had to be a role model for the rest of the Iranian people to follow.[175] Although the office of president was retained, the Supreme Leader had ultimate power.[176]

Khomeini had spoken earlier in his life about the "jurist" in his lectures called *Islamic Government: The Stewardship of the Jurist.*[177] In these, Khomeini stated that it was the Islamic Shiite clergy who were to govern Iran because such clergy were "heirs to the Prophet and to the imams."[178] He asserted that the Quran and the Tradi-tions of the Prophet were the only law needed in Iran.[179] Therefore the sole requirement for the ruler of Iran was "knowledge of the law" and a "just character."[180] Khomeini stated that if an individual had these two qualities, "then he will enjoy the same authority as God's Most Noble Prophet . . . in the administration of society and it will be the duty of all people to obey him."[181] Although a group possessed of such qualities could rule collectively, Khomeini stated that a single person could be given such power.[182]

This "jurist" doctrine is found nowhere else in the world but Shiite Iran.[183] Khomeini's vision for Iran was of a nation that would be truly different from the rest of the Islamic world. But this dis-tinction was not just for the sake of being different. Iran needed to be different in order for Khomeini's ultimate plans of pan-Islamism to be realized. His vision was fulfilled when he received authority to rule Iran as imam and the new Islamic Republic was founded on the "Stewardship of the Jurist." He finally had the opportunity to export his ideas to the rest of the world.

Exporting Terror

It is a fundamental part of human nature to follow a leader. When a charismatic leader arises who speaks to the hearts of the people, he can command tremendous support and power. Leaders such as Khomeini and those following him leveraged this tendency of human nature and the collective Shiite wrath against injustice and oppression to motivate hatred for the West. It explains why Shiite-majority Iran and many Sunni terrorist organizations have developed into a powerhouse of anti-Western jihad. When America and the West are painted as oppressors and powers of injustice, a deep-seated religious fervor is ignited.

Following the model of the Iranian Revolution, Sunni groups developed and harnessed a hatred of the West as well, using Iran's tactic of religious motivation to inspire suicide martyrdom. The same fervor that incites men to beat and slice themselves in religious processions on Ashura is exploited to inspire jihadist martyrdom against the West, because Muslims view it as a fight against the oppression that has plagued their people for centuries.

Iran by no means invented or pioneered the use of suicide tactics in warfare. But in a very real sense, Khomeini and his followers reinvented suicide attack strategies and developed a way to use them effectively for their goals.[184] Khomeini mixed Quranic jihadist doctrine, Islamic glorification of martyrdom, revolutionary rhetoric, and historical Shiite propensities toward martyrdom to develop a new and potent ideological motivation for suicide bombings. The Ayatollah even issued a fatwa during the Iran-Iraq War to encourage soldiers to rush toward certain death against the enemy.[185] The reinvention of this tactic was not used only in the Iranian Revolution and Iran-Iraq War, however. It has been exported from Iran and has become the primary modus operandi of Islamic terror organizations worldwide, both Sunni and Shiite.

After the 1979 revolution, the history of Khomeini and the

revolution was rewritten in the preamble to the new constitution to affirm the power of Shiite Islam in Iran and Khomeini as its new leader.[186] It named him imam and praised him for leading the people both in 1963 and 1979 against the United States and its conspiracy against the Iranian people.[187] It affirmed that the Iranian people had finally purified themselves of all foreign influences, especially from the United States, and that they were now able to return to the traditions of Islam in Iran.[188]

Iran was to create a model government and, by its example, to then create "a single community worldwide . . . within this century."[189] To accomplish this, Khomeini created an "ideological army" in the Army of Guardians of the Islamic Revolution (Revolutionary Guards).[190] He created the Revolutionary Guards originally as a counterweight to the regular military and leftist militias.[191] It was a "people's army" made up of those loyal to Khomeini's cause.[192] He did not want another military coup like that of 1953.[193]

The Revolutionary Guards, unlike the regular military, reported directly to Khomeini and the Revolutionary Council rather than to Iran's government, giving Khomeini ultimate control.[194] Although it began as an internal military force to protect the new Islamic Republic, the Revolutionary Guards would become Iran's main tool in spreading Islamic revolution across the globe.[195]

The Iran-Iraq War is a prime example of Khomeini's attempt to spread his Islamic doctrine to other parts of the world. Although Iraq started the war,[196] Khomeini used the conflict to unify the Iranian people behind his desire to spread Shiism. The book *Two Years of War*, published by the Political Office of the Revolutionary Guards, stated that the war had been a blessing by Allah himself.[197] It showed the strength of the new Islamic Republic to the rest of the world and had "struck fear into the bullies of West and East, [and the] capitalists."[198] Through its victories, Iran was preventing the establishment of a "new Israel on the Persian gulf" through the "lackey Saddam" and had turned the "sweet dreams of America into a nightmare."[199] What had started as Iraqi aggression turned into an Iranian holy war where Iranian holy warriors went into battle armed with "trust in Allah and a devotion to self-sacrifice."[200]

Thousands of Iranian volunteers, including children, physically threw themselves against the Iraqi defenses.[201] They willingly went to their deaths, with units suffering over 70 percent casualties,[202] and some even walked straight into minefields to clear the way for other units.[203] One such martyr wrote in his will before going to the minefield: "The Imam has opened my eyes. . . . How sweet, sweet, sweet, is death. It is like a blessing that Allah has bestowed upon his favorites."[204]

Despite tremendous losses, morale remained high, and volunteers continued to flood the army.[205] Serving in the army took on a religious character, with soldiers dreaming of their chance for martyrdom.[206] It explains why Iran refused Saddam's offer for peace after two years of struggle. Khomeini, broadcasting his response, called for Saddam's overthrow.[207] Khomeini warned other Arab nations that Iran would "establish Islamic government" and "if Iran and Iraq unite, the other nations of the region will join with them."[208] The Political Office of the Revolutionary Guards wrote, "We realized that the only way to rescue the region from the clutches of America was to overthrow Saddam's regime and replace it with an Islamic and popular regime in Iraq."[209] Khomeini saw the Iran-Iraq War not as a defensive war, but as an instrument for Iran to further its divine mission to bring true Islamic rule to the rest of the world.[210]

Khomeini used Lebanon as another staging ground for the spread of Islamic revolution and jihadist martyrdom. Israel, the "Little Satan," had invaded and occupied southern Lebanon.[211] Worse still, the "Great Satan," America, had sent Marines to assist the Israelis.[212] Through the efforts of the Revolutionary Guards, Hezbollah was established in Lebanon and funded directly by Iran to drive the United States and Israeli forces from the Islamic land.[213]

Hezbollah waged a war against Israel and the U.S. forces through direct engagements, kidnappings, and suicide bombings, including bombing the U.S. Marines barracks in Beirut on October 23, 1983.[214]

Lebanon became Iran's first major international operation. Even after Israel and the United States left, Iran continued its support for Hezbollah. One particular figure involved was the Revolutionary Guards general Qasem Soleimani. Soleimani took control in 1998 of the Quds Force, a lethal special operations and espionage unit within the Revolutionary Guards.[215] The Quds Force has been known to work closely with the Special Security Apparatus, an elite wing of Hezbollah formed by Imad Mughniyah.[216] Soleimani has been described as the "single most powerful operative in the Middle East today."[217] Although the clandestine nature of Soleimani and the Quds Force's operations makes them difficult to track with accuracy, his influence and direction have been linked to several terror incidents involving Hezbollah and Lebanon.[218]

For instance, in 2005 the former Lebanese prime minister and Sunni Muslim leader Rafic Hariri was assassinated in a bombing of his motorcade.[219] The United Nations Special Tribunal for Lebanon charged Hezbollah with this assassination, and many members of the Tribunal believed that Iran had supported Hezbollah.[220] Former senior CIA official Robert Baer stated, "If indeed Iran was involved, Suleimani [Soleimani] was undoubtedly at the center of this."[221]

John Bolton, former United States ambassador to the United Nations, said, "Iran is the world's central banker to international terrorism. It funds Hamas, Hezbollah terrorists in Afghanistan and Iraq and around the world."[222] The funding of Hamas and Hezbollah has global significance. Shia Iran funding Shia Hezbollah is dangerous but doctrinally consistent. But Shia Iran funding Sunni Hamas breaks the typical Shia-Sunni paradigm of conflict. What makes this so significant is that Iranians' hatred of Israel and the United States is so pronounced that they will give millions of dollars to a group that is their historic rival in so many ways. This reveals how the unholy alliance desires to export its Islamic conquest.

On February 1, 1979, the day Khomeini arrived in Iran to lead the Iranian Revolution, he said in a speech at Behesht-e Zahra cemetery in Tehran: "Islam has been moribund for almost fourteen hundred years; we have returned it to life with the blood of our youth. . . . Very soon we will liberate Jerusalem and pray there."[223] Indeed, within a quarter century, Khomeini and his Islamic regime—with their revolutionary ideology and tangible, material support—turned the entire scheme of terrorist machinery against America and Israel. The Sunnis and Shiites now faced a common foe, becoming unlikely allies in the export of terror around the world.

7

Exporting the Revolution

Ronen Bergman, Israel's leading investigative journalist, has said that Iran's foreign policy is based upon two main paths, two legs.

> The first is the attempt to support jihadist proxy groups. I don't know if Khomeini read or did not read Trotsky. Trotsky said, "A revolution that does not export itself is doomed to collapse from the inside." And from Day One, Khomeini and his followers were trying to export the revolution to other countries. That's one leg. The other leg is the attempt to acquire nuclear military capability. This is the insurance policy of the regime. However, the first leg uses a bargaining chip to threaten Israel and the United States: Do not dare to attack our facilities, our nuclear facilities, because if you do, we would launch a world campaign of terrorism against your targets. And therefore, you should not even dare—even think—of launching such an [aerial strike]. So these two legs are defending each other.[1]

Bergman appears to be right. One of the results of the Islamic Revolution spreading outside Iran was the creation of Hezbollah, a Shiite terrorist organization in Lebanon. The organization's name declares its dedication and commitment to Islam. The word *Hezbollah* is derived from the Arabic *Hizb Allah*, which means "party or fellowship of Allah."[2] This phrase comes from a Quranic verse (*Surah al-Ma'idah*, 5:56), which appears in red letters at the top of Hezbollah's yellow-and-green flag: "The fellowship of Allah that must certainly triumph."[3]

At its formation in 1982, Hezbollah was inspired by the ideology behind the Iranian Revolution and its principal leader, Ayatollah Khomeini.[4] It adheres to Khomeini's vision of an Islamic cleric-ruled state,[5] *vilayat-e-faqih*, and thus views Iran as the ultimate example of the successful implementation of that vision. The group reveres Khomeini as the "divinely inspired ruler" of the community of true Muslim believers and Ayatollah Ali Khamenei, Iran's current Supreme Leader, as the modern "Legal Guardian of Muslims."[6] Hezbollah believes that Allah has established Iran as the "nucleus of the world's central Islamic state."[7]

The History of Lebanon and Hezbollah: A Cocktail for Conflict

Hezbollah operates primarily out of southern Lebanon,[8] an area that once was part of the Ottoman Empire.[9] Following World War I, in the spring of 1920, the League of Nations divided the territories of this region between France and Great Britain under the system of Mandates.[10] The Mandate for Syria was given to France to prepare the people of that region for independence. The Syrian Mandate consisted of present-day Syria and Lebanon. Two separate Mandates were given to Great Britain: the Mandate for Palestine and the Mandate for Mesopotamia. The division of territories was not based on preexisting borders or cultural communities, but rather was primarily intended to accommodate European interests in oil resources and control of trade routes.[11]

In September 1920, the French annexed Mount Lebanon, the cities of Beirut, Sidon, Tyre, and Tripoli, and the four Ottoman provinces of Hasbaya, Rashaya, Baalbek, and Akkar, declaring all to constitute the unified state of Greater Lebanon.[12] The new state of Greater Lebanon was created at the request of the Maronite Christian community, which was dominant in the Mount Lebanon province. As such, the new state was primarily controlled by the Maronites.[13] Greater Lebanon went on to become the modern Lebanese Republic after the adoption of its constitution on May 23, 1926.[14]

Prior to the French creation of Greater Lebanon in 1920, the area had never been unified as a single political unit in modern times. Because of this, the area was made up of several disparate communities and ethnicities rather than a single homogeneous population. Unfortunately for the region, these were the ingredients for civil war, unrest, and instability.[15] The communities were separate from each other in many ways, and they represented a diversity of religions, such as the Christian Maronites, Catholics, and Greek Orthodox; the Druze; as well as Sunni and Shiite Muslims.[16]

Prior to the League of Nations Mandate, Lebanon had simply been a small part of a larger area known as Greater Syria, which also included modern-day Syria.[17] Yet the idea of an independent Lebanon, separate from Syria, was not uniformly accepted by all of the cultural communities that made Lebanon their home. Nearly all of the Maronites and Catholics desired an independent Lebanon; the Greek Orthodox community was divided on the issue but generally opposed uniting with Syria for fear of Muslim dominance.[18] Further, the separation of predominantly Christian Lebanon from predominantly Muslim Syria was vehemently opposed by Arab nationalists of Syria and surrounding Arab territories, as well as by Muslims within Greater Lebanon. While the new state was under the protection of the French Mandate, the underlying sectarian tension remained. Once Greater Lebanon became its own political unit, the destabilizing effects of the division surfaced.[19]

Political discord was somewhat abated in 1943, when the Maronite Christians and the Sunni Muslims reached an agreement referred to as the "National Pact."[20] This agreement represented the Muslims' acceptance of Greater Lebanon as an independent state separate from Syria and provided government offices that were fairly distributed among the diverse religious sects of Lebanon.[21] The pact resulted in a political system that recognized seventeen different religious sects, each of which was granted a position in the Lebanese government, more or less proportional to the respective size of each sect's portion of the population at the time.[22]

The Christian Maronites had control of the presidency due to their status as the largest sect; the Sunni Muslims (the second-largest group) gained control of the office of the prime minister, and the Shiite Muslims (the third-largest group) were given control of the speaker of the Parliament.[23] This proportional sectarian division of power also existed in the cabinet and other public offices. The seats in Parliament were divided similarly, although the Christian sects combined comprised 55 percent of the seats in accordance with an electoral law that maintained this allocation.[24] Because of the substantial executive powers of the presidency, the Maronite Christians became the strongest religious community in the era spanning from 1943 to 1975.[25] The last vestiges of French control disappeared in 1946, and "Lebanon was launched onto its multi-confessional independence."[26]

The Lebanese Shiites

Of the three main groups (Maronites, Sunnis, and Shiites), the Shiites were the least powerful politically. Not only was the speakership of the Parliament a much less powerful position than either the presidency or the premiership, but the Shiite community (mostly located in southern Lebanon and in the Bekaa Valley of northern Lebanon) was also poor and underdeveloped.[27] In the decades following the National Pact, however, the Shiite community began to mobilize politically and slowly transformed from passivity to activism.[28]

During and after the time of the Ottoman Empire, a few powerful families predominantly controlled Shiite politics. This continued until the 1960s, when young Shiites became disillusioned with the old style of politics and were attracted to new political parties advocating radical change. The parties included leftist and communist parties and Palestinian resistance movements,[29] but the primary ideological stance they shared was a condemnation of ethnic or religious-based discrimination.[30]

Imam Musa al-Sadr, a Muslim cleric born in Iran but of Lebanese descent, was instrumental in transforming the Lebanese Shiite community from a passive and poor minority into an active politicized force.[31] Al-Sadr encouraged Shiites to rise above the economic deprivation and social underdevelopment that characterized their community.[32]

In the late 1960s, al-Sadr created the Supreme Islamic Shiite Council of Lebanon, the first representative body for Shiite Muslims of Lebanon.[33] The Shiite Council worked to improve the social and economic conditions of the Shiite-dominated region of southern Lebanon by getting government development funds to construct schools and hospitals and by increasing the number of governmental positions held by Shiites.[34]

Al-Sadr also created the first Shiite political organization, Harakat al-Mahrumin, or the "Movement of the Disinherited," in 1974.[35] This movement included an armed militia branch known as Amal.[36] It received military training from Fatah, a militia branch of the Palestine Liberation Organization (PLO).[37] Although originally only a militia branch of the Movement of the Disinherited,

Amal eventually evolved into a separate political reformist party of its own.[38]

Amal's purpose was to improve the economic and political position of the Shiite community in Lebanon's sectarian government. It also developed into a force opposing the influence of the Palestinians in southern Lebanon.[39]

Anti-Israel Palestinian Militia in Lebanon

The presence of Palestinian groups, especially the Palestinian resistance movements, including the PLO, had a huge impact on the political climate of Lebanon throughout the latter half of the twentieth century. Palestinian refugees began to arrive in Lebanon by the thousands as a result of the 1948 Arab-Israeli War.[40] Then from 1970 to 1971, Palestinian fighters poured into Lebanon, after being expelled from Jordan.[41]

The Palestinian expulsion from Jordan transformed southern Lebanon into the only base of operations for the PLO from which it could launch actions against Israel.[42] Thus, armed Palestinian resistance groups—dedicated to the cause of "reclaiming" Palestine from the Israelis—grew strong in Lebanon.[43]

The Shiites generally supported the Palestinian cause, and many young Shiites joined the armed Palestinian militias, due in part to ideological agreement and in part to the fact that these Palestinian guerrilla forces offered substantial compensation to their fighters.[44] Thus the Palestinian resistance movement had significant influence in Lebanon and directly challenged the traditional political leaders of Lebanon.[45] In May 1973, there were several military clashes between the Palestinian resistance guerrilla forces and the Lebanese Army, foreshadowing the Lebanese Civil War, which would come only a few years later.[46]

The relationship between Imam Musa al-Sadr and the Palestinians was a complicated one, reflecting the instability and uncertainty that come from an unholy alliance between unusual partners. Although al-Sadr sympathized with their cause, he believed the growth of their movement in Lebanon would bring only further suffering to Lebanese Shiites, and thus he warned the PLO not to establish itself in southern Lebanon.[47] The PLO did not heed his warning and eventually there was a severe break of relations between the Palestinians and al-Sadr in the early years of the Lebanese Civil War.[48]

Lebanese Civil War (1975–1990) and the Birth of Hezbollah

The underlying contention between sectarian groups in Lebanon, since the nation's very inception, led to the Lebanese Civil War, beginning in 1975.[49] On one side of the conflict was the Lebanese National Movement (LNM), an umbrella organization consisting of a majority of the radical leftist and Muslim reform groups and Palestinian resistance groups, supported by the PLO and Arab states such as Syria and Libya.[50] The LNM sought radical political change in Lebanon, supported the presence of the PLO militia, and opposed the political dominance of the Christian Maronites.[51] On the other side, the conservative Christian parties consolidated as the Lebanese Front,[52] which supported the established political system and opposed the radical reform goals of the LNM and Palestinians, stood in opposition.[53] The military branches of the various Lebanese Front parties were united in a single armed body, the Lebanese Armed Forces.

At the beginning of the Lebanese Civil War, al-Sadr's reformist Amal party was aligned with the LNM.[54] But al-Sadr disliked the LNM's Druze leader, Kamal Jumblatt, because he believed that Jumblatt was exploiting the Shiites and recklessly expending Shiite lives in the war.[55] Because of his opposition to the PLO in Lebanon, al-Sadr and his Shiite Amal militia eventually supported the Syrian intervention against the LNM and the PLO in 1976.[56] Thus Amal became Syria's main proxy force throughout the civil war.[57]

In the years leading up to the Iranian Revolution, Amal and Fatah trained more than seven hundred of Khomeini's followers, who would eventually form the earliest incarnation of the Iranian Revolutionary Guards and Ministry of Intelligence after the Revolution.[58] Even Khomeini's two sons frequently visited Lebanon during the 1970s and received training in Amal and Fatah training camps.[59]

In 1976 and 1977, while Khomeini was in exile, Fatah hosted Khomeini's forces and provided them with advanced warfare training.[60] So even before the Islamic Republic and Hezbollah came into being, a strong alliance existed between these factions. As one historian stated, "The nucleus of the Revolutionary Guards and the intelligence apparatuses of the Islamic Republic were formed" in Lebanon during the mid-1970s.[61]

The strong influence that the Palestinian resistance movement wielded over the Lebanese Shiite community, as well as al-Sadr's distaste for the LNM and eventual opposition to the PLO, led to the development of a rift in the ranks of Amal.[62] In 1982, when the IDF invaded southern Lebanon in order to aid the Lebanese Armed Forces in fighting the PLO, the leader of Amal's political party (Nabih Berri, who had succeeded al-Sadr after his death in 1978) ordered the Amal militia not to resist the Israeli advancement.[63] Many of the Amal fighters disobeyed the order and joined the Palestinian resistance against Israel. The chief military commander of Amal's militia, Husayn al-Musawi, officially disassociated himself from Berri and called for resistance against the Israeli invasion,[64] forming the breakaway group Islamic Amal.[65]

Although Israel's 1982 invasion and occupation of southern Lebanon was executed to address the threat the PLO posed to northern Israel, the combination of that invasion, the vacuum created by the PLO's expulsion, and the subsequent split of Amal created the circumstances that led to the creation of a more radical group, Hezbollah.[66] Many of Hezbollah's original members had gained their military experience during the Lebanese Civil War fighting for Amal.[67]

At the same time, Iran was looking to export its radical revolution to the rest of the world. The expulsion of the PLO from Lebanon laid the "foundation . . . for the establishment in Lebanon of Iran's long arm of terror and dissemination of its Islamic Revolution."[68] Lebanese Shiites in need of help, coupled with Iran's desire to support the PLO against its enemy, Israel, would be a good testing ground for the revolution. As such, Iran and its Revolutionary Guards, many of whom had themselves been trained in Lebanon in the previous decade, radicalized Shiites in the aftermath of Israel's invasion of Lebanon.

Soon after the Islamic Revolution in 1979, the senior Shiite clerics of Lebanon had "officially declared their loyalty to the Imam Khomeini."[69] Sadeq Tabatabaei, the deputy head of the Iranian defense council and a distant relative of Ayatollah Khomeini by marriage, arrived in southern Lebanon dressed in the uniform of Amal and was enthusiastically welcomed by the Shiites.[70]

Early in Hezbollah's development, three Lebanese clerics traveled to Tehran to request Iran's support for a Lebanese Islamic resistance movement.[71] The generals of the Iranian Revolutionary Guards were eager to deploy troops to stop Israel from occupying Beirut. A documentary by BBC claims that because Iran was at the time embroiled in war with Iraq, Ayatollah Khomeini initially did not want to send any troops to Lebanon.[72] He believed the war in Lebanon might be a distraction and a trap engineered by the West to create a second front and divert Iranian troops from Iraq.[73]

The Iranian generals convinced the Ayatollah, however, that sending troops to Lebanon would "spread the Islamic Revolution."[74] Even so, the Ayatollah did not want to use Iranian troops directly to fight a revolution in Lebanon. Instead, he decided to train and support local Shiite soldiers to do the fighting. Those trainees eventually became Hezbollah.[75] Although Hezbollah was managed by a deliberative body known as the Shura Council, Ayatollah Khomeini remained the ultimate leader of the organization.[76] According to its founding constitution, whenever the council could not reach an agreement by majority vote, Khomeini would have the final say.[77] Khomeini also installed a representative on the council, Hojat al-Islam Ali Akbar Mohtashemi-Pour, to guide and form Hezbollah according to Iran's wishes.[78]

> "[t]he aims of Hizballah . . . were predictable: the ejection of foreign forces, primarily those of Israel, the United States, and France; the final eradication of the Jewish State; the liberation of Jerusalem; and the subjection of the Lebanese Christians to Islamic law."[79]

On June 6, 1982, when Israeli forces entered Lebanon, Iran sent a delegation of senior-ranking military officials to Damascus, offering assistance to the Syrians, the Lebanese Shiites, and the Palestinians.[80] According to a report published by *Middle Eastern Military Studies*, "It is almost certain that even minus the Israeli invasion Iran would have been seeking ways to channel its attention to the Lebanese arena," but the invasion provided Iran with the convenient opportunity to "establish its own foothold in Lebanon."[81] According to another report, Hezbollah would not have come into existence without Iran's political, financial, and logistical support.[82] Once established, "[t]he aims of Hizballah . . . were predictable: the ejection of foreign forces, primarily those of Israel, the United States, and France; the final eradication of the Jewish State; the liberation of Jerusalem; and the subjection of the Lebanese Christians to Islamic law."[83]

Even in the beginning, as Iran was exporting its model of radical jihadist terror, the proxy wars became the stark reality we still face today, in which global powers train, support, and finance smaller nations and militias to battle one another for land, resources, and influence. Disillusionment with the old Amal organization among the Shiite community led to the emergence of clandestine radical Islamist factions in the early 1980s, which focused their attacks against the United States and other multinational forces that had come to aid the Lebanese Armed Forces.[84] These groups had ties to Iran and were under Syria's protection.[85] In 1985, several of these radical Shiite groups joined together in the Syrian-controlled Bekaa Valley to sign the 1985 Open Letter,[86] which has been referred to as the founding act of Hezbollah.[87]

The 1985 Open Letter claimed that Israel was "the American spearhead in our Islamic world. It is a usurping enemy that must be fought until the usurped right is returned to its owners. . . . Therefore, our confrontation of this entity must end with its obliteration from existence."[88] Accordingly, with its historic and ideological roots emerging from such diverse groups and places as the PLO, the LNM, Amal, Syria, and Iran, Hezbollah became the new rallying point for Shiite Muslims in Lebanon and a fierce competitor with the original Amal party for the hearts and minds of the Shiite people.

Iran provided Hezbollah with several forms of support. Early in its formational years, Hezbollah members traveled to Iran to study religion.[89] Iran sent a contingent of the Revolutionary Guards to train the Lebanese movement's militia and to manage its incoming financial support.[90] It also used the economic influence of an oil subsidy to persuade Syria to allow the resistance movement to use the Bekaa Valley, which was under Syrian occupation, as a haven to gather and organize the anti-Israel movement.[91]

Sheikh Subhi al-Tufayli, a founding member and former secretary general of Hezbollah, said, "[The Iranian Revolutionary Guard] helped to get us established. We made good use of their training. The Iranians inspired our young men. That helped us confront Israel's armies."[92] Mohsen Rafiqdoost, a Revolutionary Guard commander, boasted, "We did it. We set up the holy and respectable Hezbollah force."[93]

Supporting Hezbollah

Iran has provided approximately $140 million of support to Hezbollah annually.[94] In a 2003 case related to the 1983 bombing of the U.S. embassy in Beirut, the United States District Court for the District of Columbia found that although support for Hezbollah "was not specifically provided for in Iran's annual budget, 'the supreme religious leader and the president openly acknowledged that Iran was providing financial support, in fact proudly acknowledged that Iran was providing financial support' for [Hezbollah]."[95] Iran's Martyrs Foundation[96] has financed Hezbollah's welfare initiatives designed to encourage the families of Hezbollah militants to support their family members' decisions to join Hezbollah's fight.[97]

As of 1988, the Martyrs Foundation was paying "100 per cent of the medical expenses for Hezbollah's injured fighters and 70 per cent of the cost of caring for injured civilians," and in that year, the foundation built a hospital in Beirut to facilitate its medical support.[98] In the early 1990s, Hezbollah focused efforts on agricultural development in the Shiite-dominated Bekaa Valley of northern Lebanon, which Iran facilitated by donating tractors, digging wells, and providing agricultural training to the group.[99]

> According to a case study published by the Terrorism Research Initiative, it is doubtful whether Hezbollah would have developed the centralized decision-making structures needed to formulate . . . [its long-term strategy] had Iran not provided it with political support and a sanctuary in the Beka'a Valley. Likewise, the group's "hearts and minds" campaign, which was predicated on the provision of a wide-

range of social services, depended on generous long-term Iranian funding.[100]

In August 2011, the foreign minister of Turkey said that an arms shipment from Iran to Syria was intercepted by Turkish authorities, and it was believed that Hezbollah was the intended recipient.[101] Hezbollah also maintains a representative office in Tehran to help coordinate Iranian support.[102]

In a 2011 interview, Hezbollah's chief of media relations, Ibrahim Moussawi, "conceded that the organization's provision of social services depended on the generosity of both Iran's government and its principal Ayatollahs, who contribute independently of the state." [103]

Iran's Use of Hezbollah as Its Proxy of Terror

On several occasions, Iran has directly influenced Hezbollah's decision making, using the group as a tool to further its own goals.[104] An early instance of this was the April 18, 1983, bombing of the U.S. embassy in Beirut.[105] An explosive-laden vehicle crashed into the front entrance of the embassy, destroying seven floors of the building's center section, killing sixty-three people, and injuring more than a hundred.[106] Hezbollah carried out the attack, but it was directed and supported by Iran. One expert on Iranian sponsorship of terrorism, Patrick Clawson,[107] testified in *Dammarell v. Islamic Republic of Iran* (a class-action suit brought by survivors of and estates of those killed in the 1983 bombing) that "[t]here's no question that Iran was responsible for the selection of the target, provided much of the information for how to carry out the bombing, the expertise for how to build the bomb . . . [and] provided financial support for the bombers. It has the Iranians' fingerprints all over it." [108]

Ambassador Robert Oakley was assigned the task of determining who was responsible for the 1983 U.S. embassy attack, and he testified that it was "very clear that Islamic Jihad [Hezbollah] was behind the bombing," and he was confident "that the government of Iran was involved directly in the [Hezbollah] organization, which was created, armed, trained, protected, [and] provided technical assistance by the Iranian Revolutionary Guards."[109] In *Dammarell*, the D.C. District Court also found that the Iranian Ministry of Intelligence and Security (MOIS) was responsible for training Hezbollah operatives to be "one of the most capable and professional terrorist organizations in the world."[110]

Later that same year, Hezbollah attacked American and French forces participating in the four-nation Multinational Force (MNF).[111] The MNF was a United Nations–authorized peacekeeping force sent to Lebanon for the purpose of stabilizing the region after Israel invaded Lebanon in an effort to eradicate the PLO, which had taken refuge there.[112] The Iranian ambassador to Syria sent a request to Ahmad Kan'ani, the commander of the Iranian Revolutionary Guard contingent stationed in the Bekaa Valley, for Hezbollah to attack the MNF. Kan'ani then met with the leaders of Hezbollah to plan the attack.[113] Part of this attack included an Iranian-trained suicide bomber who drove a truck into the U.S. Marine barracks in Beirut, killing 246 people.[114] Another bomber killed fifty-eight French soldiers the same day.[115]

In a civil case against the Iranian government brought by the victims of the bombing and their estates, the D.C. District Court found that "[b]ased on the evidence presented at trial, . . . [the Iranian Ministry of Information and Security] acted as a conduit for the Islamic Republic of Iran's provision of funds to Hezbollah, provided explosives to Hezbollah and, at all times relevant to these proceedings, exercised operational control over Hezbollah."[116]

Another instance of Iran's use of Hezbollah was the Lebanon hostage crisis from 1982 to 1991, a period during which Shiite radicals kidnapped several foreigners.[117] The hostage-taking spree began when three Iranian diplomats were killed by Christian Lebanese forces in northern Lebanon. Iran held the United States responsible for these murders because of American support of the Christian Lebanese forces, and so Iran targeted the United States by kidnapping Americans and other Westerners and holding them hostage.[118]

The first hostage taken was David Dodge, the president of the American University of Beirut. He was kidnapped directly by Iranian agents and then smuggled into Iran via Syria.[119] Once the United States determined Iran's involvement, it used Syria to pressure Iran into releasing Dodge a year later.[120] Publicly, no demands were made in exchange for Dodge's release. It has been reported, however, that the American forces unofficially agreed not to work against the establishment of the fledgling Hezbollah organization, which was just beginning to form at that time.[121] After the first kidnapping, Iran switched to indirect tactics, using local proxies to carry out its operations instead of direct involvement.[122] Its main proxy in Lebanon, of course, was the newly formed Hezbollah.[123]

Over the course of a decade, 110 Westerners were kidnapped.[124] Strong evidence suggests that Hezbollah was involved in a majority of those abductions, that the kidnappings were masterminded by two Hezbollah military commanders (Imad Mughniyah and Husayn Al-Musawi), and that the hostages were primarily held in Hezbollah and Iranian Revolutionary Guard facilities.[125] Hezbollah's decision-making council frequently criticized the kidnappings, believing the strategy would backfire and "[ruin] the image of the resistance."[126] Hezbollah's secretary general, Hassan Nasrallah, stated with regret that the fallout of the hostage situation had landed completely on Hezbollah.[127]

The statements of the party leaders contrasted with the evidence that Hezbollah's forces were instrumental in the kidnappings, indicating that Iran either bypassed Hezbollah's leaders, directly instructing the military commanders to carry out these kidnappings, or forced Hezbollah's leadership to do its bidding despite the council's distaste for the campaign.[128] Throughout the hostage operation, it was clear that Iran was calling the shots, making demands, and incrementally releasing hostages as those demands were met.[129]

The longest-held hostage was Associated Press correspondent Terry A. Anderson, who was in captivity from March 1985 until December 1991.[130] Anderson was treated terribly during his captivity. He was kept in chains and shackles, fed meagerly with bread and water, denied basic hygiene and medical needs, and subjected to psychological and emotional abuse by way of threats of execution and false promises of release.[131]

After his release, Anderson brought a lawsuit against Iran and its Ministry of Intelligence and Security, alleging that Iran had backed and supported the Hezbollah terrorists who held him captive.[132] Anderson offered evidence of this at trial, which included his own extensive personal knowledge of Hezbollah, and his eyewitness account of the Iranian troops training Hezbollah recruits in the Bekaa Valley that enabled him to identify his captors. Further, during his captivity, Anderson was visited once by the self-identified Iranian liaison between Hezbollah and Iran. Additionally, at one point in his captivity, Anderson was held in a basement beneath barracks occupied by Iranian Revolutionary Guard troops.[133]

In light of the substantial evidence provided, the district court found in Anderson's favor and granted a judgment of more than $300 million in compensatory and punitive damages against Iran and the Ministry of Intelligence and Security.[134] Similar cases were brought by other hostages, with similar results.[135]

Iran's use of Hezbollah as a tool of terror extends beyond the Middle East to other parts of the world. In 1992, for example, the Israeli embassy in Buenos Aires, Argentina, was bombed,[136] and two years later a Jewish community center in Buenos Aires was also bombed.[137] In both cases, a terrorist drove a vehicle containing explosives into the buildings, killing several people and injuring hundreds. Although hard evidence was scant, both American and Argentine officials have suspected that Iran sponsored the 1992 attack.[138] The Argentine chief prosecutor, Alberto Nisman, formally charged Hezbollah and Iran with the 1994 bombing.[139] Four days after he had accused high-level Argentine officials of covering up Hezbollah and Iran's involvement in the attack, Nisman was found dead under mysterious circumstances.[140]

The Anti-Defamation League reported on an investigation by the Argentine Intelligence Service into the 1994 Argentina incident, which concluded that Iran had instigated the attack. The ADL stated that the Iranian intelligence minister, Ali Fallahian, oversaw the operation.[141] The investigation also concluded that the actual execution of the 1994 attack was carried out by Hezbollah and led by military commander Imad Mughniyah.[142] The local Hezbollah cell in Argentina that carried out the attack had been carefully established and maintained by the Iranian embassy for more than a decade before the attack.[143]

Leading up to the attack, the number of Iranian diplomats visiting the Iranian embassy increased dramatically, perhaps delivering equipment, intelligence, or communications in preparation for the attack.[144] The investigation concluded that several Iranian governmental agencies, including the Iranian Islamic Guidance Ministry, the Revolutionary Guards, and the Intelligence Ministry, were involved in preparing for the attack and supporting Hezbollah's actions.[145]

There is no doubt that Iran has been the principal inspiration, supporter, mentor, and guide to Hezbollah. History does not hide the fact that Iran has "played the leading role" in creating and sponsoring Hezbollah.[146] Iran is clearly Hezbollah's ideological parent. From Iran's perspective, Hezbollah is the realization of Iran's "zealous campaign to spread the message" of the Islamic Revolution.[147] In fact, in March 2016, Iran broke with other Arab states when the Gulf Cooperation Council—a regional governing coalition including Saudi Arabia, the UAE, Qatar, Oman, Kuwait, and Bahrain—designated Hezbollah as a terrorist organization.[148] Iranian leaders issued a series of statements condemning the GCC move, blaming Israel, and reiterating Hezbollah's place as integral to Muslim ideals and integrity standing against what they refer to as the "Zionist regime."[149]

Raanan Gissin, senior advisor to the late Israeli prime minister Ariel Sharon, said,

> There's peace now. It's a fragile peace, a deceptive peace. . . . It's deceptive because at any moment, these 40,000 rockets and missiles on the border with Lebanon could be sprung and fired against Israel. We have a [Shiite] village here . . . on the border. . . . [T]here is clearly an understanding and orders from Hezbollah not to start anything right now because it doesn't suit either Hezbollah or Iran, but on every September 11, they fire rockets into Israel. Why? To commemorate 9/11. . . . Which, in a sense, shows you what has changed, from the first Lebanese war, to the second Lebanese war, and which requires us to be on guard 24/7.[150]

While Iran uses Hezbollah to spread its anti-Israel and anti-U.S. terrorist attacks around the world, it is only the beginning of Iranian influence on jihadists and terrorist organizations. The Ayatollah's radical Islamic ideology requires attacks against Israel to wipe it off the map, attacks against the United States to knock us out of position as the global superpower, and attacks against anyone who refuses to bow a knee to Iran. In fact, Iranian terror will stop at nothing short of global domination.

There is no doubt that Iran has been the principal inspiration, supporter, mentor, and guide to Hezbollah.

8

Beyond Terrorism

A Much Larger Goal

Iran's zeal to export the Islamic Revolution and expand its network of terror did not end with the creation of Hezbollah. That was simply the beginning. A much larger and more sinister goal is afoot. And in order to achieve this goal, Iran is creating a network of terror with a global geographic reach. In order to defeat Israel and the United States, Iran is working with its centuries-old rivals, even funding certain terrorist groups in some regions while battling those same entities in other regions. These unholy alliances between Iran, the Muslim Brotherhood, and Hamas destabilize communities, murder countless humans, and endanger our national security.

> In order to defeat Israel and the United States, Iran is working with its centuries-old rivals, even funding certain terrorist groups in some regions while battling with those same entities in other regions.

The Iranian regime strictly follows Twelver Shiism, the dominant branch of Shiite Islam.[1] The Twelvers believe in twelve imams who are directly descended from Muhammad through his daughter Fatima and her husband, Ali (the first imam).[2] Fatima and Ali's two sons were the second and the third imams, and so it continued through the family lineage. Shiites believe all but the twelfth imam were martyred by the Sunnis.[3]

The twelfth imam, Abu Al Qasim Muhammad ibn Hasan ibn Ali, called *al-Mahdi* (the Guided One), went into occultation[4] (*ghayba*; disappearance or hiding) when he was five years old. Shiites believe that the Mahdi "disappeared down a well in what is now a golden-domed [Shiite] shrine called Al []Askariyyayn, in Samarra, Iraq."[5] The Mahdi will reappear sometime near the end of the world. Shiites further believe that Jesus will also return and assist the Mahdi to convert the world to Shiite Islam.[6] "'The Imam Mahdi will lead the forces of righteousness against the forces of evil in one final apocalyptic battle in which the enemies of the Imam will be defeated.'"[7] Accordingly, Shiites believe they must hasten the Mahdi's return. Once he returns, the Mahdi will rule from Jerusalem.[8]

Jerusalem, a place of great historic and spiritual significance to Judaism and Christianity, is also extremely important to both Sunni and Shiite Muslims. It was the first *Qibla*, or the direction in which early Muslims would face during prayer, until Allah commanded that the *Qibla* be changed to Mecca.[9] Sometime around the year AD 622,[10] Muhammad is said to have taken "a Journey by night . . . To the Farthest Mosque."[11] Muslim scholars believe that his journey took him to the site of Solomon's temple in Jerusalem, and thus the Al-Aqsa Mosque was later built on the Temple Mount to commemorate that journey, making Jerusalem the third holiest city in Islam after Mecca and Medina.[12] "It is this deep conviction and celebration of the Prophet's Night Journey that manifests itself in scholarship, art, and architecture, but mostly in praying at Al-Aqsa Mosque."[13] Further, Jerusalem is especially important to Shiite Islam followers because they believe that the Mahdi, the twelfth imam, who is expected to return at the end of time and establish a worldwide Islamic Caliphate, will rule from Jerusalem.[14]

Because of Jerusalem's importance to the Shiite faith, when

Iran established Hezbollah in Lebanon in the early 1980s, Ayatollah Khomeini's purpose was to achieve "a forward strategic position which makes proximity to Jerusalem possible."[15]

In addition to exporting the Islamic Revolution around the world, the 1979 Iranian Revolution created a different focus for Iran. Rather than concentrate on the division between Sunnis and Shiites, Iran revived the fight between *dar al-Islam* and *dar al-harb*.[16] As mentioned earlier, this fight is primarily against Western influence, specifically the United States and Israel. Dan Meridor, deputy prime minister of Israel, has noted:

> Iran uses rhetoric that we haven't heard for decades. . . . Israel should not exist, has no right to exist. Israel, I quote, is a "cancerous tumor that should be removed from the Middle East." It's said again and again. So when you see a country that says you're not legitimate, you will not exist in the end of the game here, and we go nuclear and are involved in terror like no other country, to put it in an understatement, it's a cause for concern. . . . I don't have the luxury not to believe it. It was a mistake that we made in our history where we thought: "Yeah, they only say it; they don't mean it. How can they really do this thing like this? Can they really eliminate the people? Can they destroy people? Can they build extermination camps?" But we don't take things easily anymore.[17]

Despite centuries of division and hatred between Sunnis and Shiites, what is often overlooked is that both Sunnis and Shiites claim the same religion. They have the same prophet, the same basic teachings, and the same concept of jihad against nonbelievers. One thing is vitally important to remember: Sunnis and Shiites have more in common among themselves than with the rest of the world's religious traditions.

What the Western world does not understand about Islam is that its adherents' first and foremost identity is being a Muslim, without the limitations of national boundaries or allegiances. There is no such thing called Sunni *dar al-Islam* and Shiite *dar al-Islam*. There is only one *dar al-Islam* and then there is the rest of the world, *dar al-harb*, or the house of war.

Sunnis and Shiites understand this basic distinction and easily set aside internal conflict to deal with an external power. That is to say, the Sunni-Shiite conflict is secondary only to the Muslim–non-Muslim conflict. According to one author, "One of the myths of modern Islamist terrorism is that Sunni and Shi'a do not get along; but when it comes to common enemies or objectives or using force to replicate the Iranian revolution in other localities, they work together quite frequently."[18]

> **Sunnis and Shiites have more in common among themselves than with the rest of the world's religious traditions.**

There is no better example of such a display of unity against the Western influence, the external power, than the Iranian Revolution of 1979. The doctrine of jihad against nonbelievers coupled with the model of the Iranian Revolution has been a strong impetus for both Sunni as well as Shiite jihadist organizations.[19] Iran sees the United States and Israel as such grave, existential, external threats to Islam that thwarting and ultimately destroying both the United States and Israel are important enough to temporarily put aside theological differences with heretical Sunni organizations, such as the Muslim Brotherhood and Hamas, making these some of the scariest partnerships in the unholy alliance.

Iran and the Muslim Brotherhood

Al-Ikhwan al-Muslimun, the Muslim Brotherhood, was founded in Egypt in 1928 by a Sunni Islamist revivalist named Hassan al-Banna.[20] It is Egypt's oldest and largest Islamist organization.[21]

The group's purpose was to revive traditional Sharia principles in Egypt and to cleanse the nation of the Western influences that had come with British imperialism.[22] It began not as a political movement, but as a socioreligious movement that sought to improve the morality and religiosity of the Muslim community in Egypt.[23] The Muslim Brotherhood's early projects were focused on social welfare, such as building schools and mosques. This was an effort to draw the general population to its side before beginning its real work toward its bigger and more sinister goals.

Though the Muslim Brotherhood is considered to have spawned many of the Islamist revivalist parties throughout the Middle East, for most of its existence, the Brotherhood did not have legal status as an authorized political party in Egypt.[24] In fact, it had been banned in Egypt (and elsewhere in the Arab world) for many years. The group was not legalized in Egypt until after the Egyptian Revolution in 2011.[25] Its legalization was short-lived because the Egyptian government reimposed the ban after the 2013 coup, which overthrew Muslim Brotherhood–supported President Mohamed Morsi.[26]

Although a fundamental doctrinal disagreement exists between the Islamic Republic of Iran and the Muslim Brotherhood because the Muslim Brotherhood is a Sunni organization, a closer look at the relationship between the two reveals that both are willing and able to set aside their differences when needed to form an unholy alliance to fight their common enemies: Israel, the United States, and the rest of the free and prosperous Western civilization.[27]

Iran's Ties to the Muslim Brotherhood

Iran's direct ties to the Muslim Brotherhood are less visible than its ties to Hezbollah, but they do exist. Historically, the Muslim Brotherhood played an integral part in spawning the Islamic revivalism movement in Iran long before the Iranian Revolution of 1979.[28]

The Society of Islamic Devotees,[29] founded by Iranian cleric Navvab Safavi in 1945, greatly influenced the proponents of the Islamic revolution that followed decades later. It was "the first organized attempt to break away from the traditional quietism of the Shi'ite clergy in Iran. It opened the way for the next generation of radical clergy who finally succeeded in . . . establishing an Islamic government."[30]

Although the Society of Islamic Devotees was a Shiite organization, its founders believed that the sectarian contentions between Shiites and Sunnis had to be set aside in order to fight the greater enemy of Islam, the West.[31] That belief had also been held by Hassan al-Banna, the founder of the Muslim Brotherhood, and Ayatollah Khomeini—both of whom were Safavi's friends.[32] In 1954, Safavi met with Muslim Brotherhood leaders and, through their influence, became a strong supporter of the Palestinian cause.[33] Safavi also inspired Ayatollah Khamenei, the current Supreme Leader of Iran, to become involved in politics, and Khamenei even spent time translating two books into Farsi written by a prominent member of the Muslim Brotherhood, Sayyid Qutb.[34] Qutb's books have been widely read in Iran and have been referred to as "the most circulated Islamist tracts."[35] Khamenei referred to Qutb as one of only three "great thinkers of importance" in modern Islam.[36]

At the start of the 1979 revolution, the Muslim Brotherhood offered support to the Iranian revolutionaries.[37] But the Brotherhood was temporarily forced to publicly distance itself from the Iranian Revolution when, in 1981, Egyptian president Anwar al-Sadat was assassinated by an Islamic radical.[38] Though this event led the Brotherhood to be more cautious, it continued to build bridges between itself and Iran. During the Iran-Iraq War in the late 1980s, Iran's ambassador to the Vatican established ties with some figures of the Muslim Brotherhood throughout Europe.[39] The Iranian embassy in the Vatican even began publishing some Muslim Brotherhood literature.[40]

Another connection between Iran and the Muslim Brotherhood exists in the friendship between Iran and Hassan al-Turabi, a Brotherhood-linked leader in Sudan.[41] In 1985, Turabi founded the National Islamic Front (NIF) in Sudan.[42] The NIF is an outgrowth of the Muslim Brotherhood, with the same "pan-Islamic" goals and aspirations.[43] After leading a coup and assuming control of the government of Sudan in 1989,[44] Sudan's leadership decided to "transform Sudan into a base and safe haven for Islamist movements."[45] Turabi also developed close ties with Iran's political and intelligence leaders in the early 1990s.

Iranian president Akbar Hashemi Rafsanjani called Sudan the "vanguard of the Islamic revolution [on] the African continent."[46] He sent several hundred Revolutionary Guards and Quds Force soldiers to train the Islamist Sudanese forces and also offered to provide tens of millions of dollars in financial aid.[47] Further, Iran installed a man named Majid Kamel as the Iranian representative to Sudan. Kamel had previously served in Lebanon, where he played an important role in the formation of Hezbollah.[48]

Through his close ties to both the Muslim Brotherhood and to Iran, Turabi acted as the go-between for Sunni al-Qaeda, Shiite Hezbollah, and the Iranian intelligence service, brokering meetings and cooperative training between al-Qaeda and Hezbollah.[49] In fact, since the early 1990s, the Sudanese government has provided a safe haven for Islamist groups—especially those Iran funded and influenced—to conduct training camps, transport supplies and valuables, and shelter operatives.[50] The world's most dangerous Sunni terrorist organizations, Shiite Lebanese terrorist organizations, and the world's largest exporter of terror, Shiite Iran, are joining to train together, support one another, and plot together. What are they plotting? Global takeover.

Iran was also indirectly involved in Sudan's use of a nonprofit charity to sponsor terrorism. The Third World Relief Agency (TWRA), which brought together Sunni and Shiite Muslims to provide weapons to the Muslim fighters in Bosnia, was created and administered by Sudanese citizens.[51] A Bosnian politician named Hasan Cengic played an instrumental role in generating funding from the Shiite community, while al-Qaeda was the bridge to the Sunni community.[52] Cengic, the former Bosnian deputy minister of defense, was accused in 1996 of being an Iranian agent. He had maintained "close personal ties" to Iran, which led to his dismissal from the Bosnian government in 1996 due to pressure from the United States.[53]

Iran has also supported other branches of the Muslim Brotherhood. In 1993, Iran and Algeria temporarily broke off diplomatic relations when Algeria accused Iran of supporting an Algerian Muslim Brotherhood offshoot, the Islamic Salvation Front.[54] Although it denied providing such support, evidence had surfaced that Iran had supplied the organization with more than $7 million.[55] Iran also financially supported the Turkish branch of the Muslim Brotherhood in the 1990s to help it win elections. Additionally, Iran formed a close alliance with Brotherhood member Necmettin Erbakan after he became prime minister of Turkey in 1996.[56]

In January 2009, Mohammad Mahdi Akef, then the Muslim Brotherhood's leader, said about Iran's former Supreme Leader, Ayatollah Khomeini: "The Muslim Brotherhood supports the ideas and thoughts of the founder of the Islamic Republic. . . . Khomeini's idea, especially with regard to the Palestinian issue, is the continuation of the Muslim Brotherhood's attitude toward fighting occupation."[57] Iran has also made recent favorable public statements toward the Brotherhood. In early 2012, after the Egyptian Revolution afforded the Muslim Brotherhood more power in the Egyptian government, the Iranian foreign minister, Ali Akbar Salehi, stated that "Tehran is in constant contact with the Muslim Brotherhood."[58]

When Sunni Foes Become Friendly:
Saudi Arabia and the Muslim Brotherhood

Saudi Arabia's attempts to draw the Brotherhood away from Iran in the wake of the Iran nuclear deal further demonstrate the significance of the relationship between Iran and the Muslim Brotherhood.[59] In June 2015, Saudi Arabia, a longtime enemy of Iran, hosted delegations of several Hamas and Muslim Brotherhood leaders in an effort to contain a newly emboldened Iran and try to use the Muslim Brotherhood to counter increasing Iranian influence in the region.[60] Seeking closer cooperation with the Muslim Brotherhood is an anomaly, however, because Saudi Arabia has historically opposed the Muslim Brotherhood, despite the fact that both belong to the Sunni Muslim sect.[61] In July 2013, for example, Saudi Arabia joined the United Arab Emirates in pledging $12 billion of aid to Egypt, apparently for the purpose of helping the nation eliminate the Muslim Brotherhood.[62]

Egypt is a vital ally of the Saudi kingdom, and the Brotherhood openly opposes the Egyptian government. The friendship between Saudi Arabia and Egypt is not only political; it's personal. In 2003, the Egyptian military helped prevent an assassination attempt against Saudi Arabia's King Abdullah (then crown prince).[63] Saudi Arabia also fears that a Muslim Brotherhood–controlled Egypt would slip into political anarchy, and that the Egyptian military is the only force capable of maintaining stability in the country.[64] The bad blood between the Brotherhood and Saudi Arabia extends even further into their past history because the Brotherhood supported Saddam Hussein, who had made threats against Saudi Arabia during the Gulf War.[65] In addition to regional political reasons, the Muslim Brotherhood also resents Saudi Arabia because Saudis are too close to the West. Furthermore, the Brotherhood believes that the Saudi Arabian royal family is not a legitimate regime.[66]

The fact that Saudi Arabia has now turned around and offered a hand of friendship to the Muslim Brotherhood is incredibly significant. According to Mustafa Alani, the director of defense studies at the Gulf Research Center, Saudi Arabia desires "to distance the Muslim Brotherhood from Iran" and then "to use the Muslim Brotherhood to counter Iranian influence."[67] The mounting tension between Saudi Arabia and Iran is further evidenced by Saudi Arabia's complete severing of diplomatic relations with Iran in January 2016.[68] It is clear from this behavior that Saudi Arabia considers an Iran–Muslim Brotherhood alliance not only possible, but a likely and substantial threat.

Iran's Relationship with Hamas

Iran's number-one enemy is Israel. So it's no surprise that the clearest ties between Iran and the Muslim Brotherhood are to be found in Harkat al-Muqawamah al-Islamiyyah (Islamic Resistance Movement), more commonly known as Hamas, which is a Palestinian offshoot of the Muslim Brotherhood. The United States and several other countries and entities have officially designated Hamas as a terrorist organization.[69] When conflict between Israel and Hamas arose in the Gaza Strip after Hamas came to power in 2006, Iran strongly supported Hamas.[70]

Despite sectarian differences, Iran has a strong incentive to maintain friendship with Hamas because, through Gaza, Iran gains access to the southern border of its enemy, Israel. Iran and Hamas share the long-term goal of seeing Israel completely destroyed, and this is the foundation of their relationship.[71] Former Iranian president Mahmoud Ahmadinejad stated in 2005 that Israel "must be wiped out from the map of the world," echoing similar statements made by Iran's former Supreme Leader, Ayatollah Ruhollah Khomeini.[72]

Efraim Halevy, Mossad's ninth director, said:

Ahmadinejad[, as] I've often said, is one of the greatest Israeli assets we could ever have thought of because he's so clear in what he is saying, and he's so offensive in what he's saying, that we don't have to explain to the world at large what it is the Iranians are about. We don't have to explain to the world what the Iranian threat is.[73]

In a meeting with Hamas leaders in 2008, Iran's current Supreme Leader, Ayatollah Ali Khamenei, said, "God's greetings be upon the Palestinian nation who [is] firmly resisting against these unique and unprecedented crimes [of Israel]."[74] He continued: "The stance of Hamas and its Prime Minister Mr. Ismail Haniyeh, who has been elected by the Palestinian people, are very brave and strong and this is a source of joy."[75]

In another speech in March 2009, the Ayatollah referred to Hamas's anti-Israel actions as constituting "the brightest page in Palestinian history of the last hundred years."[76] He also made a statement that may have been indirectly addressed to the Muslim Brotherhood in Egypt: "It will be appropriate for the Egyptian brothers to open the way for aid to move [into Gaza] and allow Muslim countries and nations to carry out their duty in this regard."[77]

In December 2009, Khamenei met with Hamas's political leader, Khaled Meshaal, and stated that "[t]he Islamic Republic of Iran considers the issue of Palestine as a domestic issue and views supporting the Palestinian people as a religious and Islamic duty."[78] In 2015, Khamenei predicted that Israel's demise will come in the near future: "I'd say [to Israel] that they will not see [the end] of these 25 years. . . . God willing, there will be no such thing as a Zionist regime in 25 years. Until then, struggling, heroic and jihadi morale will leave no moment of serenity for Zionists."[79]

The Muslim Brotherhood has been no less vocal about its desire to see Israel destroyed. The Egyptian Muslim Brotherhood's general guide, Mohammed Badie, stated in a speech in 2012 posted to the Brotherhood's website: "[T]he sole goal for [all Muslims is] the recovery of al Aqsa Mosque, freeing it from the filth of the Zionists, and imposing Muslim rule throughout beloved Palestine." [80]

In spite of their shared hatred of Israel, the relationship between Iran and Hamas has been anything but smooth, due to the underlying sectarian differences between Shiite Iran and Sunni Hamas. When Hamas supported the Sunni forces opposing Iran-supported Bashar al-Assad in the Syrian Civil War, Iran ceased supporting Hamas. [81] Yet, when fighting between Hamas and Israel resumed in July 2014, Iran eventually returned to supporting Hamas. On August 4, 2014, Major General Mohammad Ali Jafari stated that the Iranian Revolutionary Guards were "ready to support the Palestinian resistance in different dimensions. . . . When speaking about defending the Muslims, Shiites and Sunnis are of no difference to us, and our devotion and dedication goes to all the Muslim world and the oppressed." [82]

In April 2015, Western intelligence officials reported that the Revolutionary Guards had transferred tens of millions of dollars to Hamas by order of Qasem Soleimani, commander of the Quds Force. [83] In July 2014, Iran's Supreme Leader, Ayatollah Khamenei, and General Soleimani publicly praised Palestinian resistance in general, and Hamas in particular, the latter stating that Iran would "continue to perform our religious duty to support and help the resistance till the moment of victory when the resistance will turn the earth, the air and the sea into hell for Zionists." [84]

Yet in August 2015, a senior Hamas official stated that "all assistance [from Iran] has stopped—both civilian aid to the Gaza Strip and military assistance to Hamas. . . . The relations between Hamas and Iran are not advancing in a direction in which [Hamas] is interested and aren't improving to the degree the organization wants in order to help the Palestinian issue." [85] That very same month, Iranian Foreign Ministry spokeswoman Marzieh Afkham said, "Iran's support for all resistance groups continues similar to the past."[86]

Several other Iranian officials have since given statements supporting Hamas, praising its efforts in fighting Israel and promising Hamas weapons and ammunition.[87] However, Palestinian media have reported that senior Hamas officials have traveled to Lebanon to meet with Iranian Revolutionary Guard officers,[88] because they (Hamas) have had difficulty in arranging meetings with high-ranking Iranian diplomats inside Iran to solidify the agreement.[89]

Despite the conflicting reports of the Iranian-Hamas relationship, there is ample recent evidence to support the conclusion that, in practice, Iran continues to support Hamas in Gaza. In August 2015, a report surfaced that a Hamas soldier named Ibraheem Adel Shehadeh Shaer was arrested by Israeli security while trying to cross into Israel from Gaza.[90] While in custody, he gave substantial information about Hamas's activities and the Iranian support that Hamas is receiving.[91] Shaer stated that Iran is supporting Hamas by providing "cash, advanced weapons and sophisticated electronic equipment."[92] Shaer also said that Hamas fighters had received Iranian training on the use of paragliders to infiltrate Israeli airspace.[93]

On February 8, 2016, Iranian Foreign Ministry spokesman Hossein Jaberi Ansari said that supporting Palestinian resistance groups, including Hamas, has been a "fixed policy" of Tehran ever since the 1979 revolution.[94] That same month, a senior Hamas leader, Khalil Abu Leila, said that Iran is providing help to Hamas, that the group was very grateful for this aid, and that any reports claiming that Iran was no longer assisting Hamas were false propaganda published by those who oppose the Palestinian cause.[95]

With Iranian support, Hamas has carried out its terrorism against Israel, from launching missiles at schools and civilian areas to terrorist attacks in the form of shooting or stabbing sprees, including one in early March 2016 that resulted in the death of a U.S.

citizen and veteran of the wars in Afghanistan and Iraq.[96] Hamas has continued to build tunnels through which it can attack Israel.[97] After a number of tunnels collapsed in early 2016 due to heavy rainfall, killing Hamas members in the process, Ismail Haniyeh, the Hamas prime minister, openly referred to the tunnel building as an effort "to defend Gaza and become a jumping-off point to all Palestine."[98]

Foreseeing a renewed attempt to use an underground tunnel network as a weapon against Israel, Israeli prime minister Benjamin Netanyahu publicly warned Hamas in January 2016 that Israel is "operating systematically and calmly against all threats, including those from Hamas, both with defensive and offensive means, and of course in the event we are attacked by tunnels in Gaza we will operate with great force against Hamas, with much greater force than what we used in [the 2014 conflict]."[99]

Iran's support for the Muslim Brotherhood and Hamas is disturbing and detrimental to our security and global stability. It results in the bloodshed of innocent men, women, and children in Israel, in Africa, and in other parts of the world. It results in countless international legal violations. But Iran is cozying up to more regimes of terror around the world. In just the last twenty-four months, we have seen a newly muscular Russia engaging the Middle East, a nuclear-capable Iran with an influx of cash, and terrorist partners who previously would not engage with each other. This is an unholy alliance with global implications.

9

Iran and al-Qaeda

When Iran exported its jihad to Hezbollah in Lebanon, Hamas in Palestine, and the Muslim Brotherhood in several regions around the world, these all indirectly threatened the United States. These terrorists threatened our greatest ally in the region, Israel, while destabilizing countries we depend on to help bring security to that area. These terrorists harm our allies with violence while sowing hatred for our values, thus hurting our national interests abroad. Until 2001, these organizations had not historically attempted to carry out terrorist attacks on the American homeland.

> Yet the most interesting trait common to ISIS, al-Qaeda, Iran, and every other Islamic terrorist group is this: they are all motivated by the same anti-Western, jihadist ideology.

With the Sunni-Shiite divide once again put on the back burner to tackle a bigger enemy, the relationship between al-Qaeda, another Sunni terrorist organization, and the Shiite regime in Iran is all about destroying the United States of America. Their relationship began a long time before the United States even knew about al-Qaeda and Osama bin Laden as public enemy number one.[1]

Today, ISIS is perhaps public enemy number one. Yet the most interesting trait common to ISIS, al-Qaeda, Iran, and every other Islamic terrorist group is this: they are all motivated by the same anti-Western, jihadist ideology.

The Birth of al-Qaeda

Al-Qaeda arose out of the ashes of the Soviet-Afghan War, a bloody ten-year conflict between the Afghanistan mujahideen and the USSR.[2] In 1978, the Communist People's Democratic Party of Afghanistan seized control of the country through a coup that installed Nur Muhammad Taraki as president.[3] Taraki was a friend of the Soviet Union, and he instituted brutal and oppressive policies on the Afghani people, including the execution of three thousand political prisoners and the imprisonment of another seventy thousand.[4] Civil war continued despite the success of the coup, resulting in the deaths of nearly a hundred thousand civilians.[5] Taraki also initiated communist land and social reforms that the Islamic population, notably its rural tribal leaders, fiercely opposed.[6] In response, insurgent groups rose up against Taraki in eastern Afghanistan, and eventually this revolution spread to the rest of the country.[7] These devoutly Islamic insurgents became known collectively as the *mujahideen*, or "those who engage in jihad."[8]

> **Al-Qaeda arose out of the ashes of the Soviet-Afghan War.**

This uprising, which led to Taraki's assassination in a palace shoot-out with the mujahideen, prompted the Soviet Union to invade Afghanistan in 1979 to secure its political and economic interests.[9] Conditions in Afghanistan, however, did not improve. The Soviet Union alienated the Afghan people by implementing more communist land and economic policies, which worsened living conditions for the poor.[10] In response to the Soviets' carrying out mass arrests, torture, and executions to suppress the insurgency, the mujahideen waged active war against the Soviet invaders.[11]

Volunteers, including Osama bin Laden, came from around the world to wage jihad against the Soviets.[12] From mid-1985 to early 1987, the Soviets pulled back from major operations, instead providing artillery and aviation support to the Afghan government forces.[13] In April 1988, after nearly one million civilian deaths and fifty-five thousand Soviet casualties, the Soviet Union signed the Geneva Accords and effectively ended the war.[14] By February 1989, the last Soviet forces had left Afghanistan.[15]

Osama bin Laden entered the Soviet-Afghan War in 1980.[16] It was in the mountains of Afghanistan that bin Laden found his purpose in life: to wage jihad against the two superpowers of the day, Soviet Russia and the United States.[17] But before he could take on the United States, he first needed to defeat the Soviet Union in Afghanistan. Although bin Laden participated in at least one battle, his primary role was financing the Afghan fighters.[18] Using his experience in his family's construction business, he helped design, finance, and construct roads, bunkers, and other facilities.[19] He also assembled the Golden Chain, a complex international financial network including financiers from Saudi Arabia and the Persian Gulf states.[20] Additionally, bin Laden was instrumental in creating the Services Bureau, which funneled recruits from abroad into Afghanistan.[21] After the Soviets withdrew, bin Laden used his troops of Afghan extremists, his financial donors, and his international recruitment network to create al-Qaeda.[22] Its purpose was to further jihad around the world.[23] Bin Laden later stated that during the war, he "felt closer to God than ever."[24] After achieving victory against the Soviets, bin Laden turned his sights toward the United States: "We have defeated the world's great infidel power. Now the effeminate Americans will be easy," bin Laden said.[25]

While al-Qaeda was born from the Soviet-Afghan War, much of

the credit for its strength must be given to the Ayatollah's regime in Iran, its Revolutionary Guards, and its Ministry of Intelligence and Security, which provided material support and training to al-Qaeda in Sudan during its infancy. As Colonel Oliver North pointed out about the true roots of al-Qaeda, "If you look at what we've been up against, not really since 2001, actually going back to 1979, [it all stems from] when the Ayatollah Khomeini goes back to Qom [a holy city in Iran] from Paris and begins to organize not the Iranian revolution, but the Islamic Revolution."[26]

How the Iranian Revolution
Led to al-Qaeda and September 11

Decades before 9/11, Iran was breeding terrorists under the tutelage of Hassan al-Turabi, a graduate of Oxford University and leader of the National Islamic Front in Sudan, a country that had become a terrorist incubator by the early 1980s.[27] Turabi advocated that Sunnis and Shiites should put aside their divisions and join hands against the common enemy,[28] a theology that was consistent with that of the Iranian regime. When Sudanese general Omar al-Bashir seized power in a military coup in 1989, Iran upgraded its diplomatic relations with Sudan to ambassadorial level.[29] Soon after, in October 1991, Tehran held an international conference to support the Palestinian cause. One of the four-hundred-plus delegates who attended the conference was Turabi.[30] Upon his return to Sudan, Turabi and Bashir began boosting "the operational capabilities of the Islamic guerrilla and terror movements based there" with Iranian aid.[31] Turabi and Bashir had given refuge to many terrorists from organizations such as Palestinian

> While al-Qaeda was born from the Soviet-Afghan War, much of the credit for its strength must be given to the Ayatollah's regime in Iran, its Revolutionary Guards, and its Ministry of Intelligence and Security, which provided material support and training to al-Qaeda in Sudan during its infancy.

Islamic Jihad, Hamas, Hezbollah, al-Qaeda, and others,[32] while the Revolutionary Guards and the Ministry of Intelligence provided training to these terrorists.[33] While Sudan provided these extremists a safe haven and a base for training, the logistical support and training came from Iran.[34]

One of the terrorists Iran supported during that time was Ayman al-Zawahiri, the current leader of al-Qaeda, who had also taken refuge in Sudan in the 1990s along with Osama bin Laden.[35] Zawahiri is an Egyptian-born physician who started the Egyptian Islamic Jihad (EIJ) and is currently on the FBI's Most Wanted Terrorists list.[36] EIJ later merged with al-Qaeda,[37] and Zawahiri became the group's number-two man. In April 1991, Zawahiri went to Tehran seeking help to overthrow the Egyptian government.[38] In response, Tehran promised to fund him and train his men.[39] With the Iranian help, Zawahiri carried out several attacks in Egypt, including the attempt to assassinate Egyptian president Hosni Mubarak in 1995.[40] The attacks prompted an Israeli investigation that found Zawahiri, bin Laden, and others were "part of a large group of Islamic extremists: veterans of the guerrilla war against the Soviets in Afghanistan who shared the goal of carrying out Islamic action all over the world."[41]

Between 1991 and 1996, bin Laden also lived in Sudan.[42] It was there that Zawahiri and bin Laden formed a close alliance, and Zawahiri encouraged bin Laden to form ties with Iran.[43] Said the *9/11 Commission Report*:

In late 1991 or 1992, discussions in Sudan between al Qaeda and Iranian operatives led to an informal agreement to co-operate in providing support—even if only training—for actions carried out primarily against Israel and the United States. Not long afterward, senior al Qaeda operatives and trainers traveled to Iran to receive training in explosives. In the fall of 1993, another such delegation went to the

Bekaa Valley in Lebanon for further training in explosives as well as in intelligence and security. Bin [Laden] reportedly showed particular interest in learning how to use truck bombs such as the one that had killed 241 U.S. Marines in Lebanon in 1983.[44]

One important tie between al-Qaeda and Iran was Imad Mughniyah, who met with bin Laden several times in Sudan in the early 1990s and facilitated Iran's supplying of bombs and explosives training to al-Qaeda through Hezbollah.[45]

The year 1996 brought an end to Sudanese hospitality for Zawahiri and bin Laden.[46] Civil war raged in southern Sudan, and Egypt threatened to take military action against Sudan if it continued to harbor its enemy Zawahiri. It was then that Sudan forced both Zawahiri and bin Laden to close up shop and leave, despite Iran's intercession on Zawahiri's behalf.[47]

The loss of asylum in Sudan did not harm the relationship between Iran and al-Qaeda. While bin Laden moved to Afghanistan to continue his work, Iranian intelligence assisted other al-Qaeda members and affiliates to relocate in Yemen, Pakistan, Afghanistan, Iran, and Lebanon.[48] According to the *9/11 Commission Report*, "Intelligence indicates the persistence of contacts between Iranian security officials and senior al Qaeda figures after Bin [Laden's] return to Afghanistan."[49]

One example of the continuing cooperation between Iran and al-Qaeda was the June 1996 bombing in Dhahran, Saudi Arabia, that killed nineteen Americans and wounded 372 others.[50] This attack was orchestrated by an Iranian-supported Saudi branch of Hezbollah, and there was evidence that al-Qaeda played a role in the attack as well.[51]

The connection between Iran and al-Qaeda grew even stronger when Zawahiri's Egyptian Islamic Jihad assimilated into al-Qaeda in 1998 as a result of Zawahiri's connections with Iran.[52] Zawahiri became "the chief go-between for [al-Qaeda] and Iran."[53] Through this relationship and using Hezbollah as a mediator, Iran provided materials, manpower, finances, and other support for al-Qaeda in Afghanistan, in the Middle East, and in Europe.[54] Iran proved to be one of al-Qaeda's most reliable sources of support, in contrast to Pakistan, which usually supported al-Qaeda but occasionally arrested and turned over al-Qaeda members in an attempt to appease Western powers.[55]

Another example of persistent friendliness between Iranian officials and al-Qaeda was the arrangements made with Iranian border police. Border police were instructed to give special treatment to al-Qaeda members traveling through Iran by not stamping their passports, facilitating covert movement to and from bin Laden's training camps in Afghanistan.[56] Among the al-Qaeda members who repeatedly traveled through Iran during this time, taking advantage of the Iranians' favorable treatment, were several of the operatives later involved in the 9/11 attack.[57]

Saif al-Adel, a senior-ranking al-Qaeda leader, later proclaimed the important role that Iran played in al-Qaeda's plans leading up to 9/11:

> This passage [through Iran] was new and important to us in the al-Qa'ida. We took advantage of it later on. We used it instead of the old route through Pakistan, particularly for the passage of Arab brothers. This issue prompted us to think of building good relations with some virtuous people in Iran to pave the way and coordinate regarding issues of mutual interest. Coordination with the Iranians was achieved later.[58]

Roughly a year before the 9/11 attacks, five of the 9/11 hijackers traveled to Iran under the close attention of senior Hezbollah officials.[59] The *9/11 Commission Report* concluded, "There is strong evidence that Iran facilitated the transit of al Qaeda members into and out of Afghanistan before 9/11, and that some of these were future 9/11 hijackers."[60] Other sources indicated that Hezbollah security chief Imad Mughniyah directly facilitated the travel of the 9/11 hijackers through Iran, utilizing his close relationship with high-ranking Iranian Revolutionary Guard members.[61] The 9/11 Commission reported that there was no evidence that Iran or Hezbollah was involved in actually planning the 9/11 attacks, but it also noted that the operatives themselves were most likely in the dark about the highly secretive specific details of the operation during the time they were traveling through Iran.[62] What cannot be denied, however, is that Iran aided al-Qaeda significantly by giving it unhindered access to clandestinely move operatives in and out of Afghanistan through the back door of Iran.

In 2003, a London-based Saudi periodical published an interview with Hamid Reza Zakiri, an alleged defector from the Iranian Revolutionary Guards.[63] Zakiri claimed that the relationship between "the intelligence of the [Revolutionary] Guards, not of the [Iranian] government, with the Al-Qai'da [sic] organization . . . goes back to the 1980s."[64] He further claimed that prior to 9/11, Imad Mugniyah delivered a letter to Ayatollah Khamenei from al-Qaeda leader Zawahiri, requesting Iranian assistance "to carry out a most important mission in the land of the 'Great Satan.' "[65] Zakiri stated that the request for assistance was denied, but that Mugniyah was instructed to maintain friendly relations with Zawahiri, and that Mugniyah most likely helped "plan[] the escape of dozens of Al-Qai'da men to Iran" from Afghanistan immediately following the 9/11 attacks.[66]

> What cannot be denied, however, is that Iran aided al-Qaeda significantly by giving it unhindered access to clandestinely move operatives in and out of Afghanistan through the back door of Iran.

After 9/11, Iran's connection with al-Qaeda became much less visible, as Iranians had no desire to be labeled as aiders and abettors to the most deadly attack on the American homeland since Pearl Harbor.[67]

Iran's relationship with al-Qaeda has been somewhat negatively colored since 1998 due to Iran's hatred of the Taliban, al-Qaeda's former host in Afghanistan. Iran's animosity toward the Taliban began in 1998, when nine Iranian diplomats were killed in northern Afghanistan.[68] Although the Taliban disclaimed its involvement, Iran held it responsible.[69] When U.S. forces toppled the Taliban in 2001, many al-Qaeda members, including some of Osama bin Laden's family and inner circle, fled across the border to Iran.[70] Iran placed these members under house arrest, possibly hoping to extract intelligence to gain leverage against the U.S.-led coalition.[71] For a while this system seemed to work as Tehran deported most of the low-level al-Qaeda members, copying their passports and other valuable documents beforehand, and then handing some of the members over to the U.S.-led coalition.[72]

When President George W. Bush labeled Iran part of the "axis of evil" in his 2002 State of the Union address, however, Tehran refused to continue cooperating with Western nations and began to fear what the U.S. military might do to Iran in the future.[73] The breakdown in cooperation between Tehran and the United States once again paved the way for al-Qaeda members to gain a stronger standing with Iran, based on their shared hatred for a mutual enemy—the United States.[74]

The long-standing friendship between Iran and Zawahiri was somewhat tarnished in early 2003, when reformist president Mohammad Khatami ordered Zawahiri's arrest.[75] According to reports, Zawahiri was at that time living in a government-owned house with the tacit approval of the Revolutionary Guards' intelligence arm, but Khatami ordered Zawahiri's arrest and the expulsion of many other al-Qaeda–linked operatives.[76] With the help of his sympathizers in the Revolutionary Guards, Zawahiri managed to evade capture and escape Iran.[77]

In 2006, Sunni jihadists in Iraq published a document alleged to be a classified Iranian intelligence order from May 2001.[78] Although the authenticity of the document is not certain, American and Israeli intelligence believed it to be authentic and that it was published with the intent of embarrassing Iran in retaliation for its cessation of support for al-Qaeda that occurred around that time.[79] The document purports to be from the office of Supreme Leader Ali Khamenei's chief intelligence advisor, Ali Akbar Nategh-Nouri, addressed to a subordinate head of an Iranian intelligence unit, and outlines the Iranian government's desire to support and collaborate with al-Qaeda in the common fight against the United States and Israel.[80]

The U.S. government also learned many things about al-Qaeda's operations around the globe after U.S. Navy SEALs raided bin Laden's compound in Pakistan on May 2, 2011, and killed him.[81] Although the documents captured in that raid have not been released publicly, several current and former intelligence officials have stated that they contain important information regarding Iran's relationship with al-Qaeda.[82] For instance, Lieutenant General Michael Flynn, the former director of the Defense Intelligence Agency, claimed:

> There are letters about Iran's role, influence, and acknowledgment of enabling al Qaeda operatives to pass through Iran as long as al Qaeda did [its] dirty work against the Americans in Iraq and Afghanistan. . . . Congress should demand to see all the [Osama bin Laden] documents related to Iran and all the documents related to intentions of [al-Qaeda] in the future—they are very telling.[83]

Former senior Defense Intelligence Agency official Derek Harvey similarly stated that these documents "almost certainly [contain] extremely valuable, insightful information, and potentially explosive, that would illuminate the duplicitous Iran relationship with Osama Bin Laden and al Qaeda writ large."[84] What is known about these documents is that after 9/11, some senior al-Qaeda leaders had chosen to escape Afghanistan by heading west to Iran. In June 2010, Younis al-Mauritani, one of these top al-Qaeda operatives, requested permission to relocate to Iran, where he could safely plot attacks around the globe.[85] Sulaiman Abu Ghaith, one of Osama bin Laden's sons-in-law, also sought refuge within Iran after the Taliban fell.[86] For reasons unknown, Abu Ghaith eventually left the safety of Iran and traveled to Turkey, where the FBI was able to track him down and capture him in 2013.[87]

Saif al-Adel, another member of al-Qaeda's senior personnel, was trained by Iran and Hezbollah in the 1990s[88] and is thought to have been involved in planning the bomb attacks on the U.S. embassies in East Africa in 1998.[89] Adel is also important because in 2010 he aided Iran by using his contacts and influence in Pakistan to help free a kidnapped Iranian diplomat, Heshmatollah Attarzadeh-Niyaki,[90] who had been taken captive in an ambush by Islamic militants, likely linked to the Taliban, on the Pakistani side of the Khyber Pass in 2008.[91] After this event, many of the restrictions placed on al-Qaeda operatives in Iran were loosened, allowing them to move around more freely and reach out to contact more people within and outside the country.[92]

Al-Qaeda members operating out of Iran have also been problematic for the Kingdom of Saudi Arabia. Saad, one of Osama bin Laden's sons, was in Iran for years after 9/11, specifically in 2003, when he was in contact with the terrorists responsible for the 2003 Riyadh bombings.[93] Al-Qaeda's presence in Iran was significant enough in 2009 to warrant dozens of spots on Saudi Arabia's most wanted list, which held only eighty-five names in total.[94] One of the names on the 2009 list was Abdullah al-Qarawi,[95] code-named "the star," who led al-Qaeda's operations in the Persian Gulf and Iran.[96] In order to fully command these operations, al-Qarawi had free movement and dozens of Saudis working for him, all within Iran.[97]

Top-ranking al-Qaeda commanders still within Iran continue to conduct their day-to-day operations with little interference from Iran's government and with complete assurance that no U.S. drone will kill them, as often happens to their brothers in Pakistan.[98] According to a 2011 statement made by David S. Cohen, the former undersecretary of the U.S. Treasury and current deputy director of the CIA, "There is an agreement between the Iranian government and al Qaeda to allow this network to operate [within Iran]. There's no dispute in the intelligence community on this."[99] In early 2015, U.S. intelligence officials reportedly confirmed that cooperation between Iran and al-Qaeda was "still critical to al Qaeda['s] operations."[100]

> **Top-ranking al-Qaeda commanders still within Iran continue to conduct their day-to-day operations with little interference from Iran's government.**

Iran's Quds Force and al-Qaeda

In May 2011, Kronos, a U.S. strategic advisory firm, published a report to the Congressional Anti-Terrorism Caucus exposing the connection between al-Qaeda and the Iranian Revolutionary Guards' elite special forces unit, known as the Quds Force.[101] The Quds Force, which the United States has designated as a supporter of international terrorism since 2007,[102] is a shadowy and highly specialized unit that has existed in an official capacity since 1990, although there is evidence that it may have been conducting covert operations as far back as the early 1980s.[103] Intriguingly, the name *Quds* is the Arabic word for Jerusalem, which is highly suggestive of the group's ultimate goal.[104] The Quds Force reports directly and solely to Supreme Leader Ayatollah Khamenei, is headquartered in the former U.S. embassy in Tehran, and manages most of the

Iranian Revolutionary Guards' international operations around the globe.[105]

According to the Kronos report, there is substantial evidence that the Quds Force has provided support for not only Shiite terrorist groups, but Sunni groups as well, including al-Qaeda.[106] The report claims that Iranians arrested in Iraq in 2006 were carrying materials indicating that the Quds Force had provided support for al-Qaeda affiliates in Iraq.[107] The capture of a senior Taliban official in Afghanistan in January 2011, a man who had connections with the Quds Force, revealed "a Q[u]ds Force-supported Taliban and al Qaeda network . . . operating in the remote western [Afghan] province of Farah."[108] Further evidence in the form of leaked classified intelligence documents "also point to Iranian relationships with militants under the command of a well-known al-Qa'ida-affiliated jihadi in Afghanistan," Gulbuddin Hekmatyar.[109] Hekmatyar is an Afghani warlord and Sunni Muslim with strong ties to al-Qaeda.[110] These leaked documents describe how the Revolutionary Guards transferred $212,000 to Hekmatyar's Sunni terrorist group, Hezb-e Islami Gulbuddin (HIG).[111]

Iran and al-Qaeda Affiliates in Syria

Iran has given al-Qaeda extensive freedom to operate within its own borders, even allowing al-Qaeda to fund its operations within Syria in order to challenge Iranian ally President Bashar al-Assad.[112] It is unknown why Iran would allow al-Qaeda to fund its affiliate, al-Nusra, directly against President al-Assad's Alawite and Hezbollah allies.[113]

When the civil war started in Syria, many of the original fighters were secular. Yet when the secularists failed to defeat the regime, radical Islamic groups like the Muslim Brotherhood and al-Qaeda filled the vacuum and took up the fight.[114] The substantial financial support flowing from the Gulf states into the hands of these radical rebel groups incentivized other rebel groups to become more radical in their stated purposes and ideology in order to receive a share of the coveted funding.[115] The funding shifted the focus of the resistance from nationalism toward pan-Islamic ideology, which led to the sectarian conflict currently playing itself out in the country.[116]

> The substantial financial support flowing from the Gulf states into the hands of these radical rebel groups incentivized other rebel groups to become more radical in their stated purposes and ideology in order to receive a share of the coveted funding.

After it became clear that Assad could not maintain control of Syria without Iranian support, Iran ordered Hezbollah forces to prop up Syria's faltering regime by fighting against the rebels, including al-Nusra.[117]

Once Hezbollah joined the conflict, Mohammad al-Shalabi, al-Nusra's leader in Jordan, shifted his focus toward eliminating Hezbollah forces to pave the way for total conquest of Syria.[118] While al-Nusra is not as organized as Hezbollah, the probability of this fight spilling over into Lebanon and further igniting an increasingly volatile Sunni-Shiite divide is at an all-time high. Yet Iran continues to allow al-Qaeda to run its operations abroad from within Iran, seemingly unabated.[119]

How the United States Targets al-Qaeda in Iran

Al-Qaeda's presence in Iran was significant enough that the United States had a (now declassified) CIA program to study whether it could track and kill terrorists in Iran, most notably al-Qaeda operatives, until CIA director Leon Panetta canceled it in 2009.[120]

In 2011, the U.S. Department of the Treasury found that al-Qaeda members based in Iran were using it as a transit point to funnel funding and foreign fighters into Syria, Afghanistan, and Pakistan.[121] That July, the Treasury Department added six al-Qaeda operatives to the designated foreign terrorists list,[122] chiefly Yasin al-Suri, a prominent al-Qaeda leader operating within Iran since

2005.[123] In 2012, the Treasury Department designated the Iranian Ministry of Intelligence and Security (MOIS) a terror-sponsoring organization for aiding al-Qaeda operatives with passports, money, weapons, and other necessary supplies for terrorist operations.[124] In October 2012 the Treasury Department reported that al-Suri had been replaced by Muhsin al-Fadhli,[125] a Kuwaiti long wanted by the U.S. government for an attack against U.S. Marines on Kuwait's Failaka Island in 2002, for fund-raising for al-Qaeda, and for his involvement in an attack on a French ship off the coast of Yemen.[126] Al-Fadhli eventually became the leader of the Khorasan Group, a high-level al-Qaeda cell in Syria focused primarily on carrying out attacks on U.S. soil, further highlighting his profile.[127] It is rumored that al-Fadhli was killed in Syria by an American air strike in September 2014.[128] After al-Fadhli's death (or disappearance), al-Suri eventually resumed his role as al-Qaeda's head man in Iran, partially due to the help he received from another top member, Sanafi al-Nasr.[129]

Al-Nasr is significant because he served in early 2013 as chief of al-Qaeda's Iran-based extremist and financial facilitation network before relocating to Syria to join the Khorasan Group.[130] While Iran's relationship with the Khorasan Group is not clear, Iran has worked with al-Fadhli and al-Nasr for some time.[131] According to the Pentagon, al-Nasr was killed in October 2015 by an air strike in northwest Syria, highlighting how seriously the U.S. military has been hunting for members of this shadowy group.[132]

> While Iran may not be al-Qaeda's direct sponsor, the country has been a safe haven for the infamous terrorist organization and has permitted al-Qaeda to operate in a way that has enabled its operatives to flourish and continue their mission even after a decade of war with the world's mightiest military force.

While Iran may not be al-Qaeda's direct sponsor, the country has been a safe haven for the infamous terrorist organization and has permitted al-Qaeda to operate in a way that has enabled its operatives to flourish and continue their mission even after a decade of war with the world's mightiest military force. Iran's goal of spreading terrorism against the West is not limited to overcoming the Sunni-Shiite divide, however. It goes much further. In fact, to truly subvert the West and try to destroy America, Iran is teaming up with non-Muslims. It seems to radical jihadists, all infidels are not created equal. Some of them may be useful in destroying more powerful infidels. That's why Iran has teamed up with Russia.

10

Strange Bedfellows

The Russia-Syria-Iran Alliance

In December 2010, a young man set himself on fire to protest the oppressive regime in Tunisia.[1] That moment sparked the first Arab Spring uprising—an attempt to replace dictatorships with democracy throughout the Middle East in countries such as Tunisia, Egypt, Yemen, Libya, and others.[2] At its inception, the media covered the relatively peaceful revolutions as a history-changing moment. They spread from country to country, utilizing social media to give power to the masses who had previously been oppressed. Would freedom finally come to the Middle East? Was stability possible if these despots could be overthrown?

For those who studied the Middle East and knew its socioeconomic, religious, and political makeup, the Arab Spring was cause for concern. In fact, it had the potential to create more instability, chaos, and persecution than ever before. For example, it led to the Muslim Brotherhood's takeover of Egypt.

Following its literally incendiary origin, the movement spread throughout the Middle East like a wildfire. It arrived in Syria in March 2011, after government forces shot and killed demonstrators who were protesting the government's arrest and alleged torture of fifteen Syrian teenagers.[3] The teenagers' only crime was posting anti-Assad graffiti on school walls.[4] The Assad government's heavy-handed use of force against the teenagers caused thousands of Syrians to protest against the government and demand Syrian president Bashar al-Assad's ouster.[5]

Demanding the resignation of a dictator whose family had been ruling the country for decades was a bold move that the regime could not ignore.[6] Violence rapidly spread throughout Syria, and the country erupted into civil war.[7] In the intervening four years, more than three hundred thousand Syrians have been killed,[8] and almost half of the Syrian population has been forced to flee from their homes in search of refuge,[9] seeking to escape a war that has been called the "worst humanitarian crisis" since World War II.[10] It's easy for Americans to overlook the historic nature of this crisis. It's easy for us to miss the nuance in the ever-shifting coalitions that defy typical religious rivalries and geopolitical posturing. But the deaths are all too real and the crisis is all too consequential. Look no further than the various players engaged in the conflict on all sides.

During the ebb and flow of the war, the Assad regime has relied on external support to retain power. It has sought help from Russia and Iran, two countries competing to expand their power and influence in the Middle East.[11] Despite conflicting regional goals and many years of uneasy relations, Russia and Iran are now working together to keep the Assad regime in power in Syria.[12] It is said that politics makes strange bedfellows. This statement could not be more accurate as the Syrian Civil War has brought together, at least temporarily, historical foes—Iran and Russia—as allies.

Russia and Iran

While Syria's bilateral relationships with both Iran and Russia have been relatively stable, Iran and Russia have a complicated and turbulent historical relationship. Following World War I and the Russian Revolution, Soviet Russia and Iran signed the Russo-Persian Treaty of Friendship in 1921.[13] This treaty granted the newly established Soviet government the authority to enter Iran to deal with anti-Soviet activities or threats.[14] The Soviets used the treaty to compel Iranians to declare their "friendship" with the Soviet Union and later cited the treaty as justification for the Soviets' refusal to withdraw their troops from Iran.[15]

By the early 1940s, the relationship between the Soviet Union and Iran was strained.[16] During World War II, the Soviet Union and Great Britain had jointly occupied Iran to prevent Germany from using Iran as a strategic platform to attack the Soviet Union.[17] After World War II the British withdrew from Iran, but the Soviet Union refused to withdraw its troops.[18] The Soviet Union kept troops in Iran in an attempt to bring Azerbaijan, the northern province of Iran, under Soviet domination through its support of Iran's pro-Soviet party, the Tudeh.[19] Only in 1946, after heavy pressure from the United States, did the Soviets withdraw their troops from Iran.[20]

Although the Anglo-Iranian Oil Company held a monopoly on Iranian oil, the Iranians tentatively agreed to share their oil resources with the Soviets.[21] That agreement never materialized.[22] As mentioned in chapter 5, by the early 1950s, then–prime minister Mohammad Mosaddegh took action to regain control of Iranian natural resources and nationalized the oil company.[23] As this was occurring during the height of the Cold War, Britain and the United States feared that Mosaddegh's nationalization of the company would be the first step toward Iran's aligning with the Soviet Union.[24] At the time, the United States wanted to stem Soviet influence in Iran. To accomplish this, the United States assisted Great Britain in working with Reza Shah Pahlavi to remove Mosaddegh from power.[25]

With pro-Western Reza Shah again in control of the country in 1953, relations between the Soviet Union and Iran quickly deteriorated. In 1955, over strong objections from the Soviet Union, the Iranians signed the Baghdad Pact, a treaty between Iran, Iraq, Turkey, Pakistan, and Great Britain, designed to "prevent communist incursions and foster peace in the Middle East."[26] Iran once again disregarded Soviet concerns in 1959 when the Shah, a Western-oriented autocrat who feared and distrusted the Soviets, began negotiating a security pact with the United States.[27] After considerable pressure and promises of economic and military aid from the United States, the Iranians entered into the Iranian-American treaty.[28]

By the late 1970s, Iran was experiencing increasing civil unrest against the Shah's oppressive regime, which ultimately led to the Iranian Revolution and the Shah's ouster.[29] The Soviet Union initially hoped that the fall of the Shah, a strong ally of the United States, would lead to the rise of a regime friendly to the USSR.[30]

Once Ayatollah Khomeini came to power, the Soviets' hope for a friend in Iran didn't come true. Khomeini, who, as we've seen, referred to America as the "Great Satan," labeled Soviet Russia a "Lesser Satan" and an oppressive imperial power.[31] Iran criticized the dispatch of Soviet forces to Afghanistan in late 1979.[32] Despite these differences, however, Tehran and Moscow maintained diplomatic relations.[33]

The current alliance between Iran and Russia appears even more counterintuitive, considering the religious differences between the two countries that have played a major role in the governments and policies of both nations.[34] Under the Soviets, Russia repressed the Russian Orthodox Church, a pillar of government legitimacy and national identity under the czars.[35] But with the fall of communism, the Orthodox Church regained its central role in society and much of the power it enjoyed under the czarist regime.[36] Ninety percent of the Russian population identifies as Russian Orthodox, and by embracing and helping the Orthodox Church, Putin gains not only political capital but also the possibility to gain support in other areas in the region he wishes to control.[37] As mentioned, Iran, on the other hand, is a radical Shiite nation dedicated to the concept of Islamic religious supremacy and world dominance.[38]

With these opposing faith foundations in mind, the Iranian and Russian alliance can be understood only in the context of both nations' desires to increase their own power and influence in the Middle East. Russia seeks to reestablish itself as a world power on par with the United States.[39] According to one Russian scholar, "Since 2000, Putin has sought to restore Russia as a Great Power, shaping its policy as an anti-American zero-sum game in order to position the country as a counterweight to the West in the Middle East."[40] As the United States has withdrawn from the Middle East, the Russians have stepped in.[41] For example, in 2012, President Obama drew a "red line" against President Assad's use of chemical weapons, but Obama declined to act when Assad crossed that line.[42] Rather than take military action against the Syrian government for its use of chemical weapons, the United States turned to Russia to negotiate a disarmament plan with President Assad, thereby diminishing U.S. influence and benefiting Russia.[43] This cannot be overstated: as the United States, under President Obama, has chosen to withdraw from leadership in the region, Russia has had one opportunity after another to flex its muscle and increase its influence. Iran is doing the same thing in the vacuum being left by the United States.

Iran's goal has also been to achieve regional hegemony over the Middle East, to ultimately counter American and Western influence, and to expand the Islamic Revolution.[44] As the descendant of the once-proud Persian Empire, Iran desires to regain dominance in the Middle East.[45] An advisor to Iranian president Hassan Rou-

> **Russia seeks to re-establish itself as a world power on par with the United States.**

hani even went so far as to identify Baghdad as the capital of the new Persian Empire,[46] asserting, "All of the Middle East is Iranian, and this region will be strongly defended because it is part of Iran."[47]

To this end, Iran's strategy is to establish a Greater Iran, "reaching from the borders of China and including the Indian subcontinent, the north and south Caucasus and the Persian Gulf."[48]

> As the United States, under President Obama, has chosen to withdraw from leadership in the region, Russia has had one opportunity after another to flex its muscle and increase its influence.

Moreover, as the United States withdraws from the region, Iran's grip on the Middle East has spread to include Lebanon, Iraq, Yemen, and Syria.[49] Iran's actions in the Syrian Civil War seek to keep the Assad regime in power, to maintain Iranian influence in the country, and to establish another platform from which to attack Israel.

Further allying them, both Russia and Iran have faced similar international challenges, including severe financial sanctions from the United States and the European Union since the late 1970s.[50] Over the years, the United States has imposed varying types of sanctions on Iran, including economic and trade sanctions and limits on the development of weapons, especially the development of nuclear weapons.[51]

The United States and the European Union have also placed sanctions on Russia for its recent actions in the Ukraine.[52] In March 2014, Russia sent troops into the Crimea,[53] a peninsula in the Ukraine that has been the subject of dispute between the Ukraine and Russia.[54] Russian officials moved quickly to bring Crimea under Russian control, and Crimean voters (mostly Ukrainian citizens of Russian ethnicity) overwhelmingly agreed by referendum to join Russia.[55] In response, the United States and the European Union levied sanctions on Russia.[56] Biting external sanctions served as a strong impetus to further Russian-Iranian cooperation. It explains their current alliance in Syria and their lucrative trade in conventional military hardware.

Russia and Syria

Russia has also developed a close relationship with Syria as a means to gain and retain its influence in the Middle East.[57] To purchase access, Russia provided Syria with substantial financial and military support to counter the United States' presence in the Middle East beginning in the 1950s.[58] As early as 1955, the Soviet Union was providing Syria with military aid and encouraging it to enter a pact with the Soviet Union as a counterweight to U.S. presence in the region.[59]

After losing Iran to the United States, the Soviets turned their attention to Arab states opposing Israel. The Soviet Union backed the Syrian government military in its conflict with Israel by providing the Syrians with significant aid.[60] In return for the Soviets' supply of military equipment, Syria granted the Soviet Union permission to establish a warm-water naval base for the Soviet Navy on the Mediterranean Sea in Tartus, Syria.[61] Significantly, this is the "only naval base Russia has outside the former Soviet Union."[62] Protecting and retaining that base is of critical importance to Russia due to many of its own ports being ice-locked for part of the year and none of them providing convenient access to the Mediterranean Sea, and it is from that base that Russia began providing military support to the Assad regime during the ongoing Syrian Civil War.[63] Although some in Russia publicly minimize the naval base's importance, it is strategically important to Russia because it has the capability to dock nuclear submarines, is linked to local infrastructure, and is the "receiving point for Russian weapons shipments to Syria," which is a "multi-billion-dollar" industry for Russia.[64]

Economically, Syria provides Russia with diverse and financially profitable opportunities.[65] As a major arms supplier to Syria,[66] the Russian government has a lot to gain by keeping President Assad in power.[67] In 2012, Syria ordered "36 Yak-130 combat jets worth $550 million" from Russia.[68] Furthermore, Russia and Syria have been important economic trading partners.[69] In 2012 Syria was sanctioned, and the European Union banned imports of oil from Syria.[70] Based on this ban, many nations decided to no longer sell fuel to Syria.[71] As more and more nations refused to trade with Syria, the Russian government bucked the sanctions and continued to buy Syrian oil and sell fuel to Syria.[72]

Another reason Russia continues to support the Assad regime is to accomplish one of the Russian government's key aims—to control the oil supply to Europe.[73] By positioning itself with Assad, once the Syrian Civil War is over, Russia's presence in the Middle East is expected to lead to expanded opportunities to transact with other major oil producers in the region.[74] Russia would lose significant economic opportunities as well as political and strategic presence if Assad fell from power in Syria.[75] So in order to keep Assad in power and expand the Russian presence and control of oil supply in the region, Russia provides military support to the Assad regime by supplying weapons and training and by launching air strikes in support of Iranian and Syrian ground operations.[76]

Russia is willing to do whatever it takes to protect its interests and increase its influence.

Although it is difficult to ascertain the exact number of Russian troops deployed into Syria during its civil war, the NATO secretary-general stated in 2015 that the number of Russian troops in Syria is "substantial."[77] As of October 1, 2015, despite President Putin's denial that newly conscripted troops were related to the situation in Syria, the Russian army had "conscripted 150,000 new troops . . . as the country unleashed a new wave of airstrikes in Syria."[78] Russia also had a significant air force presence in Syria, with "over 50 warplanes and helicopters," including Su-25 and Su-24 planes,[79] which were primarily used to attack anti-Assad rebel forces.[80] Moreover, in 2015 Russia expanded its operations by developing two more Syrian military bases.[81] On March 14, 2016, President Putin announced through the state news that he is ordering the beginning of a Russian military withdrawal from Syria.[82] President Putin was quoted as saying, "I consider the objectives that have been set for the Defense Ministry to be generally accomplished. That is why I order to start withdrawal of the main part of our military group from the territory of the Syrian Arab Republic starting from tomorrow."[83] This simply confirms what has been clear all along: Russia is willing to do whatever it takes to protect its interests and increase its influence. If Assad were to begin to fall from power in Syria, the Russian military would return to Syria once again.

Iran and Syria

Iran and Syria also have a close friendship, which has been well described by one Middle East expert as a "strategic relationship, a marriage of convenience."[84] Their alliance grew out of common interests between the two countries.[85]

One significant commonality between Iran and Syria is the religious persuasion of the countries' respective leaders.[86] Iran is the largest Shiite country in the world[87] and follows Twelver Shiism. Syria is led by President Bashar al-Assad, a member of the minority Alawite Muslim sect, which also follows Twelver Shiism.[88] Of course, Sunnis consider Shiites and other non-Sunni Islamic sects to be heretics. Although the Alawites make up a mere 10–15 percent of the Syrian population,[89] for decades they have kept the majority Sunni population in Syria under control by force.[90]

In their effort to fight common enemies, Iran and Syria have provided assistance to Hezbollah.[91] Both countries were vital in helping Hezbollah fight the Israelis after Israel invaded Lebanon in 1982.[92] Although Israel's stated aim in the 1982 invasion was to clear Lebanon's southern border of Palestinian terrorists threatening Israel's northern territory, the invasion was also a severe blow to the Syrian military.[93] The Syrian military had built up a substantial presence in Lebanon since the mid-1970s to the extent that Syria was practically ruling Lebanon by 1982.[94] Syrian president Hafez al-Assad was determined to strike back at Israel, although he did not have the military strength to do so directly.[95] Instead his only option was to help establish a guerrilla warfare campaign against Israel in Lebanon to undermine Israel's occupation.[96]

Always looking for a way to destroy Israel, Iran was eager to help.[97] Top Iranian officials traveled to Syria in 1982.[98] In the words of Mohsen Rezaei, the commander of the Revolutionary Guard and a member of the delegation, their purpose was "to study the problem [in Lebanon] and to implement the principles of the true jihad and to teach the Zionists a lesson."[99] At that meeting, Syria agreed to support Iran's efforts to export its Islamic Revolution to Lebanon through the use of a new Shiite terrorist organization, which would eventually become Hezbollah.[100]

As both Iran and the Assad regime in Syria belong to minority groups, they share common enemies and common insecurities, and each uses the other to advance its respective political positions. For example, Syria and Iran had a common enemy in Saddam Hussein, Iraq's former leader, whom both Syria and Iran considered to be a national security threat.[101] Hussein was a secular Sunni Muslim who dominated and forcibly put down Iraq's sizable Shiite population.[102] Iranian leadership opposed Hussein because of what they believed to be his anti-Shiite stance and they supported Shiite protests within Iraq.[103] Hussein had hoped to make Iraq a leading Middle Eastern power.[104] To do so, he had to neutralize his Shiite neighbor Iran.[105] During the Iran-Iraq War, Syria supported Iran and provided Iran with military support.[106]

The long, friendly relationship between Iran and Syria, with their religious and ideological similarities, has created a strong bond between the two nations. Since 2012, Iran has been involved in the Syrian Civil War by providing organization, funding, and training to local pro-regime militias.[107] While Iran has denied sending troops to Syria, witnesses have nonetheless reported that "hundreds of Iranian troops had arrived in Syria,"[108] including at least seven thousand Islamic Revolutionary Guard soldiers on the ground.[109] Iranian proxy Hezbollah has been actively assisting Syrian and Iranian forces in their ground operations to help regain territory that was captured by rebel forces.[110]

When Radical Islam and Russia Meet: The Unholy Alliance

Iran and Russia share one goal in Syria—to keep the Assad regime in power.[111] In July 2015, Iran and Russia rapidly and significantly increased their political and military cooperation.[112] Iranian Quds Force commander General Qasem Soleimani traveled to Moscow[113] to conduct weapons negotiations with the Russians.[114] This meeting between Iran and Russia was later determined to have played a critical role in expediting Russia's intervention in the Syrian Civil War.[115] According to one official,

> Soleimani put the map of Syria on the table. The Russians were very alarmed[] and felt matters were in steep decline and that there were real dangers to the [Assad] regime. The Iranians assured them there [was] still the possibility to reclaim the initiative. . . . At that time, Soleimani played a role in assuring them that we haven't lost all the cards.[116]

Not only have Russian and Iranian relations warmed because of their mutual interest in keeping Assad in power, but Russia also increased the number of its troops in Syria.[117] The Russian government dispatched dozens of aircraft, tanks, armored cars, and military surveillance drones to Syria.[118] Russia also constructed a "weapons depot" in Syria to supply its forces supporting the Assad regime.[119]

Initially, under the transparent guise of fighting ISIS, Russia,

Iran, and Syria focused their attacks primarily against non-ISIS, anti-Assad rebel forces.[120] While Russia told other world leaders that it is doing the world's work by taking out ISIS in Syria, it is clear that Russia's main focus is on eliminating anti-Assad rebels who are not a part of ISIS and could, in fact, be possible allies to the anti-Assad West. Rather than direct the vast majority of its air strikes at ISIS forces, as Russia had led the United States to believe was its intent,[121] Russia has instead concentrated its bombing on non-ISIS forces.[122] At the time, according to U.S. State Department officials, more than 90 percent of the Russian strikes were targeting non-ISIS, anti-Assad opposition groups instead of ISIS or al-Qaeda–affiliated terrorists.[123]

> Iran and Russia share one goal in Syria—to keep the Assad regime in power.

On October 31, 2015, ISIS claimed responsibility for bringing down a civilian Russian airliner over Egypt in one of the deadliest terror acts in recent history.[124] The commercial plane, en route to Saint Petersburg, exploded while in flight, killing all 224 people on board.[125] Most of the plane's passengers and all of its crew were Russian.[126] ISIS claimed responsibility for the attack, saying that it targeted the Russian aircraft after Russia began launching air strikes in Syria.[127] In response, President Putin ordered that Russian troops punish all individuals responsible and issued a $50 million reward for anyone providing credible information leading to an arrest.[128] Speaking of the attack, Putin stated, "We will find [ISIS] in any place on the planet and will punish them."[129]

Russia then significantly increased its bombing of ISIS in Syria.[130] However, a spokesman for U.S. Central Command explained that while Russia has increased its bombing of ISIS targets, "the majority of Russian air strikes are still against moderate Syrian opposition forces which is clearly concerning, and those strikes are in support of the Syrian regime."[131] As such, by going after Assad's non-ISIS opponents, over time, Iran and Russia have directly and significantly aided the Assad regime in Syria. Furthermore, in October 2015, Syrian forces, aided by Hezbollah, Iranian ground troops, and Russian air forces, carried out an offensive on Aleppo, a strategically important city, which indirectly allowed ISIS to make significant gains in the region.[132]

Despite beginning a new campaign of bombing ISIS, Russia continued to bomb Assad's non-ISIS rebel opponents as well. Ultimately, if Russia and Iran continue to fight for the Assad regime in Syria, the result will be an expansion of Iran's influence in Syria. This expansion will further destabilize the Middle East by placing Iranian forces in Sunni-Arab lands as well as on the border with Israel, expanding the Iranian hegemon, and strengthening Russia's presence in the region at the United States' expense.

> It is clear that Russia's main focus is on eliminating anti-Assad rebels who are not a part of ISIS and could, in fact, be possible allies to the anti-Assad West.

One thing is clear: when the United States fails to lead, enemies of freedom will fill the vacuum and do everything they can to spread terror and oppression. This is not just a matter of geopolitical gamesmanship between global superpowers. Real lives are on the line—the lives of Christians and other religious minorities in the Middle East, women and children, and innocent people of all ethnicities and nationalities. But as history has also made clear, in a globalized world, terror and chaos are not contained in one region. What happens there will impact our lives here in the United States as well.

But all hope is not lost. The United States and our allies can defeat this wave of aggression and terror. As the former prime minister of Great Britain Benjamin Disraeli regularly stated, "Forti nihil difficile"—nothing is too difficult for the brave. But time is running out.

11

An Ideological War

What Can We Do?

The war we now face is a fundamental one. Democracy is a product of Western societal values that prize the individual and individual freedom. The very idea of a form of government in which power is vested in the people, who rule through their freely chosen representatives, is at odds with Middle Eastern and Islamic cultures in which the only sovereign is Allah. Because Allah alone is sovereign, man may not change Allah's rules. There can be no room left for religious liberty or pluralism. Contrary man-made laws have no place in such a society. Accordingly, only one ruler is needed to enforce divine law, law that may not be questioned. Democracy, on the other hand, by its very nature gives people the room to enact new laws to meet with the changing needs—whether real or merely perceived—of a given society. Thus from the Islamic perspective, a democratic system of government is a direct affront to Allah's supremacy.

The belief system based on the absolute authority of Allah and his law has been ingrained in Muslim societies for centuries. The very term *Islam* means "submission,"[1] and the term *Muslim* means "one who submits."[2] Given that tradition, it is naïve to expect that democratic institutions would function as intended in fundamentally undemocratic cultures like Islamic countries. As with the election of Mohamed Morsi in Egypt and his subsequent Islamist foreign policy, a free vote may elect a leader, but leaders in such societies do not automatically reflect traditionally understood democratic principles. As dangerous as it is to assume that an elected leader will espouse democratic values, it's equally dangerous to assume that Jeffersonian democracy can be imposed upon Muslim countries in the Middle East.

Spread of Saudi Wahhabi and Iranian Revolution Culture

Although the American presence in the Middle East has been a stabilizing one, it has been complicated because even our Sunni allies are responsible for creating an atmosphere of radicalism. The clash of civilizations currently unfolding can be attributed in part to our ally Saudi Arabia, which has expended billions in petrodollars around the world to spread its extremist Sunni Wahhabi beliefs, "a strictly orthodox Sunni Muslim sect . . . [that] advocates a return to the early Islam . . . [and] rejects later innovations."[3] It's these beliefs that serve as one of the chief ideological motivations of Islamic terrorists, such as Osama bin Laden. A large amount of Saudi money has gone to constructing radical mosques and madrassas, religious schools that propagate Wahhabi beliefs to new generations.

Moreover, we must recognize that the nuclear deal negotiated by Secretary of State John Kerry places directly into Iran's hands the means to achieve their expansionist and apocalyptic goals.[4] While the Saudis are spreading fundamentalist-Sunni-Wahhabi ideology, the ayatollahs are spreading Islamic revolutionary jihad through both Shiites and Sunnis. The Islamic Revolution that started in 1979 continues to influence the hearts and minds of Muslims today.

American Presence in the Volatile Middle East

Yet, the present dangers in the Middle East are a substantial result of the failures of recent American foreign policy. The Obama administration failed to negotiate a status of forces agreement (SOFA)[5] with Iraq when U.S. forces withdrew from Iraq in 2011.[6] Obama also refrained from engaging in significant military action in Iraq and Syria when such action had the chance of success. These omissions led to the removal of U.S. forces, leaving a power vacuum in the region.[7] Iran, Russia, and ISIS have seized the opportunity, and all have grown stronger due to America's withdrawal from the Middle East. The civil wars raging in Iraq and Syria—in which Iran, Russia, and ISIS are currently embroiled—illustrate the resulting power struggle. The instability in the Middle East has also led to a rise in refugees displaced from their homes, especially in Syria.

Tackling Islamic Cultural Influence in the West

Historically America has played a major role in providing shelter and aid for refugees forced to flee their homes due to violence and oppression, and it should continue to do so. But a true concern exists that some of these so-called refugees are in fact terrorists utilizing American goodwill for the purpose of spreading jihadist terrorism.

Abdelhamid Abaaoud, the terrorist who orchestrated the Paris attacks, reportedly boasted that it was easy for the terrorists to move throughout Europe undetected, simply by mingling with migrants.[8] By pretending to be migrants and refugees, some of these terrorists were able to plot and execute attacks, moving between countries in an attempt to evade detection and capture. If America is to continue offering asylum to the ever-growing number of refugees from the turbulent Middle East, we must adopt a sensible policy for determining whether someone is genuinely a refugee or actually a jihadist.

Immigration of Muslims to America and other Western nations is not new, but it has increased in recent times. According to a 2011 survey conducted by the Pew Research Center, 63 percent of the 2.75 million Muslims in the United States are first-generation immigrants,[9] and 45 percent arrived in the United States after 1990.[10] Islamic influence can be brought into Western culture through the rapid, violent, overt route of jihadist terrorism, or the slow, subtle, inconspicuous route of promoting Sharia and Islamic culture over time.

Some Muslims chose to bring Islam to the West through violent acts of jihadist terrorism, as with the Orlando, San Bernardino, and Chattanooga attacks, the shooting of a Philadelphia police officer, and the Paris attacks. Tashfeen Malik, one of the San Bernardino shooters, had immigrated to the United States in the summer of 2014, less than two years before she and her husband perpetrated a massacre of fourteen people in December 2015.[11] According to

> **But a true concern exists that some of these so-called refugees are in fact terrorists utilizing American goodwill for the purpose of spreading jihadist terrorism.**

reports, the gunman who shot the Philadelphia police officer at point-blank range on January 7, 2015, claimed to have done so because "he believed that the police defend laws that are contrary to the teachings of the Quran."[12] These episodes of lone-wolf jihadist terrorism create a national security concern that justifies a careful examination of U.S. policy regarding Muslim immigration.

Even those Muslims who do not embrace violent jihadist doctrine may still desire to see Islamic influence come to dominate Western civilization through a process of subtle societal change and cultural incorporation. As we have mentioned, Islam itself teaches that it is superior to all other religions. It does not compromise with other religions or allow for a peaceful pluralism of faiths to coexist equally together. As a result, many Muslims do not assimilate well into Western societies but instead retain and promote a strong Islamic cultural identity,[13] thereby subverting the values of the societ-ies that have accepted them.

Another method of importing Islam to the West is the increased use of Sharia principles in legal disputes. In comparison to violent jihadist terrorism, increasing the application of Sharia is a back-door tactic of imposing Islamic influence onto Western culture. The movement has, up to this point, gained much more ground in the United Kingdom than in the United States. Nevertheless, in a democratic Western society, where statutes must be enacted by the legislature, implementing Sharia would require the majority of the population to be Muslim. Long-term demographic shifts take place over decades and sometimes even centuries; but to Muslims focused on an intergenerational conflict and movement, this is yet another part of the plan. Thus for some who desire to see Islamic law and culture exported to the West, violent jihadist terrorism still presents the most immediate option.

Fighting the War of Ideas, Islamophobia, and Political Correctness

The influence of the Islamic Revolution must be exposed and coun-tered. Not only must the unholy alliance between Iran, Syria, and Russia be recognized and combated, but so should the alliance be-tween Iran and terrorist organizations. It is equally important to acknowledge Iran's role as a primary engine powering the spread of Islamic revolutionary jihad around the world.

The struggle between the West and Islam is, at its core, an ideological war. Those who are willing to blow themselves up and unleash terror on innocents are motivated not by mere political agendas but by a fierce religious ideology rooted in their cultural and religious history. The surprising power of this ideological form of warfare is demonstrated by how quickly it has managed to spread around the world. The influence of revolutionary jihadist doctrine is no longer contained solely in Iran, the Middle East, or even Asia. As we have seen, it has already reached the West in the form of horrendous acts of terror[14] and through the subtle and gradual attempt to establish an acceptance of Sharia principles in Western nations.[15] Additionally, it's in the constant indoctrination of the "politically correct" media narrative decrying "intolerance" or "Islamophobia" when any connection is drawn between the Islamic religion and radical terrorism.

Countering a pervasive ideology requires the willingness to speak out loud and strong. The situation is complicated because two philosophies are involved: 1) the ideology of Islamic revolutionary jihad, and 2) the Western ideology of tolerance. The heart of tolerance is the desire to not harm other people. The ideology of jihad is the exact opposite: a desire to harm billions of non-Muslims around the world. That is why this battle of philosophies is difficult, but not impossible.

Calling an act of terrorism by its name is not Islamophobia. Identifying who committed the act is not Islamophobia. Trying to understand Islam is not Islamophobia, either. We must recognize what tolerance is—and what it is not. Telling the truth about radical jihadists is not being Islamophobic, nor is it intolerant—it is being honest. It's caring about saving lives. We must distinguish between commonsense analysis and irrational hatred.

It means that when we condemn an act of terrorism committed in the name of Islam, our tone should be measured and not full of hysterics.

We must also counter the stifling censorship of "political correctness," through which the academic, political, and media elite attempt to silence any views contrary to their own. The constant refrain of calling any critiques of Islamic terror "Islamophobia" must be effectively countered by persistent witness of our Christian love and charity for our fellow man, including all Muslims. This does not mean we cannot defend ourselves. It means that when we condemn an act of terrorism committed in the name of Islam, our tone should be measured and not full of hysterics.

The liberal left must be made to recognize the fundamental difference between calling an act of terrorism what it is and Islamophobia. Their, shall we say, phobia of reality gets in the way of seeing things as they are. They are well aware, as they constantly remind us, that our fight is not with the entire Islamic faith. But they forget that our fight *is* with the radical Muslim who uses that faith and parts of Islamic texts that *do* command Muslims to fight and kill non-Muslims to justify their violent and abhorrent actions. We must show the American public that we can develop effective strategies to counter evil only when we are able to accurately identify such evil and its source.

So what can we do? The responsibility of raising a voice against revolutionary jihad does not primarily rest on non-Muslims. Muslims who oppose it also have an obligation to speak up. After all, if the jihadists are misinterpreting Islam, it is the reformers within Islam whose religion is being tarnished. They are in a better position to defend their religion, condemn religiously based terrorism, and fight those who kill in its name. We must encourage them to do more than simply hold antiterrorism vigils as a show of solidarity with our fellow Muslims in Dearborn, Michigan, the city with America's highest proportion of Muslims.[16] We must encourage reformers within Islam to actively fight the jihadists, and we must assist them when and where we can. Probably the greatest aid we can give reformers is that of mere friendship. These reformers are fighting the war of ideas in the *ummah* against the jihadists, and our words can support them.

> After all, if the jihadists are misinterpreting Islam, it is the reformers within Islam whose religion is being tarnished.

The Four Madrassa Teachings

On June 6, 2015, Javed Ahmad Ghamidi, founding president of Al-Mawrid Institute and a Muslim scholar from Pakistan, said that Muslims are becoming terrorists because of the religious thought and teachings they are receiving in the madrassas (Islamic seminaries) and in their political movements.[17] According to Ghamidi, every madrassa is teaching four ideas, if not openly, then behind closed doors.[18]

The first idea is that if *kufr* (disbelief, denial of Islam), *shirk* (saying anything against the oneness of Allah), or *irtidad* (apostasy) occurs anywhere in the world, the punishment is death and Muslims must enforce that punishment.[19] The second idea is that non-Muslims are born to be subjugated. Only Muslims have the right to rule the world. Every non-Muslim government is illegitimate. When Muslims have power, they must take over that government.[20] The third idea is that the world must have one government of Muslims, called *Khilafah* (Caliphate). There is no need for separate governments.[21] And the fourth idea is that the concept of modern nation-states is *kufr*, which has no place in Islam.[22]

Ghamidi says too many Muslims are being taught this narrative about Islam. He suggests that a counternarrative must be taught. Otherwise Muslims will continue to become terrorists, one after another, and the Middle East will become a living hell.[23] It is Muslims like Ghamidi—who maintain that the jihadists misinterpret the Quran—who have the greatest interest and duty to promote a narrative of peace. Ideas affect behavior, and acts pursuant to jihadist ideas should be prosecuted. At this point, we must also recognize that Pakistani madrassas are overwhelmingly supported by petrodollars from our "ally" Saudi Arabia. The U.S. government must recognize this fact and develop a policy to confront Saudi Arabia and pressure it to stop such support.

A war of ideas is won not only by exposing the other side's

wrong ideas but also by presenting the truthfulness of the ideas and principles we fight for. From the ideas of Aristotle, Plato, Augustine, and Thomas Aquinas that informed our Founding Fathers to the literature of Western civilization, we must embrace our cultural heritage. By understanding our past and the values of Western civilization, we can better understand who we are and so defend our traditions against attacks from both without and within.

The Western Conundrum: How to React to Jihadist Atrocities

The United States was founded on the Judeo-Christian principles that undergird Western civilization. Those principles are expounded in our founding documents and embedded in our national institutions. Those principles respect and honor the inherent dignity of every person and seek to magnify and expand individual liberty. Our political system consciously and intentionally distributes political power to avoid the tyranny that so often accompanies centralization of power in the hands of a few, thereby protecting the liberty of our people. As Americans, each of us must recognize that the fundamental beliefs underlying the Judeo-Christian worldview stand in stark contrast to fundamental beliefs of the Islamic worldview. While the Judeo-Christian worldview seeks to preserve individual liberty for each person, the Islamic worldview seeks to bring all persons—Muslims and non-Muslims alike—into submission to Allah. While the Judeo-Christian worldview tolerates individual thought, opinion, and choices, the Islamic worldview demands conformity by everyone—Muslims and non-Muslims alike—to the socially accepted norms of Islam. Until we as a nation recognize such differences, Americans will never fully understand the challenges we face. Nor will we ever be able to craft an effective strategy to meaningfully confront such challenges.

The Western cultural values that underlie our political system remain strong and have withstood the test of time. The society we have built on such principles is the envy of mankind. Persons from every corner of the world—from every ethnic, racial, and religious group—continue to flock to our shores to avail themselves of the blessings God has bestowed upon us. Although Christian believers are called to "love your enemies"[24] and to "bless them that persecute you,"[25] the same is not required of government. Government serves as the agent of God to protect society from evildoers. As St. Paul noted in the Book of Romans, "[R]ulers are not a cause of fear for good behavior, but for evil. Do you want to have no fear of authority? Do what is good and you will have praise from the same. . . . But if you do what is evil, be afraid; for it does not bear the sword for nothing; for it is a minister of God, an avenger who brings wrath on the one who practices evil."[26] We clearly must understand the differing roles of the individual believer and of our government in dealing with radical Islamists, their worldview, and their ultimate goals.

Our national security is also paramount. We must look for and support political candidates who recognize the danger of the unholy alliance and inform our current representatives of the importance of this issue. Share what you've learned in this book. Ask your representatives to make sacrifices in order to defeat evil and stand up for what is good. Vote for candidates who are willing to do whatever it takes to defeat radical Islamic terrorists. This support must cross party lines. There's no reason both political parties can't be against the historic evils being perpetrated by violent jihadists around the world and on our home front. I'm friends with members of Congress from both parties who are engaged passionately in this fight. We must inform our fellow Americans about the issue and urge them to participate as well. If the informed American dutifully and

> If the informed American dutifully and courageously engages society on this issue, the ideological battle will be won, and the jihadists will ultimately be defeated.

courageously engages society on this issue, the ideological battle will be won, and the jihadists will ultimately be defeated.

This is a fight that can and must be won. But it won't be won overnight. None of the battles and wars fought and won by Americans have been quick or easy. They required sacrifice, grit, and unparalleled moral clarity. From Lexington and Concord to Gettysburg, Normandy, and Vietnam, to Afghanistan and Iraq, our country has fought evil and defended the oppressed. In order to do so again, we must realize the true nature of the enemies who stand against us and proclaim the shared values that have made America so exceptional all along.

ACKNOWLEDGMENTS

I have said before that books are team efforts. That is certainly true with this book. I would like to thank my colleagues at the Oxford Centre for the Study of Law & Public Policy—Andrew Ekonomou, Harry Hutchison, and Skip Ash. Our time at Oxford is one of research, writing, and reflection. This book is the culmination of the last three years of research and participation in various academic programs at Oxford. Shaheryar Gill, Joseph Williams, John Monaghan, and Marshall Goldman, all associated with our Oxford Centre, provided invaluable service in the compilation of this book. The team at Simon & Schuster's Howard Books, led by my publisher, Jonathan Merck, is always enthusiastic about our projects. That enthusiasm was shared by my agent, Curtis Wallace. This book benefited from the excellent skills of Howard Books' Ami McConnell, as well as Becky Nesbitt. Their editing made this a better book.

I truly believe we have to understand the motivating ideology, theology, and history of those who seek to destroy our Western concept of ordered liberty. By understanding these motivations, we are in a better place to deal with the export of their dangerous and deadly ideologies. That is what I have attempted to do here.

APPENDIX A

Comparative Chart

The following chart sets forth specific Islamic criminal and civil laws and compares them with U.S. laws, showing the inherent conflict between U.S. and Islamic standards of justice, punishments, and resolution of disputes.

Crimes and Punishments	Islamic Sharia	United States Law
Conversion from Islam (Apostasy)	Punished by death.[1]	Protected under the First Amendment's Free Exercise Clause.[2]
Blaspheming Muhammad	Punished by death.[3]	Protected under the First Amendment as free speech or expressive conduct.[4]
Consuming Alcohol	Punished by flogging of forty lashes.[5]	Allowed by state law upon reaching legal age.[6]
Female Genital Mutilation/Female Circumcision	Required under strict, traditional Sharia; generally done to promote women's chastity.[7]	Illegal.[8]

Crimes and Punishments	Islamic Sharia	United States Law
Marital Rape	A wife must have sex with her husband upon the husband's demand; if the wife refuses, the husband may take disciplinary steps (verbal admonition to physical beating).[9]	Forced sexual intercourse, even of a spouse, is punishable as domestic violence or marital rape.[10]
Polygamy	Men may take up to four wives; women may marry only one man.[11]	Illegal.[12]
Fornication	Punishable by one hundred lashes;[13] if an unmarried woman is raped but cannot provide the necessary witnesses, she will be lashed as a fornicator.[14]	Under the Supreme Court's interpretation of the Due Process Clause, fornication is legal for consenting individuals (subject to certain age restrictions prescribed by the states);[15] U.S. laws do not prescribe severe criminal penalties for unlawful fornication.
Short-term Contracted Sexual Relationships (mut'ah), or simply, prostitution	Permitted under the Shiite school of Islamic thought.[16]	Illegal in most states.[17]
Rape	If rape is proven, the rapist may either have to pay a marriage payment to the woman[18] or be punished as a fornicator or adulterer and receive lashes;[19] women who are raped may be convicted of *zina* (unlawful sexual intercourse),[20] punishable by stoning (if married) or lashes (if not married), unless they can produce four male Muslim eyewitnesses to prove they were raped.[21]	Perpetrator is punished by imprisonment; a woman's testimony is valid to establish rape, and the judge or jury decides based on all the evidence whether the sexual intercourse was forced or consensual; women are not punished for unlawful sexual intercourse if they cannot prove rape; evidence rules are designed to protect rape victims.[22]
Theft	Punished by amputation.[23]	Punished by fine or imprisonment.[24]

Family Law	Islamic Sharia	United States Law
Domestic Violence	The Quran allows a husband to beat his wife (or wives) to compel her to obey the husband's commands.[25]	Punishable by imprisonment; state protection is offered to the victim.[24]
Interfaith Marriage	Muslim women may only marry Muslim men; Muslim men may marry only Muslim, Jewish, or Christian women.[26]	With minor exceptions (e.g., age, consanguinity, etc.), everyone is free to marry the person of his or her choosing, regardless of religion, under the First and Fourteenth Amendments, and men and women must be treated equally by the law.[27]
Child Custody	Depending on whether the mother remarries or leaves Islam, custody will default to the father or mother.[28]	The child's interests are the determining factor;[29] whatever is in the "child's best interests" will generally determine the outcome of the custody proceeding.
Divorce	Generally, a husband may divorce his wife without cause by merely declaring his desire for a divorce to his wife three times, after which a Sharia court will finalize the divorce;[30] women do not obtain legal divorces on their own initiative, but merely *dissolve* their marriages and become lawfully separated from their husbands.[31] These dissolutions (*khula*) are limited to the grounds of lunacy, chronic disease, impotence, unchastity, and apostasy, and if women do choose to dissolve the marriage, they forfeit their financial security.[32]	Men and women have equal rights under the Fourteenth Amendment; both men and women may divorce each other and must do so through a judicial process that requires giving the other party notice and opportunity to be heard.[33]

Family Law	Islamic Sharia	United States Law
Forced Marriage	Parents, usually fathers, or *wali* (guardian), such as grandfathers, have the power to force their minor daughters to marry the men of the parent's choosing.[34]	Marriage is by the mutual consent of both parties (subject to minimum-age and consanguinity requirements prescribed by state law); marriages procured by force or duress are voidable.[35]
Testifying Witnesses: Men and Women	A woman's testimony is equal to half that of a man because of the supposed "deficiency of a woman's mind."[36]	Men and women must be treated equally under the Fourteenth Amendment's Equal Protection Clause.[37]

Glossary

Different authors spell Arabic words differently. We will use the following spellings unless the word appears in a direct quote.

Ahl al Bait: literally translated, "People of the House" or "Family of the House"; refers to the family of the Prophet Muhammad.

Aisha: one of Muhammad's wives; she was six years old when Muhammad married her and nine years old when the marriage was consummated.

Al-Ikhwan al-Muslimun: Muslim Brotherhood.

Al-Kitab: literally translated, "the Book"; a reference to the Quran, Islam's holy book and the primary source of Sharia.

Allah: the sole deity in Islam.

Al-Qaeda: the terrorist organization that orchestrated and carried out the 9/11 attacks and supports violent jihad for the global advancement of Islam.

Cairo Declaration on Human Rights: a declaration adopted in 1990 and submitted to the United Nations by the Member States of the Organisation of the Islamic Cooperation (OIC); declares the official Islamic perspective on human rights and guarantees freedom and the right to dignified life only in accordance with Sharia.

Caliph: term referring to those who succeeded Muhammad and served as head of the global Islamic community.

Caliphate: divinely instituted Islamic government run by a caliph.

Dar al harb: literally "territory of war"; constitutes all territories not under Islamic control.

Dar al Islam: territory under Islamic control.

Diaspora: the scattering of a people who were once in a small geographic area; applies to the Jewish people living outside Israel.

Diya: monetary compensation the perpetrator of a murder or bodily injury pays to the victim or his family in lieu of punishment.

Fatah: the military arm of the Palestinian Liberation Organization (PLO).

Fatwa: a religious edict or religio-legal opinion given by an Islamic cleric.

Fiqh: Islamic jurisprudence; the science of Islamic religious law.

Ghayba: a Shiite Islamic belief that the Mahdi, or messianic figure of Islam, has been born, but disappeared and is in hiding until the time comes for him to return and rule the world.

Hadd (Hadood): offenses against Allah for which the Quran and Sunnah prescribe severe penalties that often involve loss of life or limb.

Hadith: the second primary source of Islamic law recounting the Sunnah (actions and sayings of Muhammad); considered second in authority to the Quran.

Hamas: Palestinian organization that maintains power in the Gaza Strip, is devoted to the destruction of Israel, and believes in violent Islamic conquest; regards peaceful solutions to be in contradiction to the Islamic Resistance Movement; designated a foreign terrorist organization by the U.S. Department of State.

Hanafi: a school of Sunni jurisprudence that purportedly takes a moderate approach in applying Sharia principles to contemporary legal issues but nonetheless calls for total subjugation of the world under Sharia; prominent in Pakistan and Afghanistan.

Hanbali: the most rigid of the four schools of Sunni jurisprudence; stresses the puritanical aspects of Islam and is uncompromising in its adherence to orthodoxy; forms the basis of law in Saudi Arabia.

Harkat al Muqawamah al Islamiyah: Islamic Resistance Movement; commonly known as Hamas.

Hezbollah/Hizballah: militant Shiite group in Lebanon that maintains strong ties with both Iran and Syria.

Hijra: Muhammad's migration from Mecca to Medina, which signifies the beginning of the Islamic calendar.

Ijma: a consensus of Islamic jurists on Islamic legal issues arising after Muhammad's death.

Ijtihad: the hermeneutical efforts made by jurists in seeking knowledge of the rules of the Sharia through interpretation and to discover Allah's intention with respect to the rules of conduct.

Imam: spiritual and religious leader of a mosque and Islamic community.

Jafari: Shiite school of jurisprudence developed by Jafar as-Sadiq.

Jihad: struggle, holy war; includes greater jihad—fighting with the inner sinful self, and lesser jihad—outward violent struggle to establish Islam.

Jizyah: a poll tax that Jews and Christians who live in the territory of Islam must pay to maintain practice of their faith; otherwise, they must convert to Islam or fight and die.

Kaaba: the cube-shaped building at the center of Islam's sacred mosque, al-Masijd al-Haram, in Mecca. Muslims pray facing the Kaaba.

Lebanese National Movement (LMN): an umbrella organization of radical leftist groups, Muslim reform groups, and Palestinian resistance groups, which is supported by the PLO and various Arab states.

Mahr: dower or marriage payment to women; serves as a sort of spousal support when a husband divorces his wife but generally must be forfeited when a woman initiates dissolution of her marriage.

Maliki: one of the four schools of Sunni jurisprudence; prioritizes Islamic tenets in applying Sharia but allows for some consideration of local customs and equitable and practical concerns; prevalent in northern and western Africa, including Sudan.

Maronite: a member of the Maronite Church, a sect of Christianity; most adherents are from Mount Lebanon and surrounding areas.

Mossad: the Institute for Intelligence and Special Operations; the national intelligence agency of Israel.

Muhammad: Islam's founder and prophet.

Mujahedeen: persons engaged in jihad.

Murtad: an individual who willfully gives up the Islamic faith.

Muslim: a believer in or follower of Islam; generally, Muslims identify themselves with either Sunni or Shiite Islam.

Muslim Brotherhood: a fundamentalist Islamic movement, also known as the al-Ikhwan al-Muslimun, dedicated to resurrecting the true Islamic caliphate (divinely instituted Islamic government) based on Sharia; parent organization of Hamas; its political party was founded in Egypt in 1928 and introduced the party slogan, "Islam is the solution."

Muta: a legally permissible form of temporary, contract-based marriage with monetary payment as consideration; instituted by Muhammad but now endorsed only by Shiite Islam.

Naskh: the doctrine of abrogation or repeal of an earlier verse in the Quran by a later verse. (**Nasikh:** abrogating rule; **Mansukh:** abrogated rule.)

Nikah: contract of Islamic marriage.

Organisation of the Islamic Cooperation: the second largest international organization, second only to the United Nations; comprised of fifty-seven Islamic nations; its stated purposes include "to safeguard and protect the interests of the Muslim world" at the United Nations and "to defend the universality of [the] Islamic religion."

Palestine Liberation Organization (PLO): an umbrella organization of six Palestinian groups formed in 1964, dedicated to liberating Palestine through armed struggle; responsible for numerous terrorist attacks against Israelis since its inception.

Qadi: a Sharia judge.

Qibla: literally "direction"; the direction a Muslim should face during prayer.

Qisas: the equality in punishment; the "eye for an eye" retaliation prescribed by Sharia; the principle that the offender of a crime against a person should be punished in kind.

Qiyas: commonly recognized secondary sources of Sharia; the application of analogized rationalizations of Sharia principles to novel legal issues; limited to Sharia jurists.

Quran: Islam's holy book and the primary source of Sharia.

Riddah: apostasy; leaving Islam.

Sahih Bukhāri: one of Sunni Muslims' most trusted collections of hadith.

Shafi'i: school of Sunni jurisprudence; it is reluctant to create new legal principles for modern contexts and defers to those already existing in the Quran and Sunnah.

Sharia: Islamic law.

Shiite: one of the two major sects of Islam, accounting for approximately 10 to 15 percent of the world's Muslim population; follows the Jafari school of jurisprudence; has historically been at odds with the Sunni sect.

Shura Council: consultative body.

Status of Forces Agreement: an agreement between a host country and a foreign nation that is stationing military forces within the host country.

Sunnah: words, actions, approvals, silence, and customs ascribed to Muhammad; collected in hadiths.

Sunni: the more prominent of the two major sects of Islam, accounting for approximately 85 to 90 percent of the world's Muslim population.

Surah: the term for "chapters" in the Quran.

Talak (talaq): divorce.

Taliban: Islamic terrorists in Afghanistan who adhere to a strict interpretation of Islam.

Tazir: offenses against society; penalties are left to the discretion of the qadi (Sharia judge) because Sharia provides no specific punishment; distinct from *hadd* offenses and penalties.

Torah: literally "instruction" or "teaching"; is the foundational scripture of the Jewish people and consists of the first five books of the Old Testament.

Ummah: the global Islamic community that encompasses all Muslims, regardless of their geographical location or country of citizenship.

Vilayat-e-faqih: the guardianship of the Islamic Jurist; a doctrine of Shiite Islam, in which the jurist has custodianship over the Islamic people; the concept forms the basis of the Iranian government.

Wali: guardian or protector.

Waqf: a required religious endowment under Islamic law; the donation can be land, money, or a building given for charitable or religious purposes.

Zina: unlawful sexual intercourse, including adultery and fornication, for which Sharia prescribes harsh penalties (generally flogging or stoning).

Zionist: a political and nationalist movement of the Jewish diaspora; supports the re-establishment of a Jewish homeland in Israel's historic boundaries.

Zoroastrianism: a religion that follows the teachings of Zoroaster, a Persian prophet.

APPENDIX C

Constitution of the Islamic Republic of Iran*

Preamble

The Constitution of the Islamic Republic of Iran advances the cultural, social, political, and economic institutions of Iranian society based on Islamic principles and norms, which represent an honest aspiration of the Islamic Ummah. This aspiration was exemplified by the nature of the great Islamic Revolution of Iran, and by the course of the Muslim people's struggle, from its beginning until victory, as reflected in the decisive and forceful calls raised by all segments of the populations. Now, at the threshold of this great victory, our nation, with all its beings, seeks its fulfillment.

The basic characteristic of this revolution, which distinguishes it from other movements that have taken place in Iran during the past hundred years, is its ideological and Islamic nature. After experiencing the anti-despotic constitutional movement and the anti-colonialist movement centered on the nationalization of the oil industry, the Muslim people of Iran learned from this costly

* QANUNI ASSASSI JUMHURRI ISLAMAI IRAN [CONSTITUTION OF THE ISLAMIC REPUBLIC OF IRAN] 1358 [1980], http://www.servat.unibe.ch/icl/ir00000_.html. Only relevant parts of the constitution are printed here.

experience that the obvious and fundamental reason for the failure of those movements was their lack of an ideological basis. Although the Islamic line of thought and the direction provided by militant religious leaders played an essential role in the recent movements, nonetheless, the struggles waged in the course of those movements quickly fell into stagnation due to departure from genuine Islamic positions. Thus it was that the awakened conscience of the nation, under the leadership of Imam Khumayni, came to perceive the necessity of pursuing a genuinely Islamic and ideological line in its struggles. And this time, the militant *ulama* of the country, who had always been in the forefront of popular movements, together with the committed writers and intellectuals, found new impetus by following his leadership.

The Dawn of the Movement

The devastating protest of Imam Khumayni against the American conspiracy known as the "White Revolution," which was a step intended to stabilize the foundations of despotic rule and to reinforce the political, cultural, and economic dependence of Iran on world imperialism, brought into being a united movement of the people and, immediately afterwards, a momentous revolution of the Muslim nation in June 1963. Although this revolution was drowned in blood, in reality it heralded the beginning of the blossoming of a glorious and massive uprising, which confirmed the central role of Imam Khumayni as an Islamic leader. Despite his exile from Iran after his protest against the humiliating law of capitulation (which provided legal immunity for American advisers), the firm bond between the Imam and the people endured, and the Muslim nation, particularly committed intellectuals and militant *ulama*, continued their struggle in the face of banishment and imprisonment, torture and execution.

Throughout this time, the conscious and responsible segment of society was bringing enlightenment to the people from the strong-holds of the mosques, centers of religious teaching, and universities. Drawing inspiration from the revolutionary and fertile teachings of Islam, they began the unrelenting yet fruitful struggle of raising the level of ideological awareness and revolutionary consciousness of the Muslim people. The despotic regime which had begun the suppression of the Islamic movement with barbaric attacks on the Faydiyyah Madrasah, Tehran University, and all other active cen-ters of revolution, in an effort to evade the revolutionary anger of the people, resorted to the most savage and brutal measures. And in these circumstances, execution by firing squads, endurance of medieval tortures, and long terms of imprisonment were the price our Muslim nation had to pay to prove its firm resolve to continue the struggle. The Islamic Revolution of Iran was nurtured by the blood of hundreds of young men and women, infused with faith, who raised their cries of *"Allahu Akbar"* at daybreak in execution yards, or were gunned down by the enemy in streets and market-places. Meanwhile, the continuing declarations and messages of the Imam that were issued on various occasions, extended and deep-ened the consciousness and determination of the Muslim nation to the utmost.

Islamic Government

The plan of the Islamic government as proposed by Imam Khu-mayni at the height of the period of repression and strangulation practiced by the despotic regime produced a new, specific, and streamlined motive for the Muslim people, opening up before them the true path of Islamic ideological struggle, and giving greater intensity to the struggle of militant and committed Muslims both within the country and abroad.

The Form of Government in Islam

In the view of Islam, government does not derive from the interests of a class, nor does it serve the domination of an individual or a group. Rather, it represents the fulfillment of the political ideal of a people who bear a common faith and common outlook, taking an organized form in order to initiate the process of intellectual and ideological evolution towards the final goal, i.e., movement toward Allah. Our nation, in the course of its revolutionary developments, has cleansed itself of the dust and impurities that accumulated during the past and purged itself of foreign ideological influences, returning to authentic intellectual standpoints and worldview of Islam. It now intends to establish an ideal and model society on the basis of Islamic norms. The mission of the Constitution is to realize the ideological objectives of the movement and to create conditions conducive to the development of man in accordance with the noble and universal values of Islam.

With due attention to the Islamic content of the Iranian Revolution, the Constitution provides the necessary basis for ensuring the continuation of the Revolution at home and abroad. In particular, in the development of international relations, the Constitution will strive with other Islamic and popular movements to prepare the way for the formation of a single world community (in accordance with the Koranic verse *"This your community is a single community, and I am your Lord, so worship Me"* [21:92]), and to assure the continuation of the struggle for the liberation of all deprived and oppressed peoples in the world.

With due attention to the essential character of this great movement, the Constitution guarantees the rejection of all forms of intellectual and social tyranny and economic monopoly, and aims at entrusting the destinies of the people to the people themselves in order to break completely with the system of oppression. (This is in accordance with the Koranic verse *"He removes from them their burdens and the fetters that were upon them"* [7:157]).

In creating, on the basis of ideological outlook, the political infrastructures and institutions that are the foundation of society, the righteous will assume the responsibility of governing and administering the country (in accordance with the Koranic verse *"Verily My righteous servants shall inherit the earth"* [21:105]). Legislation setting forth regulations for the administration of society will revolve around the Koran and the Sunnah. Accordingly, the exercise of meticulous and earnest supervision by just, pious, and committed scholars of Islam is an absolute necessity. In addition, the aim of government is to foster the growth of man in such a way that he progresses towards the establishment of a Divine order (in accordance with the Koranic phrase *"And toward God is the journeying"* [3:28]); and to create favorable conditions for the emergence and blossoming of man's innate capacities, so that the theomorphic dimensions of the human being are manifested (in accordance with the injunction of the Prophet (S) *"Mold yourselves according to the Divine morality"*); this goal cannot be attained without the active and broad participation of all segments of society in the process of social development.

An Ideological Army

In the formation and equipping of the country's defense forces, due attention must be paid to faith and ideology as the basic criteria. Accordingly, the Army of the Islamic Republic of Iran and the Islamic Revolutionary Guards Corps are to be organized in conformity with this goal, and they will be responsible not only for guarding and preserving the frontiers of the country, but also for fulfilling the ideological mission of jihad in God's way; that is, extending the sovereignty of God's law throughout the world (this is in accordance with the Koranic verse *"Prepare against them whatever force you are able to muster, and strings of horses, striking fear into the enemy of God and your enemy, and others besides them"* [8:60]).

The Judiciary in the Constitution

The judiciary is of vital importance in the context of safeguarding the rights of the people in accordance with the line followed by the Islamic movement, and the prevention of deviations within the Islamic nation. Provision has therefore been made for the creation of a judicial system based on Islamic justice and operated by just judges with meticulous knowledge of the Islamic laws.

Executive Power

Considering the particular importance of the executive power in implementing the laws and ordinances of Islam for the sake of establishing the rule of just relations over society, and considering, too, its vital role in paving the way for the attainment of the ultimate goal of life, the executive power must work toward the creation of an Islamic society. Consequently, the confinement of the executive power within any kind of complex and inhibiting system that delays or impedes the attainment of this goal is rejected by Islam. Therefore, the system of bureaucracy, the result and product of old forms of government, will be firmly cast away, so that an executive system that functions efficiently and swiftly in the fulfillment of its administrative commitments comes into existence.

Mass-Communication Media

The mass-communication media, radio and television, must serve the diffusion of Islamic culture in pursuit of the evolutionary course of the Islamic Revolution. To this end, the media should be used as a forum for healthy encounter of different ideas, but they must strictly refrain from diffusion and propagation of destructive and anti-Islamic practices.

General Principles

Article 1 [Form of Government]

The form of government of Iran is that of an Islamic Republic, endorsed by the people of Iran on the basis of their long-standing belief in the sovereignty of truth and Koranic justice, in the referendum of 29 and 30 March 1979, through the affirmative vote of a majority of 98.2% of eligible voters, held after the victorious Islamic Revolution led by Imam Khumayni.

Article 2 [Foundational Principles]

The Islamic Republic is a system based on belief in:

1) the One God (as stated in the phrase *"There is no god except Allah"*), His exclusive sovereignty and right to legislate, and the necessity of submission to His commands;

2) Divine revelation and its fundamental role in setting forth the laws;

3) the return to God in the Hereafter, and the constructive role of this belief in the course of man's ascent towards God;

4) the justice of God in creation and legislation;

5) continuous leadership and perpetual guidance, and its fundamental role in ensuring the uninterrupted process of the revolution of Islam;

6) the exalted dignity and value of man, and his freedom coupled with responsibility before God; in which equity, justice, political, economic, social, and cultural independence, and national solidarity are secured by recourse to:

a) continuous leadership of the holy persons, possessing necessary qualifications, exercised on the basis of the Koran and the Sunnah, upon all of whom be peace;

b) sciences and arts and the most advanced results of human experience, together with the effort to advance them further;

c) negation of all forms of oppression, both the infliction of and the submission to it, and of dominance, both its imposition and its acceptance.

Article 3 [State Goals]

5) the complete elimination of imperialism and the prevention of foreign influence;

15) the expansion and strengthening of Islamic brotherhood and public cooperation among all the people;

16) framing the foreign policy of the country on the basis of Islamic criteria, fraternal commitment to all Muslims, and unsparing support to the freedom fighters of the world.

Article 5 [Office of Religious Leader]

During the occultation of the Wali al-'Asr (may God hasten his reappearance), the leadership of the Ummah devolve upon the just and pious person, who is fully aware of the circumstances of his age, courageous, resourceful, and possessed of administrative ability, will assume the responsibilities of this office in accordance with Article 107.

Article 11 [Unity of Islam Principle]

In accordance with the sacred verse of the Koran *"This your community is a single community, and I am your Lord, so worship Me"* [21:92], all Muslims form a single nation, and the government of the Islamic Republic of Iran have the duty of formulating its general policies with a view to cultivating the friendship and unity of all Muslim peoples, and it must constantly strive to bring about the political, economic, and cultural unity of the Islamic world.

Article 12 [Official Religion]

The official religion of Iran is Islam and the Twelver Ja'fari school, and this principle will remain eternally immutable.

Article 14 [Non-Muslims' Rights]

In accordance with the sacred verse "*God does not forbid you to deal kindly and justly with those who have not fought against you because of your religion and who have not expelled you from your homes*" [60:8], the government of the Islamic Republic of Iran and all Muslims are duty-bound to treat non-Muslims in conformity with ethical norms and the principles of Islamic justice and equity, and to respect their human rights. This principle applies to all who refrain from engaging in conspiracy or activity against Islam and the Islamic Republic of Iran.

The Rights of the People

Article 24 [Freedom of the Press]

Publications and the press have freedom of expression except when it is detrimental to the fundamental principles of Islam or the rights of the public. The details of this exception will be specified by law.

Article 26 [Freedom of Association]

The formation of parties, societies, political or professional associations, as well as religious societies, whether Islamic or pertaining to one of the recognized religious minorities, is permitted provided they do not violate the principles of independence, freedom, national unity, the criteria of Islam, or the basis of the Islamic Republic. No one may be prevented from participating in the aforementioned groups, or be compelled to participate in them.

Article 27 [Freedom of Assembly]

Public gatherings and marches may be freely held, provided arms are not carried and that they are not detrimental to the fundamental principles of Islam.

The Right of National Sovereignty

Article 56 [Divine Right of Sovereignty]

Absolute sovereignty over the world and man belongs to God, and it is He Who has made man master of his own social destiny. No one can deprive man of this divine right, nor subordinate it to the vested interests of a particular individual or group. The people are to exercise this divine right in the manner specified in the following articles.

Article 57 [Separation of Powers]

The powers of government in the Islamic Republic are vested in the legislature, the judiciary, and the executive powers, functioning under the supervision of the absolute religious Leader and the Leadership of the Ummah, in accordance with the forthcoming articles of this Constitution. These powers are independent of each other.

Powers and Authority of the Islamic Consultative Assembly

Article 72 [Limits]

The Islamic Consultative Assembly cannot enact laws contrary to the official religion of the country or to the Constitution. It is the duty of the Guardian Council to determine whether a violation has occurred, in accordance with Article 96.

The Army and the Islamic Revolution Guards Corps

Article 144 [Islamic Army]

The Army of the Islamic Republic of Iran must be an Islamic Army, i.e., committed to Islamic ideology and the people, and must recruit into its service individuals who have faith in the objectives of the Islamic Revolution and are devoted to the cause of realizing its goals.

Article 145 [No Foreigners]

No foreigner will be accepted into the Army or security forces of the country.

Article 146 [No Foreign Military Base]

The establishment of any kind of foreign military base in Iran, even for peaceful purposes, is forbidden.

Article 147 [Peace Functions]

In time of peace, the government must utilize the personnel and technical equipment of the Army in relief operations, and for educational and productive ends, and the Construction Jihad while fully observing the criteria of Islamic justice and ensuring that such utilization does not harm the combat-readiness of the Army.

The Army and the Islamic Revolution Guards Corps

Article 150 [Islamic Revolution Guards Corps]

The Islamic Revolution Guards Corps, organized in the early days of the triumph of the Revolution, is to be maintained so that it may continue in its role of guarding the Revolution and its achievements. The scope of the duties of this Corps, and its areas of responsibility, in relation to the duties and areas of responsibility of the other Armed Forces, are to be determined by law with emphasis on brotherly cooperation and harmony among them.

Foreign Policy

Article 152 [Principles]

The foreign policy of the Islamic Republic of Iran is based upon the rejection of all forms of domination, both the exertion of it and submission to it, the preservation of the independence of the country in all respects and its territorial integrity, the defense of the rights of all Muslims, nonalignment with respect to the hegemonist superpowers, and the maintenance of mutually peaceful relations with all non-belligerent States.

Article 153 [No Foreign Control]

Any form of agreement resulting in foreign control over the natural resources, economy, army, or culture of the country, as well as other aspects of the national life, is forbidden.

Article 154 [Independence, Support of Just Struggles]

The Islamic Republic of Iran has as its ideal human felicity throughout human society, and considers the attainment of independence, freedom, and rule of justice and truth to be the right of all people of the world. Accordingly, while scrupulously refraining from all forms of interference in the internal affairs of other nations, it supports the just struggles of the freedom fighters against the oppressors in every corner of the globe.

Radio and Television

Article 175 [Freedom of Expression, Government Control]

1) The freedom of expression and dissemination of thoughts in the Radio and Television of the Islamic Republic of Iran must be guaranteed in keeping with the Islamic criteria and the best interests of the country.

2) The appointment and dismissal of the head of the Radio and Television of the Islamic Republic of Iran rests with the Leader. A council consisting of two representatives each of the President, the head of the judiciary branch, and the Islamic Consultative Assembly shall supervise the functioning of this organization.

3) The policies and the manner of managing the organization and its supervision will be determined by law.

The Revision of the Constitution

Article 177 [Revision by Council and Referendum]

5) The contents of the articles of the Constitution related to the Islamic character of the political system; the basis of all the rules and regulations according to Islamic criteria; the religious footing; the objectives of the Islamic Republic of Iran; the democratic character of the government; the holy principle; the Imamate of Ummah; and the administration of the affairs of the country based on national referenda, official religion of Iran and the religious school are unalterable.

NOTES

CHAPTER ONE: EXPORTING TERRORISM

1. Steve Almasy et al., "Paris Massacre: At Least 128 Killed in Gunfire and Blasts, French Officials Say," CNN, November 14, 2015, http://www.cnn.com/2015/11/13/world/paris-shooting/.

2. "2015 Paris Terror Attacks Fast Facts," CNN, December 24, 2015, http://www.cnn.com/2015/12/08/europe/2015-paris-terror-attacks-fast-facts/.

3. Ibid.

4. Ibid.

5. Ibid.

6. http://www.wsj.com/articles/investigators-home-in-on-scope-of-terror-network-behind-brussels-paris-attacks-1459728742.

7. Ibid.

8. http://abcnews.go.com/International/brussels-airport-resume-flights-sunday/story?id=38104330.

9. Merrit Kennedy and Camila Domonoske, "The Victims of the Brussels Attacks: What We Know," NPR (March 31, 2016, 10:30 AM), http://www.npr.org/sections/the-two-way/2016/03/26/4719 82262/what-we-know-about-the-victims-of-the-brussels-attack.

10. "Istanbul Ataturk Airport Attack: 41 Dead and More than 230 Hurt," BBC News (June 29, 2016), http://www.bbc.com/news/world-europe-36658187.

11. Alissa J. Rubin et al., "Terrorist Attack in Nice, France, Leaves 84 Dead and 202 Injured," *New York Times* (July 15, 2016), http://www

.nytimes.com/2016/07/16/world/europe/attack-nice-bastille
-day.html?r=0.

12. Steve Almasy et al., "At Least 14 People Killed in Shooting in
San Bernardino; Suspect Identified," CNN (December 3, 2015,
12:11 PM), http://www.cnn.com/2015/12/02/us/san-bernardino
-shooting/; Michael Schmidt and Richard Perez-Pena, "F.B.I.
Treating San Bernardino Attack as Terrorism Case," *New York
Times* (December 4, 2015), http://www.nytimes.com/2015/12/05
/us/tashfeen-malik-islamic-state.html?_r=0.

13. Schmidt and Perez-Pena, "F.B.I. Treating San Bernardino Attack
as Terrorism Case."

14. Karen Leigh and Maria Abi-Habib, "Islamic State Praises Orlando,"
Wall Street Journal (June 13, 2016, 11:39 AM), http://www.wsj.com
/articles/islamic-state-praises-orlando-shooter-1465815349.

15. Ibid.

16. Emily Shapiro, "Man Accused of Shooting Philly Cop Pledged
Allegiance to ISIS, Police Say," ABC News (January 8, 2016, 5:43
PM), http://abcnews.go.com/US/man-accused-shooting-philly-cop
-confessed-committing-act/story?id=36169588.

17. Ibid.

18. Kristina Sgueglia, "Chattanooga Shootings 'Inspired' by
Terrorists, FBI Chief Says," CNN (December 16, 2016, 4:23 PM),
http://www.cnn.com/2015/12/16/us/chattanooga-shooting-terrorist
-inspiration/.

19. "Gunman Shoots Philadelphia Police Officer 'in the Name of
Islam,'" Reuters (January 9, 2016, 4:41 PM), http://www.cnbc
.com/2016/01/09/gunman-shoots-philadelphia-police-officer-in
-the-name-of-islam.html.

20. Greg Botelho et al., "Beirut Suicide Bombings Kill 43; Suspect
Claims ISIS Sent Attackers," CNN, November 16, 2015, http://
www.cnn.com/2015/11/12/middleeast/beirut-explosions/.

21. Ibid.

22. "Turkey: 'IS Suicide Bomber' Kills 10 in Istanbul Sultanahmet
District," BBC News, January 12, 2016, http://www.bbc.com
/news/world-europe-35290760; Greg Botelho et al., "ISIS
Member Behind Deadly Istanbul Suicide Blast, PM Says," CNN,
January 12, 2016, http://www.cnn.com/2016/01/12/europe/turkey-
istanbul-explosion/.

23. "'IS Suicide Bomber' Kills 10 in Istanbul."

24. Ibid.

25. Sophia Saifi and Greg Botelho, "In Pakistan School Attack, Taliban Terrorists Kill 145, Mostly Children," CNN, December 17, 2014, http://www.cnn.com/2014/12/16/world/asia/pakistan-peshawar -school-attack/.

26. "Rocket Attack on Israel from Gaza," Israel Defense Forces, https://www.idfblog.com/facts-figures/rocket-attacks-toward-israel (last visited July 15, 2016).

27. Ori Lewis, "West Bank Tensions Rise after Palestinian Stabbings in Israeli Settlements," Reuters (January 18, 2016, 12:59 PM), http://www.reuters.com/article/us-israel-palestinians-idUSKC N0UW1AG.

28. Peter L. Hahn, *Crisis and Crossfire: The United States and the Middle East Since 1945* (Washington, DC: Potomac Books, 2005), 1.

29. Ibid., 5.

30. Ibid.

31. Ibid., 5–7.

32. Ibid., 7–8.

33. Ibid., 105.

34. Ibid., 115.

35. Ibid., 120–22.

36. Yaroslav Trofimov, "America's Fading Footprint in the Middle East," *Wall Street Journal*, October 9, 2015, http://www.wsj.com /articles/americas-fading-footprint-in-the-middle-east-1444411954.

37. Ibid.

38. Ibid.

39. Ibid.

40. Ibid.

41. Ibid.

42. Maxim A. Suchkov, "Russia's Plan for the Middle East," *National Interest*, January 15, 2016, http://nationalinterest.org/feature/russias -plan-the-middle-east-14908.

43. Jonathan Saul, "Exclusive: Russia Steps Up Military Lifeline to Syria's Assad," Reuters, January 17, 2014, http://www.reuters.com /article/us-syria-russia-arms-idUSBREA0G0MN20140117.

44. Lucas Tomlinson, "Defiant Iran Ignores UN Ban, Hits Up Putin for High-Tech Tanks, Fighter Jets," Fox News, February 16, 2016, http://www.foxnews.com/world/2016/02/16/iran-s-defense-chief -meets-putin-to-discuss-controversial-sale-fighter-jets-tanks.html.

45. S.C. Res. 2231, Annex B ¶ 5, July 20, 2015.

46. Tomlinson, "Defiant Iran Ignores UN Ban."

47. "Russia, Iran to Reinforce Military Cooperation," *Al Arabiya English*, February 17, 2016, http://english.alarabiya.net/en/News /middle-east/2016/02/17/Russia-Iran-ready-to-reinforce-military -cooperation.html.

48. Antoun Issa, "Russia-Iran Ties Warm over Syria: Marriage of Convenience or Lasting Alliance?," *National*, October 20, 2015, http://www.thenational.ae/world/europe/russia-iran-ties-warm -over-syria-marriage-of-convenience-or-lasting-alliance.

49. Guide to the Syrian Rebels, BBC News, December 13, 2013, http:// www.bbc.com/news/world-middle-east-24403003.

50. Syed Kamran Hashmi, "What Do Saudis Want from Pakistan?," *Daily Times*, January 15, 2016, http://www.dailytimes.com.pk /opinion/15-Jan-2016/what-do-saudis-want-from-pakistan; Ben Hubbard, "Iranian Protestors Ransack Saudi Embassy After Execution of Shiite Cleric," *New York Times*, January 2, 2016, http:// www.nytimes.com/2016/01/03/world/middleeast/saudi-arabia -executes-47-sheikh-nimr-shiite-cleric.html.

51. Hashmi, "What Do Saudis Want from Pakistan?"

52. Ibid.

53. "Joint Comprehensive Plan of Action," U.S. Department of State, July 14, 2015, http://www.state.gov/documents/organization/245317 .pdf.

54. Kenneth Katzman and Paul K. Kerr, Congressional Research Service, R43333, Iran Nuclear Agreement 1 (2016) (hereinafter "Iran Nuclear Agreement").

55. Ibid., 17, 21.

56. Kenneth Katzman, Congressional Research Service, RS20871, Iran Sanctions 2–3 (2016).

57. Jonah Hicap, "Obama Set to Release $150-Billion Iranian Assets as US Senate Fails to Block Nuke Deal, *Christianity Today*, September 20, 2015," http://www.christiantoday.com/article/obama.set.to .order.release.of.150.b.iran.assets.as.us.senate.fails.to.block.nuke .deal/65222.htm; Tim Mak, "Obama Admin Fears Iran Deal Will Release Billions for Terror Attacks," *Daily Beast*, July 8, 2015, http://www.thedailybeast.com/articles/2015/07/08/obama-admin -fears-iran-deal-could-give-tehran-billions-for-terror.html.

58. Iran Nuclear Agreement.

59. *The Export* (ACLJ Films, 2011).

60. Ibid.

61. Ashley Collman, "How Homeland's Peter Quinn Delivered

Prophetic Speech on ISIS and America's 'Strategy' in Syria Six Weeks Ago," *Daily Mail* (November 16, 2016, 2:26 PM), http://www.dailymail.co.uk/news/article-3320487/Homeland-s-Peter-Quinn-delivers-prescient-speech-ISIS-America-s-lack-strategy-Syria.html#ixzz41DP6MveR.

62. Winston Churchill, "We Shall Fight on the Beaches" (June 4, 1940), http://www.winstonchurchill.org/resources/speeches/1940-the-finest-hour/129-we-shall-fight-on-the-beaches.

CHAPTER TWO: RISING FROM THE ASHES OF THE OTTOMAN EMPIRE

1. Mesopotamia is the ancient Greek name for the area of land stretching between the Euphrates and Tigris rivers, including land that is now within the territories of modern Syria and Iraq. Hans Jörg Nissen and Peter Heine, *From Mesopotamia to Iraq: A Concise History* (Chicago: University of Chicago Press, 2009), 1.
2. Caroline Finkel, *Osman's Dream: The History of the Ottoman Empire* (New York: Basic Books), 4–5.
3. Mehmet Sinan Birdal, *The Holy Roman Empire and the Ottomans: From Global Imperial Power to Absolutist States* (London and New York: I. B. Tauris, 2011), 118; Donald Quataert, *The Ottoman Empire, 1700–1922* (New York: Cambridge University Press, 2005), 13, 60–61.
4. Birdal, *The Holy Roman Empire and the Ottomans*, 60–61, 120.
5. Quataert, *The Ottoman Empire*, 20–24.
6. Philip K. Hitti, *History of the Arabs*, 10th ed. (Basingstoke, England: Palgrave Macmillan, 2002), 285, 286. The successor Caliphate, the Abbasids, were not full-blooded Arabs and their coup drew the "purely Arab phase of the Islamic empire . . . towards its close." Ibid., 286. The Abbasids's reign ended de jure in 1543 but the Abbasid caliph had been a puppet of the Mamluks (of Turkish and Armenian descent) since 1261. Ibid., 489, 671.
7. Scott Anderson, *Lawrence in Arabia* (New York: Doubleday 2013), 34.
8. Ibid.
9. Ibid.
10. Ibid.
11. Ibid.
12. Ibid.
13. Ibid., 34–35.
14. Ibid., 40.

15. Ibid., 55.
16. Steven Wagner, "The Zionist Movement in Search of Grand Strategy," *Journal of Military and Strategic Studies* 16 (2015): 61, 62.
17. Anderson, *Lawrence in Arabia*, 52.
18. Ibid.
19. "Dreyfus Affair," *Encyclopaedia Britannica*, http://www.britannica .com/event/Dreyfus-affair (last visited April 22, 2016).
20. Ibid.
21. Ibid.
22. Ibid.
23. Ibid.
24. Ibid.
25. Ibid.
26. Anderson, *Lawrence in Arabia*, 52.
27. Ibid.
28. Ibid.
29. Ibid.
30. Ibid.
31. Ibid., 52–53.
32. Ibid., 53.
33. Ibid., 35.
34. Ibid.
35. Ibid.
36. Ibid.
37. Ibid.
38. Quataert, 60; Dardanelles, *Encyclopaedia Britannica*, http://www .britannica.com/place/Dardanelles (last visited April 26, 2016).
39. Ibid., 61.
40. Mahdi Abdul Hadi, "The Evolution of Palestine 1," unpublished paper, (June 9, 2015), www.passia.org/about_us/MahdiPapers /15.DOC. See also Gilbert Clayton, "Arabia and the Arabs," *Journal of the Royal Institute of International Affairs* (January 1929): 8, 9, 11.
41. *Sharif* is an honorific meaning "distinguished, eminent, illustrious or noble." It is an hereditary title that connotes religious, not temporal, leadership. Avi Shlaim, *Lion of Jordan* (New York: Knopf, 2008), 4. But see Sean McMeekin, The *Berlin–Baghdad Express* (Cambridge, MA: Belknap Press of Harvard University Press, 2010), 64. ("a glorified protection racket")
42. James L. Bowden, "An Empire of the Hejaz? An Examination of

Sharif Hussein's Pre–World War I Imperial Ambitions," *World History Bulletin*, Spring 2015, 4.

43. Clayton, "Arabia and the Arabs," 9.
44. McMeekin, *The Berlin–Baghdad Express*, 64.
45. Ibid.
46. Ibid.
47. Ibid.
48. Sean McMeekin, *The Ottoman Endgame* (New York: Penguin Press, 2015), 55.
49. Shlaim, *Lion of Jordan*, 4.
50. Ibid.
51. Ibid.
52. Ibid., 3–5.
53. Shlaim, *Lion of Jordan*, 4.
54. McMeekin, *The Berlin-Baghdad Express*, 64.
55. Bowden, "An Empire of the Hejaz?", 4.
56. Shlaim, *Lion of Jordan*, 5.
57. Ibid., 6. See also McMeekin, *The Ottoman Endgame*, 304.
58. "Arabia and the Arabs," 9.
59. Ibid.
60. Ibid.
61. Ibid., 9–10. The hill tribes became Yemen and were granted freedom by the Treaty of Lausanne. Jane Smiley Hart, Supplement to the Chronology, *Middle East Journal* (Winter–Spring 1963), 148.
62. "Arabia and the Arabs," 9–10.
63. Ibid., 13.
64. Anderson, *Lawrence in Arabia*, 47.
65. Ibid.
66. Ibid.
67. Bowden, "An Empire of the Hejaz?", 5.
68. Shlaim, *Lion of Jordan*, 7.
69. Ibid., 5–6.
70. Bowden, "An Empire of the Hejaz?", 5.
71. Ibid.
72. Letter from Sharif Hussein of Mecca to Sir Henry McMahon, His Majesty's High Commissioner at Cairo (July 14, 1915), http://www.jewishvirtuallibrary.org/jsource/History/hussmac1.html#1.
73. Ibid., Letter No. 1.
74. Bowden, "An Empire of the Hejaz?", 5.
75. Ibid.

76. Hussein-McMahon Correspondence, Letter No. 3.

77. Ibid., Letter No. 2.

78. Ibid., Letter No. 4.

79. Eugene Rogan, *The Fall of the Ottomans* (New York: Basic Books, 2015), 47–48.

80. Florence Waters, "Germany's Grand First World War Jihad Experiment," *Telegraph*, August 10, 2014, 2.

81. Rogan, *The Fall of the Ottomans*, 48.

82. Tibor Krausz, "The Kaiser's Jihad," *Jerusalem Post*, February 1, 2011, 1; Rogan, *The Fall of the Ottomans*, 48.

83. Anderson, *Lawrence in Arabia*, 36.

84. Ibid., 30.

85. Ibid.

86. Ibid.

87. Krausz, "The Kaiser's Jihad," 3.

88. Ibid.

89. Ibid., 1.

90. Anderson, *Lawrence in Arabia*, 38.

91. Ibid.

92. McMeekin, *The Berlin–Baghdad Express*, 3.

93. Battle of Omdurman: *Encyclopaedia Britannica*/African History, http://www.britannica.com/event/Battle-of-Omdurman (last visited May 2, 2016). At this time, the Sudan was nominally under Egyptian control. The battle was fought between an Anglo-Egyptian army and Mahdist—i.e., Islamist (also called *dervishes*)—army at the village of Omdurman. The Mahdi was a Muslim religious leader who had declared jihad and invaded Egypt in 1884, defeating a British force at Khartoum in 1885. There were multiple skirmishes between the Anglo-Egyptians and the Mahdist forces between 1885 and 1896 along the Sudanese/Egyptian border. The British desire to protect the Suez Canal led to the campaign against the Mahdi, even though by 1896, the Mahdi had died. The "Khalifa" succeeded the Mahdi and led the dervishes at Omdurman. Harold E. Raugh, Jr., *British Military Operations in Egypt and the Sudan: A Selected Bibliography* (Lanham, MD: Scarecrow Press, 2008), xiii–xiv.

94. Krausz, "The Kaiser's Jihad," 3.

95. A fatwa is a religious ruling on Islamic law.

96. Krausz, "The Kaiser's Jihad," 3.

97. Ibid., 4.

98. Ibid.
99. Anderson, *Lawrence in Arabia*, 30.
100. Ibid.
101. Ibid., 32.
102. Ibid.
103. Ibid., 32, 37–39.
104. Krausz, "The Kaiser's Jihad," 4.
105. Yochanan Visser, "The Unlikely Founding Fathers of the Islamic State," *Western Journalism*, December 10, 2014, http://www.western journalism.com/unlikely-founding-fathers-islamic-state/; Dennis Ross, *The Missing Peace* (New York: Farrar, Straus & Giroux, 2004), 2.
106. Krausz, "The Kaiser's Jihad," 2.
107. Ibid., 3.
108. McMeekin, *The Berlin–Baghdad Express*, 273.
109. Allen, *God's Terrorists*, 267. The discovery was a fluke. A courier for the rebels visited the father of two friends who turned him.
110. McMeekin, *The Berlin–Baghdad Express*, 282.
111. Neither did the British effort have much initial success. The Arab revolt had no support outside the Hejaz. No Arab unit defected to the British after the Hashemite rebellion. Success came after the British began to win the war. Roger Ford, *Eden to Armageddon: World War I in the Middle East* (New York: Pegasus Books, 2011), 314–15.
112. U.S. Department of State, *International Boundary Study (1969)*, 7–9; Krausz, "The Kaiser's Jihad," 7.
113. Anderson, *Lawrence in Arabia*, 19.
114. Ibid., 27.
115. Ibid., 26.
116. Ibid., 26–27.
117. Ibid., 27.
118. Ibid.
119. Ibid., 32.
120. Ibid.
121. Ibid., 33.
122. Ibid.
123. Ibid.
124. Ibid., 258.
125. Rogan, *The Fall of the Ottomans*, 305.
126. Ibid.

127. Ibid.; Chaim Weizmann, *Trial and Error* (New York: Harper, 1949), 232.
128. Rogan, *The Fall of the Ottomans*, 309.
129. Ibid., 306, 308, 343.
130. Scott Anderson, "The True Story of Lawrence of Arabia," http://www.smithsonianmag.com/history/true-story-lawrence-arabia-180951857/?page=2, 2.
131. Ibid.
132. Ibid.
133. Anderson, *Lawrence in Arabia*, 335.
134. Ibid., 338.
135. Ibid., 322, 343.
136. Ibid., 425.
137. McMeekin, *The Ottoman Endgame*, 286.
138. Quataert, *The Ottoman Empire*, 61; Ian Black, "Middle East Still Rocking from First World War Pacts Made 100 Years Ago," *Guardian*, December 30, 2015, http://www.theguardian.com/world/on-the-middle-east/2015/dec/30/middle-east-still-rocking-from-first-world-war-pacts-made-100-years-ago; Sykes-Picot Agreement.
139. International Boundary Study, 8–9.
140. McMeekin, *The Ottoman Endgame*, 284–88.
141. International Boundary Study, 9.
142. T. E. Lawrence, *Seven Pillars of Wisdom* (1938), 275.
143. Ibid.
144. Ibid.
145. Ibid., 134–35.
146. Ibid., 278.
147. Ibid., 134.
148. Ibid., 555.
149. Ibid.; International Boundary Study, 9.
150. International Boundary Study, 9.
151. Balfour Declaration, http://avalon.law.yale.edu/20th_century/balfour.asp.
152. International Boundary Study, 9.
153. Rogan, *The Fall of the Ottomans*, 353.
154. Ibid.
155. International Boundary Study, 10.
156. McMeekin, *The Ottoman Endgame*, 406.
157. Ibid., 410.

158. Ibid., 408. The United States of America was never at war with the Ottoman Empire during World War I.

159. Weizmann, *Trial and Error,* 232.

160. Ibid., 235.

161. "Faysal I, King of Iraq," *Encyclopaedia Britannica,* http://www .britannica.com/biography/Faysal-I (last visited April 14, 2016).

162. Weizmann, *Trial and Error,* 234.

163. Ibid.

164. Ibid.

165. Ibid.

166. Ibid., 233–34.

167. Ibid. 235.

168. Ibid.

169. Agreement Between Emir Feisal and Dr. Weizmann, January 3, 1919, http://www.mideastweb.org/feisweiz.htm.

170. Ibid.

171. Weizmann, *Trial and Error,* 235.

172. Ibid., 245–46.

173. Ibid., 236.

174. Ibid., 235.

175. "Faysal I, King of Iraq," *Encyclopaedia Britannica.*

176. Ibid.

177. Ibid.

178. Ali A. Allawi, *Faisal I of Iraq* (New Haven, CT: Yale University Press, 2014), 324–25.

179. Alan Rush, "The Enlightened King of Iraq," *Spectator,* February 15, 2014, http://www.spectator.co.uk/2014/02/faisal-of-iraq-by-ali-a -allawi-review/.

180. Allawi, *Faisal I of Iraq,* 340.

181. D. K. Fieldhouse, *Western Imperialism in the Middle East 1914–1958* (New York: Oxford University Press, 2006), 70.

182. "The Making of Iraq: Man of the Moment," *Economist,* February 8, 2014, http://www.economist.com/news/books-and-arts/21595880 -revisionist-history-iraqi-king-man-moment.

183. Allawi, *Faisal I of Iraq,* 340.

184. "The Making of Iraq: Man of the Moment," *Economist.*

185. Ibid.

186. "Arabia and the Arabs," 14

187. Ibid., 14–15.

188. Weizmann, *Trial and Error,* 235.

189. Ibid.
190. "Treaty of Sevres Dissolves the Ottoman Empire," Center for Israel Education.
191. Ibid.; Rogan, *The Fall of the Ottomans*, 393.
192. "Treaty of Sevres Dissolves the Ottoman Empire."
193. "Forget Sykes-Picot," 3.
194. "Treaty of Sevres Dissolves the Ottoman Empire."
195. Treaty of Lausanne (1923), 1.
196. "Treaty of Sevres Dissolves the Ottoman Empire."
197. Rogan, *The Fall of the Ottomans*, 393.
198. Ibid. Then Mustafa Kemal Pasha, he did not take the name Ataturk until 1934. See "Mustafa Kemal Atatürk'ün Nüfus Hüviyet Cüzdani. (24.11.1934)," www.isteataturk.com.
199. "Treaty of Sevres Dissolves the Ottoman Empire."
200. Rogan, *The Fall of the Ottomans*, 393.
201. "Forget Sykes-Picot," 2.
202. Rogan, *The Fall of the Ottomans*, 395.
203. "Treaty of Lausanne," *Encyclopaedia Britannica*.
204. Treaty of Lausanne (1923), 2.
205. Ibid.
206. Ibid.
207. Ibid.
208. Ibid.
209. Treaty of Lausanne, Article 28, http://wwi.lib.byu.edu/index.php/Treaty_of_Lausannewi.
210. Anderson, *Lawrence in Arabia*, 32–33.
211. Treaty of Lausanne (1923), 2.
212. Ibid.
213. Rogan, *The Fall of the Ottomans*, 395.
214. James Renton, "Flawed Foundations: The Balfour Declaration and the Palestine Mandate," in *Britain, Palestine, and Empire: The Mandate Years*, Rory Miller, ed. (London and New York: Routledge, 2010), 15, 34.
215. Ruth Henig, *Makers of the Modern World: League of Nations* (London: Haus, 2010), 1.
216. Covenant of the League of Nations, http://avalon.law.yale.edu/20th_century/leagcov.asp#art22; George Antonius, *International Affairs* (Royal Institute of International Affairs, 1931–39), 13, no. 4 (July–August 1934): 523–539, 525, http://www.jstor.org/stable/2603401?&Search=yes&searchText=Mandate&search

Text=French&searchText=Syria&list=hide&searchUri=%2Faction
%2FdoBasicSearch%3FQuery%3DFrench%2BMandate%2BSyria
%26gw%3Djtx%26prq%3DMiddle%2BEast%2Bpost%2BWWI
%26Search%3DSearch%26hp%3D25%26wc%3Don&prevSearch
=&item=2&ttl=3756&returnArticleService=showFullText&seq
=3#page_scan_tab_contents; http://www.hri.org/docs/king-crane
/mesopotamia.html.

217. Covenant of the League of Nations, art. 22.

218. Ibid.

219. Ibid.

220. "San Remo Resolution," Council on Foreign Relations, http://www
.cfr.org/israel/san-remo-resolution/p15248 (last visited April 21,
2016).

221. Nele Matz, "Civilization and the Mandate System under the
League of Nations as Origin of Trusteeship," page 72, http://www
.mpil.de/files/pdf2/mpunyb_matz_9_47_95.pdf.

222. Antonius, *International Affairs*, 523–39, 525; King-Crane
Commission Report, August 28, 1919, http://www.hri.org/docs
/king-crane/mesopotamia.html.

223. Eli E. Hertz, "'Mandate for Palestine': The Legal Aspects of
Jewish Rights," http://www.mythsandfacts.org/conflict/mandate
_for_palestine/mandate_for_palestine.htm (last visited May 21,
2016); http://www.kinghussein.gov.jo/his_transjordan.html.

224. Fawwaz Traboulsi, *A History of Modern Lebanon*, second edition
(London: Pluto Press, 2012), 75.

225. Ibid., 75, 80.

226. Ibid., 79.

227. Ibid., 76.

228. Ibid., 81, 82. The Christians were divided and on all sides.

229. Ibid., 88–89.

230. Mandate for Palestine, Article 4. French Mandate for Syria and
Lebanon, Art. 1, 1922, http://www.ndu.edu.lb/Lerc/resources
/French%20Mandate%20for%20Syria%20and%20the%20Lebanon
.pdf; Draft of the Mandate for Mesopotamia, Art. 1 (submitted
December 7, 1920, to the League of Nations, not ratified), https://
archive.org/details/draftmandatesfor00leagrich; Mandate for
Palestine.

231. Ibid., Art. 6, 7.

232. Ibid.

233. Hertz, "Mandate for Palestine": The Legal Aspects of Jewish

Rights"; Regina Goff, "The Legality of Israel's Blockade of Gaza," *8 Regent Journal of International Law* (2011), 83, 85; see also Article 25 of the Palestine Mandate, memorandum by the British representative (September 16, 1922), https://www.wdl.org/en /item/11572/view/1/13/; "History: The Making of Transjordan," Hashemite Kingdom of Jordan, http://www.kinghussein.gov.jo /his_transjordan.html (last visited May 21, 2016).

234. Hertz, "'Mandate for Palestine'"

235. Mandate for Palestine, Art. 6; Jordanian Nationality Law, Official Gazette, No. 1171, Article 3(3) of Law No. 6, 1954 (February 16, 1954), 105.

236. U.N. Special Committee on Palestine, Report to the General Assembly, U.N. Doc. A/364, chapter II, 100–117 (Sept. 3, 1947) [hereinafter 1947 U.N. Report].

237. Ibid, chapter I.

238. G.A. Res. 181 (II), U.N. GAOR, 2nd Sess., U.N. Doc. A/Res/181 (II), 131 (Nov. 29, 1947).

239. Robert Bowker, *Palestinian Refugees: Mythology, Identity, and the Search for Peace* (Boulder, CO: Lynn Rienner, 2003), 88.

240. G.A. Res. 181, § II, U.N. GAOR, 2nd Sess., U.N. Doc. A/Res/181, § II (November 29, 1947), 131.

241. "The Palestine Commission reported the difficulty it had in overcoming Arab resistance to Resolution 181." U.N. Palestine Commission, Report to the General Assembly, U.N. Doc. A/532, § III, (April 10, 1948). Upon receiving this report and noting the outbreak of violence, the General Assembly shifted its focus to the war and voted to relieve the Palestine Commission of its duties to implement Resolution 181. G.A. Res. 186, (S-2), U.N. GAOR, 2nd Sess., U.N. Doc. A/Res/186, § III (May 14, 1948).

242. Declaration of the Establishment of the State of Israel, Israel Ministry of Foreign Affairs (May 14, 1948), http://www.mfa.gov .il/mfa/foreignpolicy/peace/guide/pages/declaration%20of%20 establishment%20of%20state%20of%20israel.aspx.

243. "The Arab-Israeli War of 1948," U.S. Department of State: Office of the Historian, http://history.state.gov/milestones/1945-1952/ arab-israeli-war (last visited April 27, 2016).

244. Ibid.

245. Ibid.

246. "The 1967 Arab-Israeli War," U.S. Department of State: Office of

the Historian, https://history.state.gov/milestones/1961–1968/arab
-israeli-war-1967 (last visited April 27, 2016).

247. Hussein, King of Jordan, Address to the Nation (July 31, 1988),
http://www.kinghussein.gov.jo/88_july31.html.

248. 1947 U.N. Report, 66. No sovereign Arab state existed in Palestine.
In fact, in 1947, when the U.N. conducted its report, the land of
Palestine had not been a sovereign state since 63 B.C.

249. Ibid., 16–17.

CHAPTER THREE: A CLASH OF CULTURES

1. Michael Lipka, "Muslims and Islam: Key Findings in the U.S. and
Around the World," Pew Research Center (December 7, 2015),
http://www.pewresearch.org/fact-tank/2015/12/07/muslims-and
-islam-key-findings-in-the-u-s-and-around-the-world/.

2. Stephen Kinzer, *All the Shah's Men: An American Coup and the Roots
of Middle Eastern Terror*, 2nd ed. (New York: Wiley, 2008), 24.

3. See Philip K. Hitti, *History of the Arabs*, 10th ed. (Basingstoke,
England: Palgrave Macmillan, 2002), 121–22, 136–38, 140–43.

4. Bernard Lewis, "The Ottoman Empire and Its Aftermath," *Journal
of Contemporary History* 15 (1980): 27, 28–29.

5. Abdullah Yusuf Ali, *The Meaning of the Holy Qur'an*, 10th ed.
(Beltsville, MD: Amana, 2001), 2:130–36 (hereinafter *Quran*).

6. Ibid., 2:285.

7. Ibid., 33:40.

8. *Quran* 29:46 [emphasis added]. This translation of the Quran
uses specialized capitalization. However, herein, quotations from
the Quran have been adjusted to conventional English rules of
capitalization.

9. Nabeel Qureshi, "Do Muslims and Christians Worship the Same
God?" Ravi Zacharias International Ministries, December 27, 2015,
http://rzim.org/global-blog/do-muslims-and-christians-worship
-the-same-god.

10. Ibid.

11. Ibid.

12. Matt Slick, "The Trinity," Christian Apologetics & Research
Ministry, https://carm.org/trinity.

13. Rudolph Peters et al., "Apostasy in Islam," *Die Welt des Islams* 17
(1976–77): 1, 3; Abdal-Hakim Murad, "The Trinity: A Muslim
Perspective," *Masud*, 1996, http://masud.co.uk/ISLAM/ahm/trinity
.htm.

14. Qureshi, "Do Muslims and Christians Worship the Same God?"
15. The fifth chapter of the Quran.
16. *Quran* 5:73.
17. Matthew 16:15–16; John 10:30, 38; Colossians 2:9.
18. *Quran* 5:72.
19. Matthew 6:9.
20. John 3:16.
21. John 10:30.
22. *Quran* 112:1–4 [emphasis added].
23. Qureshi, "Do Muslims and Christians Worship the Same God?";
    Peters, "Apostasy in Islam."
24. Qureshi, "Do Muslims and Christians Worship the Same God?"
25. Ibid.
26. Ephesians 2:4–5.
27. Genesis 1:26.
28. 1 Peter 3:18; 1 John 2:2, 4:10.
29. Revelation 3:20.
30. *Quran* 5:18.
31. Nabeel Qureshi, "Nabeel Qureshi Debates Muslim Apologist
    Shabir Ally," Ravi Zacharias International Ministries, April 8,
    2015, http://rzim.org/global-blog/nabeel-qureshi-debates-muslim
    -apologist-shabir-ally.
32. Ibid.
33. Ibid.; *Quran* 112:1–4.
34. Qureshi, "Do Muslims and Christians Worship the Same God?"
35. *Quran* 112:1–4, 42:11.
36. Matt Slick, "Does Islam Teach Salvation by Works?," Christian
    Apologetics & Research Ministry, https://carm.org/does-islam
    -teach-salvation-works.
37. Ibid.
38. Ibid.
39. *Quran* 4:95, 9:20.
40. Ibid., 4:74.
41. Patricia A. Santy, "Shame, Guilt, the Muslim Psyche, and the
    Danish Cartoons," Dr. Sanity, February 6, 2006, http://drsanity
    .blogspot.com/2006/02/shame-guilt-muslim-psyche-and-danish
    .html.
42. Ibid.
43. Ibid.
44. Ibid.

45. Ibid.

46. Ibid.

47. Ibid.

48. Islam's Prime Directive, "An Inquiry into Islam," http://www
.inquiryintoislam.com/2010/08/islams-prime-directive.html
(hereinafter Islam's Prime Directive); see also *Quran* 2:191
(commanding Muslims to slay nonbelievers), 18:74–81 (recounting
a story of a man who kills his disobedient son, and was justified in
doing so).

49. *Quran* 2:216.

50. Islam's Prime Directive.

51. Ibid.; Santy, "Shame, Guilt, the Muslim Psyche, and the Danish
Cartoons."

52. "Parwasha," Be Heard Project, http://beheardproject.com
/parwasha (last visited July 15, 2016).

53. Shaheryar Gill, "A Big Win for Parwasha in Pakistan," American
Center for Law and Justice, http://aclj.org/persecuted-church/a
-big-win-for-parwasha-the-8-year-old-christian-girl-brutalized-in
-pakistan (last visited July 15, 2016).

54. Santy, "Shame, Guilt, the Muslim Psyche, and the Danish
Cartoons."

55. Ibid.

56. Ibid.; see also "Muslim Fury: LIVE Anti-US Protest Timeline
[PHOTOS]," RT.com, September 13, 2002, https://www.rt.com
/news/anti-american-protests-live-updates-053/ (detailing extreme
anti-American protests throughout the Muslim world after the
online release of an American-made film that insulted the Prophet
Muhammad); "Perceived Insults to Islam Trigger Muslim Anger,"
Daily News, September 12, 2012, http://www.nydailynews.com
/news/world/perceived-insults-islam-trigger-muslim-anger
-article-1.1157564 (listing incidents of violence committed by
Muslims that were spurred by perceived insults to Islam).

57. Santy, "Shame, Guilt, the Muslim Psyche, and the Danish
Cartoons."

58. Ibid.

59. Ibid.

60. Ziad Abu-Amr, "The Significance of Jerusalem: A Muslim
Perspective," *Palestine–Israel Journal of Politics, Economics and
Culture* (1995), http://www.pij.org/details.php?id=646.

61. "Profile: Osama bin Laden," Council on Foreign Relations,

September 1, 2007, http://www.cfr.org/terrorist-leaders/profile
-osama-bin-laden/p9951#p1.

62. Richard A. Debs, *Islamic Law and Civil Code: The Law of Property in Egypt* (New York: Columbia University Press, 2010) 8–13, 16–17; see also "Hamas Covenant 1988: The Covenant of the Islamic Resistance Movement," Avalon Project: Documents in Law, History and Diplomacy, http://avalon.law.yale.edu/20th_century /hamas.asp).

63. Ibid.

64. *Quran* 17:1; Abu-Amr, "The Significance of Jerusalem: A Muslim Perspective."

65. Abu-Amr, "The Significance of Jerusalem: A Muslim Perspective."

66. Santy, "Shame, Guilt, the Muslim Psyche, and the Danish Cartoons."

67. Ibid.

68. Raymond Ibrahim, "Islamic Supremacism: The True Source of Muslim "Grievances,'" *Frontpage*, May 14, 2015, http://www .frontpagemag.com/fpm/257003/islamic-supremacism-true-source -muslim-grievances-raymond-ibrahim.

69. *Quran* 2:221.

70. Ibid., 48:29.

71. Ibrahim, "Islamic Supremacism."

72. Santy, "Shame, Guilt, the Muslim Psyche, and the Danish Cartoons."

73. Ibid.

74. Ibid.

75. Nile Gardiner and Morgan Lorraine Roach, "Barack Obama's Top 10 Apologies: How the President Has Humiliated a Superpower," Heritage Foundation, June 2, 2009, http://www.heritage.org /research/reports/2009/06/barack-obamas-top-10-apologies-how -the-president-has-humiliated-a-superpower#_ftn2.

76. Press release, Barack Obama, President, Remarks by the President at National Prayer Breakfast (February 5, 2015), https://www .whitehouse.gov/the-press-office/2015/02/05/remarks-president -national-prayer-breakfast.

77. Press release, Barack Obama, President, Remarks by the President at Cairo University, 6-04-09 (June 4, 2009), https://www.white house.gov/the-press-office/remarks-president-cairo-university -6-04-09.

78. http://cnsnews.com/news/article/susan-jones/wh-move-gitmo
    -detainees-us-so-theyre-treated-way-american-citizens-are.
79. Santy, "Shame, Guilt, the Muslim Psyche, and the Danish
    Cartoons."
80. Ibid.
81. Gerry J. Gilmore, "Cheney: America Determined to Defeat
    Terrorism," U.S. Department of Defense, September 19, 2006,
    http://archive.defense.gov/news/newsarticle.aspx?id=1023;
    "President Bush Delivers Remarks on the War on Terror,"
    Washington Post, September 5, 2006, http://www.washingtonpost
    .com/wp-dyn/content/article/2006/09/05/AR2006090500656.html.
82. *The Export* (ACLJ Films, 2011).
83. Ibid.
84. "What Is the Muslim Understanding of 'Ummah'?," Christian
    Broadcasting Network, http://www1.cbn.com/onlinediscipleship
    /what-is-the-muslim-understanding-of-%22ummah%22%3F.
85. Ibid.
86. http://www.thedailybeast.com/articles/2016/03/16/the-isis-army
    -that-s-still-unborn.html.
87. Ibid.
88. Ibid.
89. Ibid.
90. "What Is the Muslim Understanding of 'Ummah'?"
91. Qureshi debate.
92. "What Is the Muslim Understanding of 'Ummah'?"
93. Ibid.
94. Ibid.
95. Matthew 5:38–48; Luke 19:12–27.
96. Romans 13:1.
97. "What Is the Muslim Understanding of 'Ummah'?"
98. *The Export* (ACLJ Films, 2011).
99. Shadi Shakibai, "An Examination of Collectivist Cultural
    Orientation Among Middle Eastern College Students of Different
    Gender, Generation Status, and Academic Class Standing"
    (unpublished M.A. thesis, University of Maryland, May 27, 2005),
    http://drum.lib.umd.edu/handle/1903/2654.
100. Ibid.; Santy, "Shame, Guilt, the Muslim Psyche, and the Danish
     Cartoons."
101. Santy, "Shame, Guilt, the Muslim Psyche, and the Danish
     Cartoons."

CHAPTER FOUR: SHARIA LAW AND THE MUSLIM WORLD

1. Raj Bhala, *Understanding Islamic Law (Shari'a)* (New Providence, NJ: Lexis-Nexis, 2011), xxii.
2. Ibid.
3. Ibid., xxiii.
4. Ibid., xix.
5. Ibid., 1238.
6. Ibid., 1211.
7. Abdullah Yusuf Ali, *The Meaning of the Holy Qur'an*, 10th ed. (Beltsville, MD: Amana, 2001) (hereinafter *Quran*).
8. Ibid. 4:89; *Sahih Bukhari*, vol. 4, book 52, no. 260, http://www.sahih-bukhari.com; ibid., 9:83:37.
9. "The World's Muslims: Religion, Politics and Society," Pew Research Center, April 30, 2013, http://www.pewforum.org/2013/04/30/the-worlds-muslims-religion-politics-society-overview/.
10. Statistics are 84 percent in South Asia, 77 percent in Southeast Asia, 74 percent in Middle East-North Africa, 64 percent in Sub-Saharan Africa, 18 percent in Southern Eastern Europe, and 12 percent in Central Asia.
11. "The World's Muslims: Religion, Politics and Society."
12. Ibid.
13. Dalia Mogahed, "The Battle for Hearts and Minds: Moderate vs. Extremist Views in the Muslim World," Gallup Organization, 2006, http://media.gallup.com/WorldPoll/PDF/ExtremismInMuslimWorld.pdf.
14. Phillip K. Hitti, *History of the Arabs*, 10th rev. ed. (Basingstoke, England: Palgrave Macmillan, 2002), 400.
15. Bernard Lewis, *The Political Language of Islam* (Chicago: University of Chicago Press, 1991), 25.
16. Bhala, *Understanding Islamic Law (Shari'a)*, 292.
17. *Mawil Izzi Dien, Islamic Law: From Historical Foundations to Contemporary Practice 37* (2004).
18. *Imran Ahsan Khan Nyazee, Islamic Jurisprudence 394* (2000).
19. *Nyazee*, 162.
20. Bhala, *Understanding Islamic Law (Shari'a)*, 302.
21. Ibid., 307–9.
22. Ibid.
23. Ibid., 310.
24. Serdar Demirel, "The Impact of Hadith Perception on Disputes

between ahl al-Sunnah and Al-shiah al-Imamiyyah al-Ithna Ashariyyah," *Intellectual Discourse* 19 (2011): 245, 247–50.

25. Bhala, *Understanding Islamic Law (Shari'a)*, 345.
26. Ibid., 389.
27. Ibid., 207.
28. Ibid., 388.
29. One Law for All, "Sharia Law in Britain: A Threat to One Law for Law & Equal Rights," 2010, 9 (hereinafter "Sharia Law in Britain"), http://www.onelawforall.org.uk/wp-content/uploads/New-Report -Sharia-Law-in-Britain_fixed.pdf; "About Us," Islamic Sharia Council, http://www.islamic-sharia.org/aboutus/.
30. "Sharia Law in Britain," 11.
31. Ibid.
32. "Family Mediation: Sorting Out Family Disputes Without Going Through Court," Ministry of Justice, https://www.gov.uk /government/uploads/system/uploads/attachment_data/file/489124 /family-mediation-leaflet.pdf.
33. History, Muslim Arbitration Tribunal, http://www.matribunal.com /history.php.
34. "Frequently Asked Questions: Islamic Divorce," Muslim Arbitration Tribunal, http://www.matribunal.com/faqs.php.
35. "Sharia Law in Britain," 16.
36. One Law for All, "Multiculturalism and Child Protection in Britain," 2013, 13 (hereinafter "Multiculturalism and Child Protection"), http://www.onelawforall.org.uk/wp-content/uploads /Multiculturalism-and-Child-Protection-in-Britain.pdf.
37. Ibid., 13–14.
38. Ibid.
39. *BBC Panorama: Secrets of Britain's Sharia Councils*, BBC documentary, September 16, 2013, https://www.youtube.com /watch?v=-7TjzSSZUvg. See also Soeren Kern, "Britain's Sharia Courts: 'You Cannot Go Against What Islam Says,'" Gatestone Institute, April 23, 2013, http://www.gatestoneinstitute.org/3682/uk -sharia-courts.
40. Ibid.
41. Ibid.
42. Ibid.
43. "UK Imams Agree to Perform Underage Marriages," ITV October 6, 2013, http://www.itv.com/news/2013-10-06/uk-imams -agree-to-perform-underage-marriages/. (The others did refuse.)

44. Marriage Act of 1949, 13 & 14 Geo. 6 c. 76 (UK).
45. "Multiculturalism and Child Protection," 30.
46. Ibid.
47. 24 Nov. 2008 Parl. Deb. HC (2008) col. 866W (UK).
48. Ibid.
49. Home Affairs, Forced Marriage, 2015, SN/HA/1003 (UK).
50. Feisal Abdul Rauf, "What Shariah Law Is All About," *The World Post* (May 25, 2009, 5:12 AM), http://www.huffingtonpost.com /imam-feisal-abdul-rauf/what-shariah-law-is-all-a_b_190825.html.
51. *The Export* (ACLJ Films, 2011).
52. Bhala, *Understanding Islamic Law (Shari'a)*, 1262.
53. Ahmad ibn Naquib al-Misri, *Reliance of the Traveller*, rev. ed., ed. and trans. Nuh Ha Mim Keller (Beltsville, MD: Amana, 1994), 596–97.
54. *Quran* 5:33.
55. Ibid.
56. Al-Misri, *Reliance of the Traveller*, 596–98. See also Rudolph Peters, *Crime and Punishment in Islamic Law: Theory and Practice from the Sixteenth to Twenty-first Century* (Cambridge: Cambridge University Press, 2005), 65.
57. *Sahih Bukhari* 3:46:705.
58. "Saudi Arabia: Criminal Justice Strengthened," Human Rights Watch, January 14, 2010, https://www.hrw.org/news/2010/01/14 /saudi-arabia-criminal-justice-strengthened.
59. *Islamic Penal Code of the Islamic Republic of Iran: Book 5—Ta'zir and Deterring Punishments*, art. 513 (1991 as amended in 2012), Iran Human Rights Documentation Center trans., 2013, http:// iranhrdc.org/english/human-rights-documents/iranian-codes /1000000351-islamic-penal-code-of-the-islamic-republic-of-iran -book-five.html#2.
60. "Muslim Apostates Threatened Over Christianity," *Telegraph*, December 9, 2007, http://www.telegraph.co.uk/news/uknews /1571970/Muslim-apostates-threatened-over-Christianity.html.
61. Bureau of Democracy, Human Rights, and Labor, U.S. Department of State, International Religious Freedom Report 2010: Saudi Arabia, November 17, 2010, http://www.state.gov/g /drl/rls/irf/2010/148843.htm (In Saudi Arabia,"[b]lasphemy is a crime punishable by long prison terms or, in some cases, death"); Bureau of Democracy, Human Rights, and Labor, U.S. Department of State International Religious Freedom Report 2010:

Afghanistan, November 17, 2010, http://www.state.gov/g/drl/rls
/irf/2010/148786.htm ("Blasphemy is a capital crime under some
interpretations of Islamic law in [Afghanistan], and according to
such interpretations, an Islamic judge could punish blasphemy with
death, if committed by a male over age 18 or a female over age 16 of
sound mind"); Pakistan Penal Code, ch. XV, § 295-C (1860), http://
www.pakistani.org/pakistan/legislation/1860/actXLVof1860.html
(providing that "[w]hoever . . . defiles the sacred name of the Holy
Prophet Muhammad (peace be upon him) shall be punished with
death, or imprisonment for life, and shall also be liable to fine").

62. E.g., "Egypt: A Year of Attacks on Free Expression," Human
Rights Watch, February 11, 2012 (quoting Egypt's penal code
98(f): "Whoever exploits religion in order to promote extremist
ideologies by word of mouth, in writing or any other manner,
with a view to stirring up sedition, disparaging or contempt of
any divine religion or its adherents, or prejudicing national unity
shall be punished with imprisonment between six months and five
years or paying a fine of at least 500 Egyptian pounds."); Bureau
of Democracy, Human Rights, and Labor, U.S. Department
of State, International Religious Freedom Report 2005: Jordan
(2005), http://www.state.gov/g/drl/rls/hrrpt/2004/41724.htm ("[I]n
February 2003, three journalists were charged with blasphemy
and slandering the government. They received prison terms
ranging from 2 to 6 months and returned to work after their
release."); Bureau of Democracy, Human Rights, and Labor, U.S.
Department of State, International Religious Freedom Report
2005: Kuwait (2005), http://www.state.gov/g/drl/rls/irf/2005/51603
.htm ("The 1961 Press and Publications Law specifically prohibits
the publication of any material that attacks religions or incites
persons to commit crimes, create hatred, or spread dissension
among the public. There are laws against blasphemy, apostasy, and
proselytizing. These laws sometimes have been used to restrict
religious freedom."); Bureau of Democracy, Human Rights, and
Labor, U.S. Department of State, International Religious Freedom
Report 2010: Kuwait, November 17, 2010, http://www.state.gov/g
/drl/rls/irf/2010/148828.htm. Indonesia, although not an official
Islamic country, has a large Muslim population and punishes
blasphemy. Penal Code art. 156a (Indonesia) (1952) (last amended
in 1999) ("By a maximum imprisonment of five years shall be
punished any person who deliberately in public gives expression to

feelings or commits an act, which principally have the character of being at enmity with, abusing or staining a religion, adhered to in Indonesia; with the intention to prevent a person to adhere to any religion based on the belief of almighty God.").

63. Pakistan Penal Code, ch. XV (1860), § 298-A, http://www.pakistani .org/pakistan/legislation/1860/actXLVof1860.html.

64. Ibid., § 295-B.

65. Ibid., § 295-C.

66. Pakistan Constitution, art. 203(D)–(DD).

67. *Qureshi v. Pakistan*, (1990) 1991 PLD (Federal Shariat Court) 10 (Pak.) (holding alternate punishment of life imprisonment, as provided in Pakistan Penal Code, ch. XV, § 295-C (1860), repugnant to the injunctions of Islam as given in the Qur'an and Sunnah).

68. Penal Code art. 513 (Iran) ("Anyone who insults the Islamic sanctities or any of the imams or her excellency Sadigheh Tahereh should be executed if his insult equals to speaking disparagingly of Prophet Muhammad. Otherwise, [he] should be imprisoned from one to five years.").

69. Press Code art. 26 (Iran), http://www.parstimes.com/law/press_law .html.

70. Organisation of the Islamic Cooperation, Charter art. 1, para. 12.

71. Ibid. art. 15 (emphasis added) ("The Independent Permanent Commission on Human Rights shall promote the civil, political, social and economic rights enshrined in the organisation's covenants and declarations and in universally agreed human rights instruments, in conformity with Islamic values").

72. Article 19 of the ICCPR provides "the right to freedom of expression," which includes the "freedom to seek, receive and impart information and ideas of all kinds, regardless of frontiers, either orally, in writing or in print, in the form of art, or through any other media of his choice." International Covenant on Civil and Political Rights, adopted as G.A. Res. 2200A (XXI), at art. 4, opened for signature December 16, 1966, 999 U.N.T.S. 171 (in effect beginning March 23, 1976).

73. While some of the OIC member states that have ratified the ICCPR have made reservations to Article 19, their other reservations pertaining to articles that apply to all other articles (like Article 3, which requires equal treatment of men and women) or to freedom of religion in general (Article 18)

effectively limit Article 19 as well. E.g., Status of Treaties, United Nations Treaty Series: Bahrain ("The Government of the Kingdom of Bahrain interprets the Provisions of Article 3, (18) and (23) [marriage and family] as not affecting in any way the prescriptions of the Islamic Sharia.") and Mauritania ("The Mauritanian Government, while accepting the provisions set out in Article 18 concerning freedom of thought, conscience and religion, declares that their application shall be without prejudice to the Islamic Sharia.") February 4, 2011, http://treaties.un.org/Pages/ViewDetails.aspx?src=TREATY&mtdsg_no=IV-4&chapter=4&lang=en#EndDec.

74. The Cairo Declaration on Human Rights in Islam (1990), http://www.oic-oci.org/english/article/human.htm.

75. Ibid., art. 22 [emphasis added].

76. See, e.g., G.A. Res. 65/224, December 21, 2010, http://www.un.org/en/ga/search/view_doc.asp?symbol=A/RES/65/224; see also Laura MacInnis, "U.N. Body Adopts Resolution on Religious Defamation," Reuters, March 26, 2009, http://www.reuters.com/article/idUSTRE52P60220090326.

77. MacInnis, "U.N. Body Adopts Resolution on Religious Defamation."

78. Securing the Protection of our Enduring and Established Constitutional Heritage Act, Pub. L. No. 111-223, 124 Stat. 2380 (2010) (to be codified at 28 U.S.C. §§ 4101 et seq.).

79. Kimberly Railey, "More States Move to Ban Foreign Law in Courts," *USA Today*, August 4, 2013, http://www.usatoday.com/story/news/nation/2013/08/04/states-ban-foreign-law/2602511/.

80. Bhala, *Understanding Islamic Law (Shari'a)*, 866–67.

81. Ibid., 867.

82. Ibid.

83. *Quran* 5:5.

84. Ibid.

85. Ibid., 4:3.

86. Bhala, *Understanding Islamic Law (Shari'a)*, 1217.

87. *Al-Misri* 525. See also *Quran* 2:223.

88. Bhala, *Understanding Islamic Law (Shari'a)*, 886–87.

89. Ibid.

90. Ibid., 866.

91. Ibid., 867.

92. Ibid., 878.

93. *In re Marriage of Obaidi*, 226 P.3d 787 (Wash. Ct. App. 2010).
94. Ibid., 788.
95. Ibid., 790.
96. Ibid. (citing *Jones v. Wolf*, 443 U.S. 595, 602–03 (1979)).
97. *Akileh v. Elchahal*, 666 So. 2d 246 (Fla. Dist. Ct. App. 1996).
98. Ibid., 249.
99. *Rahman v. Hossain*, No. A-5191-08T3, 2010 N.J. Super. Unpub. LEXIS 1326, at *13 (Super. Ct. App. Div. June 17, 2010).
100. Ibid., 2.
101. Ibid., 13.
102. Ibid.
103. Bhala, *Understanding Islamic Law (Shari'a)*, 867.
104. *Quran* 4:34.
105. Muhammad Subhi bin Hasan Hallaq, *Fiqh: According to the Quran & Sunnah* (Riyadh: Darussalam, 2008), 2:156.
106. Muhammad Asad, *The Message of the Qur'an*, 5th ed. (Bitton, England: Book Foundation, 2003), 4:34, n.45.
107. Ibid.
108. Al-Misri, *Reliance of the Traveller*, 540–41.
109. Ibid.
110. Ibid.
111. Ibid.
112. Ibid., 541.
113. *S.D. v. M.J.R.*, 2 A.3d 412, 419–20 (N.J. Super. Ct. App. Div. 2010).
114. Ibid., 424.
115. Ibid., 422–23.
116. Ibid., 428.
117. Ibid., 429. (The wife was able to appeal because the granting of a protective order is a civil matter requiring findings of fact about criminal actions.)
118. Ibid., 442.
119. *S.D. v. M.J.R.*, 433.
120. Bhala, *Understanding Islamic Law (Shari'a)*, 878.
121. Ibid., 879.
122. Ibid.
123. Ibid., 879–80.
124. Ibid.
125. Ibid., 881.
126. Ibid., 883–84.
127. Ibid., 884–85.

128. Ibid., 882, 884–85.
129. "Comity," *Black's Law Dictionary*, 9th. ed. (St. Paul, MN: West, 2009).
130. *Chaudry v. Chaudry*, 388 A.2d 1000, 1002 (New Jersey Super. Ct. App. Div. 1978).
131. Ibid., 1007–8.
132. Ibid., 1004–5.
133. *Ashfaq v. Ashfaq*, 467 S.W.3d 539, 544 (Tex. App. 2015) (concluding that the foreign talak divorce was valid in the United States since the parties were in Pakistan at the time of the divorce); *Siddiqui v. Siddiqui*, 107 A.D.3d 974, 974–75 (NY App. Div. 2013). (The court dismissed an action to void a talaq divorce but specifically refused to decide whether talaq was offensive to public policy. The court stated that its holding was limited to the particular facts of this case.)
134. *Sheriff v. Moosa*, No. 05-13-01143-CV, 2015 Tex. App. LEXIS 8390, at *11–12 (App. Aug. 11, 2015); *Banu v. Saheb*, No. 287403, 2009 Mich. App. LEXIS 733, at *6 (Ct. App. Apr. 7, 2009).
135. *Aleem v. Aleem*, 947 A.2d 489, 501 (Md. 2008).
136. Bhala, *Understanding Islamic Law (Shari'a)*, 992–93.
137. Ibid., 993.
138. Ibid., 995.
139. Ibid.
140. Ibid.
141. Ibid., 997–98.
142. Ibid.
143. Child Custody Jurisdiction and Enforcement Act Summary, Uniform Law Commission, (N.B.: Massachusetts uses an older version of the Act.).
144. Uniform Child Custody Jurisdiction and Enforcement Act § 105(c) (1997).
145. *In re Marriage of Malak*, 227 Cal. Rptr. 841, 842 (1986).
146. Ibid., 843–44.
147. Ibid., 846.
148. Ibid., 847.
149. *S.B. v. W.A.*, 959 N.Y.S.2d 802, 808 (Sup. Ct. 2012).
150. Abu Dhabi has a dual court system of state secular courts and Sharia law courts. After a UAE Federal Supreme Court decision in 2010, Sharia law no longer applies to child custody cases.
151. *S.B. v. W.A.*, 959 N.Y.S.2d at 818–819.
152. *Charara v. Yatim*, 937 N.E.2d 490, 492 (Mass. App. Ct. 2010).

153. Ibid., 493–94.
154. Ibid.
155. Ibid.
156. Bhala, *Understanding Islamic Law (Shari'a)*, 1168.
157. Ibid.
158. Ibid., 1169.
159. Ibid., 1171.
160. Ibid., 1173–74.
161. Ibid.
162. Ibid., 1177.
163. Ibid., 1178.
164. Ibid., 1399, 1435.
165. Bhala, *Understanding Islamic Law (Shari'a)*, 1169.
166. Ibid.
167. *Quran* 8:55, 25:44, 2:171, 7:175–76, 62:5, and 5:59–60.
168. *Quran* 2:178.
169. *Sahih Bukhari* 9:89:271; 9:84:57; 9:84:58; 9:83:37.
170. Bhala, *Understanding Islamic Law (Shari'a)*, 1181.
171. Ibid.; see also *Quran* 2:282.
172. *Sahih Bukhari* 1:6:301.
173. Bhala, *Understanding Islamic Law (Shari'a)*, 1202.
174. Ibid.
175. Ibid.
176. Bhala, *Understanding Islamic Law (Shari'a)*, 1211
177. *Quran* 4:15.
178. Bhala, *Understanding Islamic Law (Shari'a)*, 1213.
179. *People v. Jones*, 697 N.E.2d 457, 459 (Ill. App. Ct. 1998).
180. Ibid., 690–91.
181. Ibid., 689.
182. Ibid., 694.
183. *E. Band of Cherokee Indians v. Sequoyah*, 3 Cher. Rep. 95, 2004 N.C. Cherokee Ct. LEXIS 564 (2004).
184. Ibid., 95–96.
185. Ibid., 96.
186. Ibid., 95–96.
187. *Reynolds v. United States*, 98 U.S. 145 (1878).
188. Ibid., 166.
189. Ibid.
190. Ibid., 167.
191. See, e.g., *Sherbert v. Verner*, 374 U.S. 398, 403–04 (1963) (a state

needs to have a compelling interest and least restrictive means when regulating religion), but see *Employment Div. v. Smith*, 494 U.S. 872, 876-89 (1990) (Sherbert does not apply to religiously neutral generally applicable laws). The limits do not concern us here.

192. See, e.g., "Shelby Lin Erdman, Pakistani Newlyweds Decapitated by Bride's Family in Honor Killing," CNN, June 29, 2014, http://www.cnn.com/2014/06/28/world/asia/pakistan-honor-murders; Mohammad Tahir, "Why Are Honor Killings Still Happening?," MSNBC,, May 30, 2014, http://www.msnbc.com/ronan-farrow-daily/why-are-honor-killings-still-happening.

193. Terrence McCoy, "In Pakistan, 1,000 Women Die in 'Honor Killings' Annually. Why is This Happening?," *Washington Post*, May 28, 2014, https://www.washingtonpost.com/news/morning-mix/wp/2014/05/28/in-pakistan-honor-killings-claim-1000-womens-lives-annually-why-is-this-still-happening/.

194. Julia Dahl, " 'Honor Killing' " Under Growing Scrutiny in the U.S.," CBS News, April 5, 2012, http://www.cbsnews.com/news/honor-killing-under-growing-scrutiny-in-the-us/.

195. Ibid.

196. Ibid.

197. Ibid.

198. Ahmed Rashid, "After 1,700 Years, Buddhas Fall to Taliban Dynamite," *Telegraph*, March 12, 2001, http://www.telegraph.co.uk/news/worldnews/asia/afghanistan/1326063/After-1700-years-Buddhas-fall-to-Taliban-dynamite.html.

199. "Iraq's Oldest Christian Monastery Destroyed by Islamic State," BBC News, January 20, 2016, http://www.bbc.com/news/world-middle-east-35360415.

200. Hitti, *History of the Arabs*, 136.

CHAPTER FIVE: ISLAM: A RELIGION OF PEACE?

1. Press release, George W. Bush, President, "'Islam Is Peace' Says President" (September 17, 2001), http://georgewbush-whitehouse.archives.gov/news/releases/2001/09/20010917-11.html.

2. Press release, Barack Obama, President, Remarks by President Obama in Address to the United Nations General Assembly (September. 24, 2014), https://www.whitehouse.gov/the-press-office/2014/09/24/remarks-president-obama-address-united-nations-general-assembly; Press release, Barack Obama, President,

Remarks by the President at Islamic Society at Baltimore (February 3, 2016), https://www.whitehouse.gov/the-press -office/2016/02/03/remarks-president-islamic-society-baltimore.

3. Philip K. Hitti, *History of the Arabs*, 10th rev. ed. (Basingstoke, England: Palgrave Macmillan, 2002), 100–101.

4. Raj Bhala, *Understanding Islamic Law (Shari'a)* (New Providence, NJ: Lexis-Nexis, 2011), 34, 76.

5. Ibid.

6. Ibid., 42, 76, 89.

7. *Abdullah Yusuf Ali, The Meaning of the Holy Qur'an*, 10th ed. (Beltsville, MD: Amana, 2001), 3:64–71, 84, 42:13 (hereinafter *Quran*); Bhala, *Understanding Islamic Law (Shari'a)*, 9–10.

8. Bhala, *Understanding Islamic Law (Shari'a)*, 75.

9. *Quran* 5:12–17; see also 4:155–56; Bhala, *Understanding Islamic Law (Shari'a)*, 18–19.

10. *Quran* 3:78, 5:14–17; see also Bhala, *Understanding Islamic Law (Shari'a)*, 18–19.

11. Fred M. Donner, "Muhammad and the Caliphate," in John L. Esposito, ed., *The Oxford History of Islam* (New York: Oxford University Press, 1999), 1, 5–6.

12. Bhala, *Understanding Islamic Law (Shari'a)*, 34.

13. Ibid.

14. Ibid., 35.

15. Ibid., 28–29.

16. Ibid.

17. Ibid., 29.

18. Ibid., 36.

19. Ibid., 35.

20. *Sahih Bukhari* 1:1:3, http://www.sahih-bukhari.com/Pages /Bukhari_1_01.php; Bhala, *Understanding Islamic Law (Shari'a)*, 35–36. See also *Quran* 7:157 n. 1127 (commenting that Muhammad is the fulfillment of Moses's prophecy in Deuteronomy 18:15 that God would send another prophet after Moses and Jesus's promise to send a comforter or paraclete in John 14:16).

21. Bhala, *Understanding Islamic Law (Shari'a)*, 35–36.

22. Ibid., 36.

23. Ibid., 193–94.

24. Ibid., 189, 194–95.

25. Ibid., 189.

26. *Quran* 7:199, 25:52, 63, 29:8–9, 41:34–36; see also Bhala,

Understanding Islamic Law (Shari'a), 85–89 (detailing in a chart whether each *surah* was revealed in Mecca or in Medina).

27. Bhala, *Understanding Islamic Law (Shari'a)*, 85.
28. *Quran* 45:16 ("We did aforetime grant to the children of Israel the Book, the power of command, and prophethood; We gave them for sustenance, things good and pure; and We favoured them above the nations."); see also ibid., 44:30–32 (speaking of the children of Israel: "We chose them aforetime above the nations, knowingly").
29. Ibid., 4:171. Ironically, Ruhallah is also the name of the former Supreme Leader of Iran.
30. Ibid., 4:155–59.
31. Ibid.
32. Jean-Pierre Filiu, *Apocalypse in Islam*, trans. M. B. DeBevoise (Berkeley: University of California Press, 2011), xi, 5, 40.
33. Hitti, *History of the Arabs*, 113 (noting that "Muhammad was gaining few converts" in Mecca besides his wife Khadija, his cousin Ali, and Abu-Bakr).
34. Francis E. Peters, *Mecca: A Literary History of the Muslim Holy Land* (Princeton, NJ: Princeton University Press, 1994), 24–25, https://books.google.com/books?id=tdb6F1qVDhkC&printsec=frontcover#v=onepage&q&f=false.
35. *Quran* 2:124–27 n. 125.
36. Hitti, *History of the Arabs*, 100, 113.
37. Bhala, *Understanding Islamic Law (Shari'a)*, 38.
38. Ibid., 24, 38; Hitti, *History of the Arabs*, 113.
39. Bhala, *Understanding Islamic Law (Shari'a)*, 42–43.
40. Ibid., 89.
41. Ibid., 89–90.
42. Ibid., 85.
43. Ibid., 1340, 1351.
44. Asma Afsaruddin, *Striving in the Path of God* (New York: Oxford University Press, 2013), 114.
45. This translation of the Quran uses specialized capitalization. Herein, quotations from the Quran have been adjusted to conventional English capitalization.
46. *Quran* 8:60.
47. Ibid., 4:95.
48. Ibid.
49. Ibid., 2:154.

50. Asma Afsaruddin, *Striving in the Path of God* (New York: Oxford University Press, 2013), 114, https://books.google.com/books?id=tp wdajIJjDUC&printsec=frontcover&source=gbs_ge_summary_r&ca d=0#v=onepage&q&f=false.

51. *Quran* 6:164, 17:13–15.

52. Imran Ahsan Khan Nyazee, *Islamic Jurisprudence* (Islamabad: International Institute of Islamic Thought: Islamic Research Institute, 2000), 318. All four schools of Sunni thought generally accept the abrogation doctrine. Ibid.

53. Bhala, *Understanding Islamic Law (Shari'a)*, 75.

54. *Quran* 3:19, 3:64–72, 4:171, 5:15–19.

55. Ibid., 15:9 ("We have, without doubt, sent down the message; and We will assuredly guard it (from corruption).")

56. Bhala, *Understanding Islamic Law (Shari'a)*, 78.

57. *Quran* 17:105–06; Bhala, *Understanding Islamic Law (Shari'a)*, 76.

58. Nyazee, *Islamic Jurisprudence*, 320.

59. Ibid., 318.

60. Hitti, *History of the Arabs*, 140–42, 169, 176; Bhala, *Understanding Islamic Law (Shari'a)*, 192–96.

61. Nyazee, *Islamic Jurisprudence*, 318.

62. Bhala, *Understanding Islamic Law (Shari'a)*, 77–78.

63. Ibid., 78.

64. Ibid.

65. *Quran* 8:38–39.

66. *Quran* 8:38–42, n.1212.

67. Ibid., 8:39.

68. *Quran* 9:29.

69. Ibid., 5:34.

70. Ibid., 5:33.

71. Julie Roys, "Interview: Former Muslim Nabeel Qureshi on 'Is Islam a Religion of Peace?' (Part 2)," *Christian Post*, December 28, 2015, http://www.christianpost.com/news/former-muslim-nabeel -qureshi-islam-religion-of-peace-interview-153539/.

72. Ibid.

73. Bhala, *Understanding Islamic Law (Shari'a)*, 1326–27.

74. Ibid., 1352.

75. Ibid., 1357.

76. *The Export* (ACLJ Films, 2011).

77. Ibid.

78. Ibid.

79. Declaration of the Muslim Reform Movement, American Islamic Forum for Democracy (December 6, 2015), http://aifdemocracy .org/declaration-of-the-muslim-reform-movement-signed-by-aifd -december-4-2015/.

80. Eliza Griswold, "Is This the End of Christianity in the Middle East?" *New York Times* (July 22, 2015), http://www.nytimes.com /2015/07/26/magazine/is-this-the-end-of-christianity-in-the -middle-east.html?_r=0.

81. Francis Phillips, "A Significant Study of the World's Disappearing Communities," *Catholic Herald* (January 20, 2015), http://www .catholicherald.co.uk/commentandblogs/2015/01/20/a-significant -study-of-the-worlds-disappearing-communities/.

82. Johnnie Moore, "ISIS's Mission: Burn Their Churches and Kill Their Pastors," *The Federalist* (March 20, 2015), http://thefederalist .com/2015/03/20/isiss-mission-burn-their-churches-and-kill-their -pastors/.

83. Griswold, "Is This the End of Christianity in the Middle East?"

84. "As ISIS Destroys Artifacts, Could Some Antiquities Have Been Saved?" NPR (Sept. 5, 2016, 9:14 AM), http://www.npr.org /sections/parallels/2015/09/05/437616132/as-isis-destroys-artifacts -could-some-antiquities-have-been-saved/.

85. Ibid.

86. Margaret Hartmann, "How ISIS Is Destroying Ancient Art in Iraq and Syria," *New York* magazine. http://nymag.com/daily /intelligencer/2015/03/isis-destroys-ancient-art.html.

CHAPTER SIX: THE SUNNI-SHIITE DIVIDE AND THE IRANIAN REVOLUTION

1. http://www.pewresearch.org/fact-tank/2015/12/07/muslims-and -islam-key-findings-in-the-u-s-and-around-the-world/.

2. Lesley Hazleton, *After the Prophet: The Epic Story of the Shia-Sunni Split in Islam* (New York: Anchor Books, 2009), 100.

3. Ibid., 11.

4. Raj Bhala, *Understanding Islamic Law (Shari'a)* (New Providence, NJ: Lexis-Nexis, 2011), 121.

5. Ibid., 122.

6. Ibid., 123–24.

7. Ibid., 124.

8. http://www.pewforum.org/2009/10/07/mapping-the-global-muslim -population/.

9. Michael Axworthy, *A History of Iran: Empire of the Mind* (New York: Basic Books, 2010), 4.
10. Ibid., 5.
11. Ibid., 12.
12. Ibid., 28–29.
13. Francis Fukuyama, *The Origins of Political Order* (New York: Farrar, Straus & Giroux, 2011), 193.
14. Stephen Kinzer, *All the Shah's Men: An American Coup and the Roots of Middle East Terror*, 2d ed. (New York: Wiley, 2008), 24–25.
15. Ibid., 20, 22.
16. Ibid., 19–20.
17. Ibid., 20–21.
18. Roger Savory, *Iran Under the Safavids* (Cambridge: Cambridge University Press, 1980), 29.
19. Kinzer, *All the Shah's Men*, 20.
20. Ibid., 22.
21. Ibid., 23.
22. Ibid., 19–20.
23. Ibid., 24.
24. Ismail, a Muslim conqueror, was the founder of the Safavid dynasty that followed Twelver Shiism.
25. Kinzer, *All the Shah's Men*, 25.
26. Ibid.
27. Ibid.
28. Ibid.
29. Ibid., 27.
30. Ibid., 27–28.
31. Ibid., 28.
32. Ibid., 42.
33. Ibid., 28.
34. Ibid.
35. Ibid.
36. Ibid., 31.
37. Ibid., 31, 48.
38. Ibid., 48.
39. Ibid.
40. Ibid.
41. Ibid., 49.
42. Ibid., 68.

43. Ibid., 50.
44. Ibid., 28.
45. Ibid., 34, 38.
46. Ibid., 41.
47. Ibid.
48. Ibid.
49. Ibid., 42.
50. Ibid., 43.
51. Ibid.
52. Ibid.
53. Ibid., 45.
54. Ibid.
55. Ibid.
56. Ibid.
57. Ibid.
58. Ibid.
59. Ibid., 66.
60. Ibid.
61. Ibid., 63.
62. Ibid., 64.
63. Ibid., 53.
64. Ibid., 57.
65. Ibid., 53, 56.
66. Ibid., 57–59.
67. Ibid., 71.
68. Ibid., 82, 93–94, 98.
69. Ibid., 98.
70. Ibid., 65.
71. Ibid., 85.
72. Ibid., 92–93.
73. Ibid., 99, 111–12.
74. Ibid., 131, 155.
75. Ibid., 132, 208.
76. Ibid., 103–4.
77. Ibid.
78. Ibid.
79. Ibid., 157–58.
80. Ibid., 158, 160.
81. Ibid., 161; Donald N. Wilber, "Overthrow of Premier Mossadeq of Iran," *C.I.A.: Clandestine Service*, 1954, iv–v, 18–21 (CIA

historical document recounting the details of Operation TPAJAX, declassified in 2013, the fiftieth anniversary of the 1953 coup).

82. Kinzer, *All the Shah's Men*, 166.
83. Ibid., 188.
84. Ibid., 193.
85. Ibid., 15, 190.
86. Ibid., 190.
87. Ibid., 191.
88. Ibid.
89. Ibid., 195–96.
90. Ibid., 196.
91. Ibid.
92. James Buchan, *Days of God: The Revolution in Iran and Its Consequences* (New York: Simon & Schuster, 2012), 104.
93. Ronen Bergman, *The Secret War with Iran*, trans. Ronnie Hope (New York: Free Press, 2008), 43; Steven Simon, "The Iran Primer: Iran and Israel," U.S. Institute of Peace, http://iranprimer.usip.org /resource/iran-and-israel.
94. Michael Zirinsky, "Riza Shah's Abrogation of Capitulations," in Stephanie Cronin, ed., *The Making of Modern Iran: State and Society Under Reza Shah, 1921–1941* (New York: Routledge, 2007), 83.
95. Ibid., 86.
96. Ibid., 83.
97. Jaleh Taheri, "Areas of Iranian Women's Voice and Influence," in Roksana Bahramitash and Eric Hooglund, eds., *Gender in Contemporary Iran: Pushing the Boundaries* (New York: Routledge, 2011), 95.
98. Ibid.
99. Zirinsky, "Riza Shah's Abrogation of Capitulations," 83.
100. *The Export* (ACLJ Films, 2011).
101. Kinzer, *All the Shah's Men*, 196.
102. Ibid.
103. Ibid.
104. Ibid.
105. Buchan, *Days of God*, 79.
106. Ibid., 252.
107. Ibid.
108. Ibid.
109. Ibid., 84.
110. Ibid.

111. Ibid., 93.
112. Ibid., 91.
113. Ibid.
114. Ibid.
115. Ibid., 92.
116. Ibid.
117. Ibid., 92, 95.
118. Ibid., 96.
119. Ibid., 97.
120. Ibid., 222.
121. Ibid., 95.
122. Ibid., 160
123. Ibid., 95.
124. Ibid., 257.
125. Ibid., 256–57.
126. Ibid., 272.
127. Ibid., 214.
128. http://www.cbsnews.com/news/iran-ayatollah-ali-khamenei-us
     -still-great-satan-israel-gone-in-25-years/.
129. Hazleton, *After the Prophet*, 183.
130. "Ashura of Muharram—A Shia and Sunni Muslim Observance,"
     IqraSense.com, http://www.iqrasense.com/islamic-history/ashura
     -of-muharram-a-shia-and-sunni-muslim-observance.html.
131. Hazleton, *After the Prophet*, 188–90.
132. Ibid.
133. Ibid., 172.
134. Ibid., 172–73.
135. Ibid., 173.
136. Ibid.
137. Ibid.
138. Ibid.
139. Ibid., 184–85.
140. Ibid.
141. Ibid., 185–88.
142. Ibid.
143. Ibid., 185.
144. Ibid., 185–86.
145. Ibid., 186.
146. Ibid.
147. Ibid., 187.

148. Ibid.
149. Ibid., 190–92.
150. Ibid., 192–94.
151. Ibid., 194.
152. Ibid., 183.
153. Ibid.
154. Ibid., 188.
155. Ibid.
156. Ibid., 189.
157. Ibid.
158. Ibid., 189–90.
159. Ibid., 197.
160. Ibid.
161. Ibid., 197–98.
162. Ibid., 181.
163. Ibid., 197.
164. Ibid., 197–98.
165. Ibid., 198.
166. Ibid., 197.
167. Bhala, *Understanding Islamic Law (Shari'a)*, 206.
168. Ibid. (quoting Professor Esposito).
169. Ibid., 206–7.
170. Hazleton, *After the Prophet*, 197.
171. Ibid., 170–71.
172. Buchan, *Days of God*, 255.
173. Ibid.
174. Ibid., 122, 255.
175. Ibid., 255.
176. Ibid., 256.
177. Ibid., 122.
178. Ibid.
179. Ibid.
180. Ibid.
181. Ibid.
182. Ibid.
183. Ibid., 123.
184. Bergman, *The Secret War with Iran*, 70–71.
185. Ibid., 70, 72.
186. Buchan, *Days of God*, 254–55.
187. Ibid., 255.

188. Ibid., 255–56.

189. Ibid., 255.

190. Ibid.

191. Ibid., 249.

192. Greg Bruno et al., "Iran's Revolutionary Guards." Council on Foreign Relations, http://www.cfr.org/iran/irans-revolutionary -guards/p14324 (last updated June 14, 2013).

193. Ibid.

194. Buchan, *Days of God*, 249.

195. Bruno et al., "Iran's Revolutionary Guards."

196. Buchan, *Days of God*, 277.

197. Ibid., 281.

198. Ibid.

199. Ibid.

200. Ibid.

201. Ibid., 302.

202. Ibid., 303.

203. Orde F. Kittrie, "Emboldened by Impunity: The History and Consequences of Failure to Enforce Iranian Violations of International Law," *Syracuse Law Review* 57 (2007): 519, 529; Bernard K. Freamon, "Martyrdom, Suicide, and the Islamic Law of War: A Short Legal History," *Fordham International Law Journal* 27 (2003): 299, 347–48.

204. Bergman, *The Secret War with Iran*, 42.

205. Buchan, *Days of God*, 304.

206. Ibid.

207. Ibid., 300–301.

208. Ibid., 301.

209. Ibid.

210. Ibid.

211. Bergman, *The Secret War with Iran*, 56.

212. Buchan, *Days of God*, 301.

213. Ibid.

214. Ibid.

215. Dexter Filkins, "The Shadow Commander," *New Yorker*, September 30, 2013, http://www.newyorker.com/magazine/2013 /09/30/the-shadow-commander.

216. Ibid.

217. Harrison Jacobs, "7 Times When Iran's Strategic Mastermind Reshaped the Middle East," *Business Insider*, April 11, 2015,

http://www.businessinsider.com/operations-by-irans-military
-mastermind-2015-4.

218. Ibid.
219. Ibid.
220. Ibid.
221. Filkins, "The Shadow Commander."
222. *The Export* (ACLJ Films, 2011).
223. Bergman, *The Secret War with Iran*, 27.

CHAPTER SEVEN: EXPORTING THE REVOLUTION

1. *The Export* (ACLJ Films, 2011).
2. Abdullah Yusuf Ali, *The Meaning of the Holy Quran*, 10th ed. (Beltsville, MD: Amana, 2001), *Surah* 5:56 (hereinafter *Quran*); see also Jonathan Masters and Zachary Laub, "Hezbollah (a.k.a. Hizbolah, Hizbu'llah)," Council on Foreign Relations, January 3, 2014, http://www.cfr.org/lebanon/hezbollah-k-hizbollah-hizbullah /p9155. Several variations of spellings are in common use, such as *Hizbullah, Hezbullah, Hizballah*, but we will use *Hezbollah* for the purposes of this book.
3. Masters, "Hezbollah (a.k.a. Hizbolah, Hizbu'llah)."
4. Augustus Richard Norton, *Hezbollah: A Short History* (Princeton, NJ: Princeton University Press, 2007), 34–37.
5. Tony Badran, "The Lebanese Civil War," Rubin Center, June 7, 2008, http://www.rubincenter.org/2008/06/badran-2008-06-07/.
6. Kim Cragin, "Hizballah, the Party of God," in *Aptitude for Destruction: Case Studies of Organizational Learning in Five Terrorist Groups* 2 (2005): 39, http://www.rand.org/content/dam/rand/pubs /monographs/2005/RAND_MG332.pdf.
7. Near East/South Asia Report, "Lebanon: Hizballah Issues 'Open Letter' on Goals, Principles," April 19, 1985, 2, (hereinafter "Open Letter").
8. Cragin, "Hizballah, the Party of God," 37.
9. Kamal Salibi, *A House of Many Mansions: The History of Lebanon Reconsidered* (Berkeley: University of California Press, 1993), 19; D. K. Fieldhouse, *Western Imperialism in the Middle East 1914–1958* (New York: Oxford University Press, 2006), 304.
10. Ibid.
11. Ibid.
12. Fawwāz Ṭarābulsī, *A History of Modern Lebanon* (London: Pluto Press, 2012), 80.

13. Fieldhouse, *Western Imperialism in the Middle East 1914–1958*, 307.
14. Ibid., 317.
15. Ibid., 305.
16. Ibid.
17. Ṭarābulsī,, *A History of Modern Lebanon*, 85.
18. Fieldhouse, *Western Imperialism in the Middle East 1914–1958*, 311–12.
19. Ibid., 314.
20. Ibid., 322; Norton, *Hezbollah*, 11.
21. Fieldhouse, *Western Imperialism in the Middle East 1914–1958*, 322.
22. Norton, *Hezbollah*, 11.
23. Ibid., 12.
24. Samir Makdisi and Richard Sadaka, "The Lebanese Civil War, 1975–1990," American University of Beirut Institute of Financial Economics, IFE Lecture and Working Paper Series No. 3, 2003, 9–10.
25. Ibid.
26. Fieldhouse, *Western Imperialism in the Middle East 1914–1958*, 327.
27. Norton, *Hezbollah*, 12.
28. Ibid., 14.
29. Ibid.
30. Ibid., 14–15.
31. Ṭarābulsī, *A History of Modern Lebanon*, 183.
32. Ibid.; Norton, *Hezbollah*, 17.
33. Norton, *Hezbollah*, 20.
34. Ibid.
35. Dominique Avon and Anais-Trissa Khatchadourian, *Hezbollah: A History of the "Party of God,"* trans. Jane Marie Todd (Cambridge, MA: Harvard University Press, 2012), 15.
36. Ibid.
37. Norton, *Hezbollah*, 17.
38. Ibid., 29.
39. Makdisi and Sadaka, "The Lebanese Civil War, 1975–1990," 12.
40. Ibid., 13.
41. Ibid at 14.
42. Makdisi and Sadaka, "The Lebanese Civil War, 1975–1990," 14; Badran, "The Lebanese Civil War."
43. Norton, *Hezbollah*, 16.
44. Ibid., 17.

45. Ibid.; Badran, "The Lebanese Civil War"; see also Makdisi and Sadaka, "The Lebanese Civil War, 1975–1990," 12–13.
46. Badran, "The Lebanese Civil War."
47. Norton, *Hezbollah*, 19.
48. Ibid., 22.
49. Marwan George Rowayheb, "Political Change and the Outbreak of Civil War: The Case of Lebanon," *Civil Wars* 13 (2011): 414, 417.
50. Ibid.
51. Norton, *Hezbollah*, 17–18.
52. Badran, "The Lebanese Civil War," 3.
53. Rowayheb, "Political Change and the Outbreak of Civil War," 417.
54. Norton, *Hezbollah*, 17–18.
55. Ibid., 19.
56. Badran, "The Lebanese Civil War."
57. Ibid.
58. Ronen Bergman, *The Secret War with Iran*, trans. Ronnie Hope (New York: Free Press, 2008), 53–54.
59. Ibid., 53.
60. Ibid., 55.
61. Ibid.
62. Marc R. DeVore, "Exploring the Iran-Hezbollah Relationship: A Case Study of How State Sponsorship Affects Terrorist Group Decision-Making," *Perspectives on Terrorism* 6 (2012): 85, 91–92.
63. Badran, "The Lebanese Civil War."
64. Ibid.
65. Ibid.
66. DeVore, "Exploring the Iran-Hezbollah Relationship," 92–93; Bergman, *The Secret War with Iran*, 57; see also Norton, *Hezbollah*, 32–34.
67. DeVore, "Exploring the Iran-Hezbollah Relationship," 91.
68. Bergman, *The Secret War with Iran*, 57.
69. Ibid., 52.
70. Ibid.
71. DeVore, "Exploring the Iran-Hezbollah Relationship," 92.
72. *Iran and the West: The Pariah State*, BBC television broadcast, February 14, 2009, https://youtube/UfuzlnB0YB8 (hereinafter *The Pariah State*).
73. Ibid.
74. Ibid.
75. Ibid.

76. Bergman, *The Secret War with Iran*, 69.
77. Ibid.
78. Ibid., 69–70.
79. Bergman, *The Secret War with Iran*, 61.
80. Daniel Sobelman, "Hizbollah—from Terror to Resistance: Towards a National Defence Strategy," in Clive Jones and Sergio Catignani, eds., *Israel and Hizbollah: An Asymmetric Conflict in Historical and Comparative Perspective* (London and New York: Routledge, 2010), 51–52.
81. Ibid.
82. Amal Saad-Ghorayeb, *Hizbu'llah Politics & Religion* (London: Pluto Press, 2001), 14.
83. Bergman, *The Secret War with Iran*, 61.
84. Badran, "The Lebanese Civil War."
85. Ibid.
86. DeVore, "Exploring the Iran-Hezbollah Relationship," 100; Robert G. Rabil, "Hezbollah: The Islamic Association and Lebanon's Confessional System Al-Infitah and Lebanonization," *Levantine Review* 1 (2012): 49, 52.
87. DeVore, "Exploring the Iran-Hezbollah Relationship," 92.
88. *Open Letter.*
89. Bergman, *The Secret War with Iran*, 69.
90. Ghorayeb, *Hizbu'llah Politics & Religion*, 14–15; Avon and Khatchadourian, *Hezbollah: A History of the "Party of God,"* 22.
91. DeVore, "Exploring the Iran-Hezbollah Relationship," 92.
92. *The Pariah State.*
93. Ibid.
94. Judith Harik, *The Public and Social Services of the Lebanese Militias*, Papers on Lebanon 14 (Oxford: Centre for Lebanese Studies, 1994), 41.
95. *Dammarell v. Islamic Republic of Iran*, 404 F. Supp. 2d 261, 273 (D.D.C. 2005).
96. Bureau of International Narcotics and Law Enforcement Affairs, U.S. Department of State, 2011 INCSR: Countries/Jurisdictions of Primary Concern—Guatemala through Mexico, March 3, 2011, http://www.state.gov/j/inl/rls/nrcrpt/2011/vol2/156375.htm. The Martyrs Foundation is "an Iranian parastatal organization that channels financial support from Iran to several terrorist organizations in the Levant, including Hizballah, Hamas, and the Palestinian Islamic Jihad." Ibid.

97. DeVore, "Exploring the Iran-Hezbollah Relationship," 93; Harik, *The Public and Social Services of the Lebanese Militias*, 40–41.
98. Harik, *The Public and Social Services of the Lebanese Militias*, 32.
99. Ibid., 37.
100. DeVore, "Exploring the Iran-Hezbollah Relationship," 95–96.
101. Associated Press, "Turkey Stops Iranian Arms Shipment to Syria," *Wall Street Journal*, August 5, 2011, http://www.wsj.com/articles/SB 10001424053111903454504576490192016253506.
102. "Health Minister Attends Hezbollah Tehran Office," Islamic Republic News Agency, January 22, 2015, http://www.irna.ir/en /News/81474594/.
103. DeVore, "Exploring the Iran-Hezbollah Relationship," 94–95.
104. Ibid.
105. *Dammarell v. Islamic Republic of Iran*, 404 F. Supp. 2d 261, 271 (D.D.C. 2005).
106. Ibid.
107. Patrick Clawson is the director for Research at the Washington Institute for Near East Policy; http://www.washingtoninstitute.org /experts/view/clawson-patrick.
108. *Dammarell*, 404 F. Supp. 2d at 272.
109. Ibid., 271–72.
110. Ibid., 273. Another case arising from the same events is *Salazar v. Islamic Republic of Iran*, 370 F. Supp. 2d 105 (D.D.C. 2005).
111. *Peterson v. Islamic Republic of Iran*, 264 F. Supp. 2d 46, 49, 56 (D.D.C. 2003); DeVore, "Exploring the Iran-Hezbollah Relationship," 97.
112. DeVore, "Exploring the Iran-Hezbollah Relationship," 97. See also "Suicide Bomber Killed 41 American Troops 25 Years Ago in Barracks," Arlington National Cemetery, October 23, 2008, http:// www.arlingtoncemetery.net/terror.htm.
113. DeVore, "Exploring the Iran-Hezbollah Relationship," 97; *Peterson*, 264 F. Supp. 2d, at 54–56.
114. *The Pariah State*.
115. Ibid.
116. *Peterson*, 264 F. Supp. 2d at 53.
117. DeVore, "Exploring the Iran-Hezbollah Relationship," 97.
118. Interview with Robert Baer, *Frontline*, PBS, March 22, 2002, http:// www.pbs.org/wgbh/pages/frontline/shows/tehran/interviews/baer .html.

119. Ibid.
120. DeVore, "Exploring the Iran-Hezbollah Relationship," 98; Baer interview.
121. Bergman, *The Secret War with Iran*, 91.
122. DeVore, "Exploring the Iran-Hezbollah Relationship," 99–100.
123. Baer interview.
124. Devore, "Exploring the Iran-Hezbollah Relationship," 97–98.
125. Ibid., 98; Jeffrey Goldberg, "In The Party of God (Part I)," *New Yorker*, October 14, 2002, http://www.newyorker.com/magazine /2002/10/14/in-the-party-of-god.
126. DeVore, "Exploring the Iran-Hezbollah Relationship," 98.
127. Ibid.
128. Ibid.
129. Ibid.
130. *Anderson v. Islamic Republic of Iran*, 90 F. Supp. 2d 107, 109 (D.D.C. 2000).
131. Ibid., 109–11.
132. Ibid., 108.
133. Ibid., 111.
134. Ibid., 114.
135. See, e.g., *Cicippio v. Islamic Republic of Iran*, 18 F. Supp. 2d 62 (D.D.C. 1998) (holding in favor of kidnapping victims Joseph J. Cicippio, David P. Jacobsen, and Frank Reed against the Islamic Republic of Iran).
136. Matthew Levitt, "Hezbollah's 1992 Attack in Argentina Is a Warning for Modern-Day Europe," *Atlantic*, March 19, 2013, http://www.theatlantic.com/international/archive/2013/03 /hezbollahs-1992-attack-in-argentina-is-a-warning-for-modern-day -europe/274160/.
137. "Investigation Finds Iranian, Hezbollah and Syrian Involvement in 1994 Bombing of Argentine Jewish Community Center," Anti-Defamation League, October 2003, http://archive.adl.org/terror /terror_buenos_aries_attack.html#.VikbF36rSUk (hereinafter Anti-Defamation League).
138. Dexter Filkins, "The Shadow Commander," *New Yorker*, September 30, 2013, http://www.newyorker.com/magazine /2013/09/30/the-shadow-commander.
139. "Iran Charged Over Argentina Bomb," *BBC News*, October 25, 2006, http://news.bbc.co.uk/2/hi/americas/6085768.stm.

140. Jonathan Blitzer, "What Happened to Alberto Nisman?," *New Yorker*, January 31, 2015, http://www.newyorker.com/news/news -desk/happened-alberto-nisman.

141. Anti-Defamation League; "Iran Charged over Argentina Bomb."

142. Anti-Defamation League.

143. Ibid.

144. Ibid.

145. Ibid.

146. Norton, *Hezbollah*, 34.

147. Ibid.

148. http://freebeacon.com/national-security/iran-breaks-with-arab -states-continues-backing-hezbollah/.

149. Ibid.

150. *The Export* (ACLJ Films, 2011).

CHAPTER EIGHT: BEYOND TERRORISM: A MUCH LARGER GOAL

1. Raj Bhala, *Understanding Islamic Law (Shari'a)* (New Providence, NJ: Lexis-Nexis, 2011), 207.

2. Ibid., 205.

3. Ibid., 207.

4. *Occultation* is a term used in astronomy. It means hiding of one object by another. Here it means the Mahdi was hidden by Allah from the eyes of men. Moojan Momen, *An Introduction to Shi'i Islam* (New Haven, CT: Yale University Press, 1985), 165.

5. Bhala, *Understanding Islamic Law (Shari'a)*, 220.

6. Ibid., 221.

7. Momen, *An Introduction to Shi'i Islam*, 166.

8. Joel Richardson, "The Mahdi: Islam's Awaited Messiah," Answering Islam, http://www.answering-islam.org/Authors/JR /Future/ch04_the_mahdi.htm (quoting Muhammad ibn Izzat and Muhammad 'Arif, *Al Mahdi and the End of Time* [London: Dar al Taqwa, 1997], 40).

9. Ziad Abu-Amr, "The Significance of Jerusalem: A Muslim Perspective, *Palestine-Israel Journal of Politics, Economics, and Culture* 2, no. 2 (1995), http://www.pij.org/details.php?id=646.

10. S. Ahmad Rahnamaei, "The Prophet's Night Journey and Ascent to Heaven," *Message of Thaqalayn* (Autumn 2009): 15–16, http:// messageofthaqalayn.com/39-prophet.pdf.

11. Abdullah Yusuf Ali, *The Meaning of the Holy Qur'an* , 10th ed. (Beltsville, MD: Amana, 2001), 17:1, n.2168 (hereinafter *Quran*).

12. Ibid.; Abu-Amr, "The Significance of Jerusalem."

13. Mustafa Abu Sway, "Al-Aqsa Mosque: Do Not Intrude!," *Palestine–Israel Journal of Politics, Economics, and Culture* 20, no. 4 (2015), http://www.pij.org/details.php?id=1644.

14. Richardson, "The Mahdi: Islam's Awaited Messiah."

15. Ronen Bergman, *The Secret War with Iran*, trans. Ronnie Hope (New York: Free Press, 2008), 59.

16. Bhala, *Understanding Islamic Law* (Shari'a), 1326–27.

17. *The Export* (ACLJ Films, 2011).

18. Bergman, *The Secret War with Iran*, 213–14.

19. Ibid., 214.

20. "Profile: Egypt's Muslim Brotherhood," BBC News, December 25, 2013, http://www.bbc.com/news/world-middle-east-12313405.

21. Zachary Laub, "Egypt's Muslim Brotherhood," Council on Foreign Relations, January 15, 2014, http://www.cfr.org/egypt/egypts-muslim-brotherhood/p23991.

22. Andrew M. Bennett, "Islamic History & Al-Qaeda: A Primer to Understanding the Rise of Islamist Movements in the Modern World," *Pace International Law Review Online Companion* 3 (2013): 316, 347, http://digitalcommons.pace.edu/cgi/viewcontent.cgi?article=1035&context=pilronline.

23. Kristen Stilt, "'Islam Is the Solution': Constitutional Visions of the Egyptian Muslim Brotherhood," *Texas International Law Journal* 46 (2010): 73, 76–77.

24. Ibid., 74.

25. İpek Yezdani, "'Shariah in Egypt Is Enough for Us,' Muslim Brotherhood Leader Says," *Hurriyet Daily News*, May 23, 2011, http://www.hurriyetdailynews.com/default.aspx?pageid=438&n=8220shari8217a-law-in-egypt-is-enough-for-us8221-tells-a-muslim-brotherhood-leader-2011-05-23.

26. Sally Nabil, "Egypt Court Bans Muslim Brotherhood Political Wing," BBC News, August 9, 2014, http://www.bbc.com/news/world-middle-east-28722935.

27. Mehdi Khalaji, "Egypt's Muslim Brotherhood and Iran," Washington Institute for Near East Policy, February 12, 2009, http://www.washingtoninstitute.org/policy-analysis/view/egypts-muslim-brotherhood-and-iran.

28. Ibid.

29. Seyed Mohammad Ali Taghavi, *The Flourishing of Islamic Reformism*

in Iran: Political Islamic Groups in Iran (1941–61) (New York: RoutledgeCurzon, 2004), 113.

30. Ibid.
31. Khalaji, "Egypt's Muslim Brotherhood and Iran."
32. Thomas Joscelyn, "Iran, the Muslim Brotherhood, and Revolution," *Long War Journal: Threat Matrix*, January 28, 2011, http://www.longwarjournal.org/archives/2011/01/iran_the_muslim _brotherhood_an.php.
33. Khalaji, "Egypt's Muslim Brotherhood and Iran."
34. Joscelyn, "Iran, the Muslim Brotherhood, and Revolution"; see Taghavi, *The Flourishing of Islamic Reformism in Iran*, 120; Amir Taheri, "Iran and the Ikhwan: The Ideological Roots of a Partnership," *Ashraq Al-Awsat*, May 31, 2014, http://english.aawsat .com/2014/05/article55332765/iran-and-the-ikhwan-the-ideological -roots-of-a-partnership.
35. Joscelyn, "Iran, the Muslim Brotherhood, and Revolution."
36. Taheri, "Iran and the Ikhwan."
37. Ibid.; Khalaji, "Egypt's Muslim Brotherhood and Iran."
38. Khalaji, "Egypt's Muslim Brotherhood and Iran."
39. Taheri, "Iran and the Ikhwan."
40. Ibid.
41. Ibid.
42. "National Islamic Front," World Public Library, http://worldlibrary .org/articles/national_islamic_front (last updated February 29, 2016).
43. Douglas Farah, "The Role of Sudan in Islamist Terrorism: A Case Study," International Assessment and Strategy Center, April 13, 2007, http://www.strategycenter.net/research/pubID.156/pub _detail.asp.
44. "National Islamic Front."
45. Farah, "The Role of Sudan in Islamist Terrorism."
46. Ibid.
47. Ibid.
48. Ibid.
49. Ibid.
50. Ibid.
51. John Pomfret, "Bosnia's Muslims Dodged Embargo," *Washington Post*, September 22, 1996, http://www.washingtonpost.com/wp-srv /inatl/longterm/bosvote/front.htm.
52. Farah, "The Role of Sudan in Islamist Terrorism."

53. Mike O'Connor, "Under U.S. Pressure, Bosnia Dismisses Official Linked to Iran," *New York Times*, November 20, 1996, http://www.nytimes.com/1996/11/20/world/under-us-pressure-bosnia-dismisses-official-linked-to-iran.html.

54. Semira N. Nikou, "Timeline of Iran's Foreign Relations," Iran Primer, http://iranprimer.usip.org/resource/timeline-irans-foreign-relations.

55. Taheri, "Iran and the Ikhwan."

56. Ibid.

57. Khalaji, "Egypt's Muslim Brotherhood and Iran."

58. Gomaa Hamadalla, "Tehran in 'Constant Contact' with Brotherhood, Says Iranian FM," *Egypt Independent*, January 31, 2012, http://www.egyptindependent.com//news/tehran-constant-contact-brotherhood-says-iranian-fm.

59. Taylor Luck, "Iran Nuclear Deal: Why Are Saudis Wooing the Muslim Brotherhood?," *Christian Science Monitor*, July 23, 2015, http://www.csmonitor.com/World/Middle-East/2015/0723/Iran-nuclear-deal-Why-are-Saudis-wooing-the-Muslim-Brotherhood.

60. Ibid.

61. Robert Baer, "Why Saudi Arabia Is Helping Crush the Muslim Brotherhood," *New Republic*, August 26, 2013, http://www.newrepublic.com/article/114468/why-saudi-arabia-helping-crush-muslim-brotherhood.

62. Ibid.

63. Ibid.

64. Ibid.

65. Shoaib, "Saudi Arabia Extends Hand to Muslim Brotherhood," *Middle East Monitor*, March 29, 2015, https://www.middleeastmonitor.com/blogs/politics/17773-saudi-arabia-extends-hand-to-muslim-brotherhood.

66. Baer, "Why Saudi Arabia Is Helping Crush the Muslim Brotherhood."

67. Luck, "Iran Nuclear Deal."

68. Syed Kamran Hashmi, "What Do Saudis Want from Pakistan?," *Daily Times*, January 15, 2016, http://www.dailytimes.com.pk/opinion/15-Jan-2016/what-do-saudis-want-from-pakistan.

69. E.g., Bureau of Counterterrorism, U.S. Department of State, Designated Foreign Terrorist Organizations, http://www.state.gov/j/ct/rls/other/des/123085.htm; Home Office of the U.K., "Proscribed Terrorist Organizations," 2015, 9.

70. Bernard Gwertzman and Karim Sadjadpour, "Iran Supports Hamas, but Hamas Is No Iranian 'Puppet,'" Council on Foreign Relations, January 8, 2009, http://www.cfr.org/israel/iran-supports -hamas-but-hamas-no-iranian-puppet/p18159.

71. Khaled Abu Toameh, "Hamas Ready to Cooperate with Iran 'to Destroy Israeli Occupation,'" *Jerusalem Post*, February 1, 2015, http://www.jpost.com/Arab-Israeli-Conflict/Hamas-ready-to -cooperate-with-Iran-to-destroy-Israeli-occupation-389655.

72. "Iranian Leader: Wipe Out Israel," CNN, October 27, 2005, http:// www.cnn.com/2005/WORLD/meast/10/26/ahmadinejad/.

73. *The Export* (ACLJ Films, 2011).

74. "Supreme Leader Meets Hamas Political Leaders," Khamenei.ir, May 27, 2008, http://farsi.khamenei.ir/print-content?id=100797.

75. Ibid.

76. "Supreme Leader's Inaugural Address to the Fourth International Conference for Support of Palestine," Khamenei.ir, March 4–6, 2009, http://farsi.khamenei.ir/speech-content?id=101052.

77. Ibid.

78. "Leader Meets Khaled Meshaal," Khamenei.ir, December 15, 2009, http://english.khamenei.ir/news/1261/Leader-Meets-Khaled -Meshaal.

79. "Leader Says Jihadi Morale Will Leave No Serenity for Zionists," Islamic Republic News Agency, September 9, 2015, http://www .irna.ir/en/News/81753808/.

80. "Exclusive: Muslim Brotherhood Preaching Israel Destruction After Election," Investigative Project on Terrorism, June 27, 2012, http://www.investigativeproject.org/3650/exclusive-muslim -brotherhood-preaching-israel#.

81. Kay Armin Serjoie, "One Result of the Gaza Conflict: Iran and Hamas Are Back Together," *Time*, August 19, 2014, http://time .com/3138366/iran-and-hamas-alliance-after-gaza-war/.

82. "Commander: IRGC Ready to Support Palestinian Resistance," FARS News Agency, August 4, 2014, http://en.farsnews.com/news text.aspx?nn=13930513001267.

83. Jagdish N. Singh, "What to Expect in Iran," Gatestone Institute, February 22, 2016, http://www.gatestoneinstitute.org/7459/iran -relations.

84. Serjoie, "One Result of the Gaza Conflict: Iran and Hamas Are Back Together."

85. Jack Moore, "Iran Ceases Financial Aid to Hamas in Gaza, Official

Claims," *Newsweek*, July 28, 2015, http://europe.newsweek.com/iran
-ceases-financial-aid-hamas-gaza-official-claims-330889.

86. "Iran Underlines Strong Support for Palestinian Hamas," FARS
News Agency, August 26, 2015, http://english.farsnews.com/news
text.aspx?nn=13940604001262.

87. Serjoie, "One Result of the Gaza Conflict: Iran and Hamas Are
Back Together."

88. Avi Issacharoff and *Times of Israel* Staff, "Hamas, Hezbollah,
Revolutionary Guards Said to Meet in Beirut," *Times of Israel*,
July 4, 2015, http://www.timesofisrael.com/hamas-hezbollah-irgc
-said-to-meet-in-beirut/.

89. Fatima Al-Smadi, "Analysis: Hamas, Islamic Jihad Redefining
Relations with Iran," Al Jazeera Center for Studies, September 20,
2015, http://studies.aljazeera.net/en/reports/2015/09/2015920843
40199169.htm.

90. Stuart Winer, "Hamas Has Dug 'Several Tunnels' into Israel, in
New Iran-Funded War Drive," *Times of Israel*, August 11, 2015,
http://www.timesofisrael.com/hamas-has-dug-several-tunnels
-into-israel-in-new-iran-funded-war-drive/; Yoav Zitun, "Arrested
Hamas Fighter Reveals Tunnel Attack Plot, Shifting Strategies,"
ynetnews.com, August 11, 2015, http://www.ynetnews.com/articles
/0,7340,L-4689765,00.html.

91. Winer, "Hamas Has Dug 'Several Tunnels' into Israel"; Zitun,
"Arrested Hamas Fighter Reveals Tunnel Attack Plot, Shifting
Strategies."

92. Winer, "Hamas Has Dug 'Several Tunnels' into Israel."

93. Ibid.

94. "Supporting Resistance Groups, Like Hamas, Iran's Principled
Policy: Spokesman," Tasnim News Agency, February 8, 2016,
http://www.tasnimnews.com/en/news/2016/02/08/995139
/supporting-resistance-groups-like-hamas-iran-s-principled-policy
-spokesman.

95. Ibid.

96. Susan Svrluga, "Vanderbilt Student Fatally Stabbed in Israel
Was West Point Grad, War Veteran," *Washington Post*, (March 9,
2016), https://www.washingtonpost.com/news/grade-point
/wp/2016/03/09/vanderbilt-student-stabbed-to-death-in-israel
-was-west-point-grad-war-veteran/.

97. Kibbutz Reim, "Fears Are Growing of Fresh Hostilities in Gaza,"
Economist, February 8, 2016, http://www.economist.com/news

/middle-east-and-africa/21690180-blockade-stays-place-while
-network-tunnels-expands-fears-are-growing.

98. Ibid.
99. "Israel's Netanyahu Warns Gaza Militants Against Attacking,"
Associated Press, January 31, 2016, 5:39 PM, http://bigstory.ap
.org/article/3c5830b9f99c42ed8a70f352b2027df0/israeli-military
-palestinian-gunmen-who-wounded-3-shot-dead.

CHAPTER NINE: IRAN AND AL-QAEDA
1. Ronen Bergman, *The Secret War with Iran*, trans. Ronnie Hope
(New York: Free Press, 2008), 218–19; National Commission on
Terrorist Attacks upon the United States, *The 9/11 Commission
Report* (Washington, DC: U.S. Government Printing Office, 2004),
61 (hereinafter *9/11 Commission Report*).
2. *9/11 Commission Report*, 55.
3. Admin, "The Soviet Occupation of Afghanistan," *PBS Newshour*,
October 10, 2006, http://www.pbs.org/newshour/updates/asia-july
-dec06-soviet_10-10/.
4. Joel C. Rosenberg, *Inside the Revolution* (Carol Stream, IL: Tyndale
House, 2009), 98.
5. Ibid.
6. "Soviet Invasion of Afghanistan," *Encyclopaedia Britannica*, http://
www.britannica.com/event/Soviet-invasion-of-Afghanistan.
7. Admin, "The Soviet Occupation of Afghanistan."
8. "Soviet Invasion of Afghanistan," *Encyclopaedia Britannica*.
9. Admin, "The Soviet Occupation of Afghanistan"; Rosenberg, *Inside
the Revolution*, 98.
10. Ibid.
11. Ibid.
12. *9/11 Commission Report*, 55.
13. Keelan Balderson, "Soviet Afghan War, Al Qaeda and the Muslim
Rebel Formula," WideShut.co.uk, September 30, 2013, http://wide
shut.co.uk/soviet-afghan-war-cia-muslim-rebels/.
14. Ibid.; Admin, "The Soviet Occupation of Afghanistan."
15. Admin, "The Soviet Occupation of Afghanistan."
16. *9/11 Commission Report*, 55.
17. Rosenberg, *Inside the Revolution*, 5, 107.
18. *9/11 Commission Report*, 55.
19. Rosenberg, *Inside the Revolution*, 109.

20. *9/11 Commission Report*, 55.
21. Ibid., 56.
22. Ibid.
23. Rosenberg, *Inside the Revolution*, 108.
24. Ibid., 107.
25. Ibid., 5.
26. *The Export* (ACLJ Films, 2011).
27. Bergman, *The Secret War with Iran*, 218–19.
28. Ibid., 218; *9/11 Commission Report*, 61.
29. Bergman, *The Secret War with Iran*, 218.
30. Ibid., 218–19.
31. Ibid., 219.
32. Ibid.
33. Ibid., 218.
34. Ibid.
35. Ibid., 220.
36. "Most Wanted Terrorists," Federal Bureau of Investigation, https://www.fbi.gov/wanted/wanted_terrorists/ayman-al-zawahiri (last visited March 9, 2016).
37. Ibid.
38. Bergman, *The Secret War with Iran*, 221.
39. Ibid.
40. Ibid., 221–22.
41. Ibid., 222.
42. "Iran's Link to Al-Qaeda," *Middle East Quarterly* 11 (2004): 71.
43. Bergman, *The Secret War with Iran*, 222–23.
44. *9/11 Commission Report*, 61.
45. Bergman, *The Secret War with Iran*, 223–24.
46. Ibid., 225–26.
47. Ibid., 226.
48. Ibid.
49. *9/11 Commission Report*, 240.
50. Ibid., 60.
51. Ibid.
52. Bergman, *The Secret War with Iran*, 231.
53. Ibid.
54. Ibid.
55. Ibid.
56. *9/11 Commission Report*, 240.

57. Ibid.

58. Kronos, "The Al-Qa'ida–Qods Force Nexus: Scratching the Surface of a 'Known Unknown,'" 2011, 15.

59. *9/11 Commission Report*, 240–41.

60. Ibid., 241.

61. Kronos, "The Al-Qa'ida–Qods Force Nexus," 15.

62. Ibid.

63. "Special Dispatch No. 473: Top Iranian Defector on Iran's Collaboration with Iraq, North Korea, Al-Qa'ida, and Hizbullah," Middle East Media Research Institute, February 20, 2003, http://www.memri.org/report/en/0/0/0/0/0/0/814.htm.

64. Ibid.

65. Ibid.

66. Ibid.

67. Bergman, *The Secret War with Iran*, 232.

68. Douglas Jehl, "For Death of Its Diplomats, Iran Vows Blood for Blood," *New York Times*, September 12, 1998, http://www.nytimes.com/1998/09/12/world/for-death-of-its-diplomats-iran-vows-blood-for-blood.html.

69. Ibid.

70. Peter Bergen, "Opinion: Strange Bedfellows—Iran and Al Qaeda," CNN, March 10, 2013, http://www.cnn.com/2013/03/10/opinion/bergen-iran-al-qaeda/index.html.

71. Ibid.

72. "Iran Gave U.S. Help on Al Qaeda After 9/11," CBS News, October 7, 2008, http://www.cbsnews.com/news/iran-gave-us-help-on-al-qaeda-after-9-11.

73. Brian Murphy, "Iran and Al Qaeda Connected? The History Behind a Complex Relationship," *World Post*, June 23, 2013, http://www.huffingtonpost.com/2013/04/23/iran-al-qaeda_n_3139749.html.

74. Daniel L. Byman, "Unlikely Alliance: Iran's Secretive Relationship with Al-Qaeda," Brookings Institution, July 2012, http://www.brookings.edu/research/articles/2012/07/iran-al-qaeda-byman.

75. Bergman, *The Secret War with Iran*, 233.

76. Ibid.

77. Ibid.

78. Will Stewart and Simon Tomlinson, "Putin Signs Decree Drafting 150,000 Conscripts into the Russian Military . . . as Iran and

Hezbollah Prepare Major Ground Offensive in Syria with Air Support from Moscow's Bombers," *Daily Mail* (Oct. 1, 2015), http://www.dailymail.co.uk/news/article-3255876/Russia-pouring -gasoline-fire-Syria-s-civil-war-says-America-Putin-defies-West -drops-bombs-non-ISIS-forces-fighting-Assad.html.

79. Ibid.

80. Ibid., 234–35.

81. Melanie Batley, "Bin Laden Papers Reveal Iranian Support for Al-Qaida," *Newsmax*, February 27, 2015, http://www.newsmax.com /Newsfront/al-qaida-iran-bin-laden-aid/2015/02/27/id/627352.

82. Stephen F. Hayes and William Kristol, "Demand the Documents," *Weekly Standard*, August 10, 2015, http://www.weeklystandard.com /article/demand-documents/1001576.

83. Ibid.

84. Ibid.

85. Batley, "Bin Laden Papers Reveal Iranian Support for Al-Qaida"; Thomas Joscelyn, "New Docs Reveal Osama Bin Laden's Secret Ties with Iran," *Weekly Standard*, February 27, 2015, http://www .weeklystandard.com/new-docs-reveal-osama-bin-ladens-secret -ties-with-iran/article/868678.

86. Bergen, "Opinion, Strange Bedfellows—Iran and Al Qaeda."

87. Ibid.

88. Abraham D. Sofaer, *Taking on Iran: Strength, Diplomacy, and the Iranian Threat* (Stanford, CA: Hoover Institution Press, 2013), 36–37.

89. Pam Benson, "Iran: Haven or Prison for Al Qaeda," *CNN: Security Clearance*, March 8, 2013, http://security.blogs.cnn.com/2013/03/08 /iran-haven-or-prison-for-al-qaeda.

90. "Top Al-Qaeda Ranks Keep Footholds in Iran," *USA Today*, July 9, 2011, http://usatoday30.usatoday.com/news/world/2011-07-09-iran -al-qaeda_n.htm.

91. "Iranian Diplomat Kidnapped, Insecurity Mounts in Pakistan," Reuters, November 13, 2008, http://www.reuters.com/article /2008/11/13/us-pakistan-kidnapped-idUSTRE4AC0SJ20081113 #CslcHm3diYsuhbyB.97; Murphy, "Iran and Al Qaeda Connected?"; Isabel Cowles, "Pakistan Arrests Five but Iranian Diplomat Still Held Captive," *Finding Dulcinea*, November 17, 2008, http://www.findingdulcinea.com/news/international/2008 /November/Pakistan-Arrests-Five-but-Iranian-Diplomat-Still -Held-Captive.html.

92. Murphy, "Iran and Al Qaeda Connected?"

93. Thomas Joscelyn, "WikiLeaks: The Iran–Al Qaeda Connection," *Weekly Standard*, December 1, 2010, http://www.weeklystandard .com/blogs/wikileaks-iran-al-qaeda-connection_520538.html.

94. Ibid.

95. Ibid.

96. Robert F. Worth, "Saudis Issue List of 86 Terrorism Suspects," *New York Times*, February 3, 2009, http://www.nytimes.com/2009 /02/04/world/middleeast/04saudi.html.

97. Joscelyn, "WikiLeaks: The Iran–Al Qaeda Connection."

98. Bergen, "Opinion, Strange Bedfellows—Iran and Al Qaeda."

99. Hayes and Kristol, "Demand the Documents."

100. Ibid.

101. Kronos, "The Al-Qa'ida–Qods Force Nexus"; Abeer Tayel, "Report from Congressional Panel Says Iran's Revolutionary Guard Helps Al-Qaeda," *Al Arabiya News*, May 5, 2011, http:// english.alarabiya.net/articles/2011/05/05/147902.html.

102. Press release, U.S. Department of the Treasury, "Fact Sheet: Designation of Iranian Entities and Individuals for Proliferation Activities and Support for Terrorism," October 25, 2007, https:// www.treasury.gov/press-center/press-releases/Pages/hp644.aspx.

103. Kronos, "The Al-Qa'ida–Qods Force Nexus," 4.

104. Ibid.

105. Ibid.

106. Ibid., 8.

107. Ibid.

108. Bill Roggio, "ISAF Captures Quds Force–Linked Taliban Leader in Afghan West," *Long War Journal*, January 10, 2011, http:// www.longwarjournal.org/archives/2011/01/isaf_captures_qods_f .php#ixzz1IIE66BXJ.

109. Kronos, "The Al-Qa'ida–Qods Force Nexus," 9.

110. Ibid., 9–10; "Hekmatyar Could Expose—As Well As Aid—Al Qaeda," Stratfor Global Intelligence, December 26, 2002, https:// www.stratfor.com/analysis/hekmatyar-could-expose-well-aid-al -qaeda.

111. Kronos, "The Al-Qa'ida–Qods Force Nexus," 9–10.

112. Thomas Joscelyn, "Doomed Diplomacy," *Weekly Standard*, March 2, 2015, http://www.weeklystandard.com/articles/doomed -diplomacy_859655.html.

113. Ibid.; Hanin Ghaddar, "The Imminent Hezbollah-Nusra War," *Now*, May 15, 2013, https://now.mmedia.me/lb/en /commentaryanalysis/the-imminent-hezbollah-nusra-war.

114. Daniel E. Rogell, "German Intel: Al-Qaida Rise in Syria," Investigative Project on Terrorism, July 30, 2012, http://www .investigativeproject.org/3689/german-intel-al-qaida-rise-in-syria#.

115. Ibid.; Neil MacFarquhar and Hwaida Saad, "As Syrian War Drags On, Jihadists Take Bigger Role," *New York Times*, July 29, 2012, http://www.nytimes.com/2012/07/30/world/middleeast/as-syrian -war-drags-on-jihad-gains-foothold.html.

116. Ibid.

117. Yochanan Visser, "An Unexpected Source Just Took a Major Stand Against ISIS," *Western Journalism*, May 12, 2015, http:// www.westernjournalism.com/syria-hezbollah-and-iran-step-in-to -rescue-assad-jabhat-al-nusra-declares-war-on-islamic-state; "Jabhat al-Nusra," Mapping Militants, Stanford University (last updated October 1, 2015), http://web.stanford.edu/group /mappingmilitants/cgi-bin/groups/view/493.

118. Ghaddar, "The Imminent Hezbollah-Nusra War."

119. Ibid.

120. Adam Goldman, "AP Exclusive: CIA Tracks Al-Qaida Moving from Iran," Boston.com, May 13, 2010, http://www.boston.com /news/nation/washington/articles/2010/05/13/ap_exclusive _iran_eases_grip_on_al_qaida; DRJ, "A New Era: Iran and Al Qaeda," Patterico's Pontifications, May 14, 2010, http://patterico .com/2010/05/14/iran-and-al-qaeda.

121. Joscelyn, "Doomed Diplomacy."

122. Ibid.

123. Ibid.

124. Ibid.; see also Office of Foreign Assets Control, U.S. Department of the Treasury, Specially Designated Nationals and Blocked Persons List 398, March 2, 2016, https://www.treasury.gov/ofac /downloads/sdnlist.pdf.

125. Joscelyn, "Doomed Diplomacy."

126. Howard Koplowitz, "Who Is Musin Al-Fadhli? Khorasan Group Leader Believed Dead in Syria Airstrike," *International Business Times*, September 24, 2014, http://www.ibtimes.com/who -muhsin-al-fadhli-khorasan-group-leader-believed-dead-syria -airstrike-1694422.

127. Ibid.
128. Joscelyn, "Doomed Diplomacy."
129. Ibid.
130. Ibid.
131. Ibid.
132. Barbara Starr and Tim Hume, "Top Al Qaeda Leader Sanafi Al-Nasr Killed in U.S. Airstrike, Pentagon Says," CNN, October 18, 2015, http://www.cnn.com/2015/10/18/middle east/syria-khorasan-leader-killed.

CHAPTER TEN: STRANGE BEDFELLOWS: THE RUSSIA-SYRIA-IRAN ALLIANCE

1. Rania Abouzeid, "Bouazizi: The Man Who Set Himself and Tunisia on Fire," *Time*, January 21, 2011, http://content.time.com /time/magazine/article/0,9171,2044723,00.html.
2. Greg Botelho, "Arab Spring Aftermath: Revolutions Give Way to Violence, More Unrest," CNN, March 28, 2015, http://www.cnn .com/2015/03/27/middleeast/arab-spring-aftermath/.
3. Joe Sterling, "Daraa: The Spark That Lit the Syrian Flame," CNN, March 1, 2012, http://www.cnn.com/2012/03/01/world/meast/syria -crisis-beginnings/.
4. Kelly McEvers, "Revisiting the Spark That Kindled the Syrian Uprising," NPR, May 23, 2012, http://www.npr.org/2012/03/16 /148719850/revisiting-the-spark-that-kindled-the-syrian-uprising; "Syria: The Story of the Conflict," BBC News, February 3, 2016, http://www.bbc.com/news/world-middle-east-26116868; "Syrian Civil War Explained: Why Did It Start, When Will It End, and Will Britain Get Involved?," *Evening Standard*, September 14, 2015, http://www.standard.co.uk/news/world/syrian-civil-war -explained-why-did-it-start-when-will-it-end-and-will-britain-get -involved-a2946741.html.
5. "Syria: The Story of the Conflict."
6. See, e.g., "Guide: Syria Crisis," BBC News, April 9, 2012, http:// www.bbc.com/news/world-middle-east-13855203.
7. "Syria: The Story of the Conflict."
8. Nick Thompson, "Syria's War: Everything You Need to Know About How We Got Here," CNN, October 11, 2015, http://www .cnn.com/2015/10/08/middleeast/syria-war-how-we-got-here/.
9. Mark Bixler and Michael Martinez, "War Has Forced Half of Syrians From Their Homes. Here's Where They've Gone," CNN,

September 11, 2015, http://www.cnn.com/2015/09/11/world/syria
-refugee-crisis-when-war-displaces-half-a-country/index.html.

10. Kathy Gilsinan, "The Confused Person's Guide to the Syrian
Civil War," *Atlantic*, October 29, 2015, http://www.theatlantic.com
/international/archive/2015/10/syrian-civil-war-guide-isis/410746/.

11. See, e.g., Antoun Issa, "Russia-Iran Ties Warm Over Syria:
Marriage of Convenience or Lasting Alliance?," *National*,
October 20, 2015, http://www.thenational.ae/world/europe/russia
-iran-ties-warm-over-syria-marriage-of-convenience-or-lasting
-alliance.

12. Dennis Ross, "Stop Playing Iran and Russia's Game in
Syria," *Washington Post*, October 9, 2015, https://www.wash
ingtonpost.com/opinions/a-syria-plan-that-uses-us-leverage
/2015/10/09/04d3ce50-6b93-11e5-aa5b-f78a98956699_story.html.

13. Ralph A. Cossa, *Iran: Soviet Interests, US Concerns* (Washington,
DC: Institute for National Strategic Studies, 1990), 21–22.

14. Ibid. The treaty gave the Soviet Union "the right to send its army
into Persia in order to take the necessary military steps in its own
defense." Ibid., 22.

15. Ibid., 21–22.

16. Mark N. Katz, "Russia and Iran," *Middle East Policy* 19 (2012): 54;
Stephen Kinzer, *All the Shah's Men: An American Coup and the Roots
of Middle East Terror* (New York: Wiley, 2003), 65–66.

17. Kinzer, *All the Shah's Men*, 45.

18. Ibid., 65.

19. Ibid., 65–66.

20. Gary R. Hess, "The Iranian Crisis of 1945–46 and the Cold War,"
Political Science Quarterly 89 (1974): 117.

21. "1946: Soviets Announce Withdrawal from Iran," History.com,
http://www.history.com/this-day-in-history/soviets-announce
-withdrawal-from-iran.

22. Ibid.

23. Kinzer, *All the Shah's Men*, 2.

24. Artemy M. Kalinovsky, "The Soviet Union and Mosaddeq:
A Research Note," *Iranian Studies* 47 (2014): 401, http://www
.tandfonline.com/doi/abs/10.1080/00210862.2014.880633.

25. Kinzer, *All the Shah's Men*, 3–4, 167–88.

26. "The Baghdad Pact (1955) and the Central Treaty Organization
(CENTO)," U.S. Department of State, http://2001-2009.state
.gov/r/pa/ho/time/lw/98683.htm (last visited Mar. 2, 2016).

27. James A. Bill, *The Eagle and the Lion: The Tragedy of American-Iranian Relations* (New Haven, CT: Yale University Press, 1989), 119.

28. Ibid.

29. Kinzer, *All the Shah's Men*, 196–97; see "In Pictures: The Iranian Revolution," BBC News, http://news.bbc.co.uk/2/shared/spl/hi /pop_ups/04/middle_east_the_iranian_revolution/html/1.stm (last visited Mar. 2, 2016).

30. Katz, "Russia and Iran," 54–55.

31. Mark N. Katz, "Iran and Russia," U.S. Institute of Peace, http:// iranprimer.usip.org/resource/iran-and-russia.

32. Ibid.

33. Ibid.

34. See, e.g., Rob Garver, "Putin's Calculated Revival of the Russian Orthodox Church," *Fiscal Times*, June 9, 2015, http://www.the fiscaltimes.com/2015/06/09/Putin-s-Calculated-Revival-Russian -Orthodox-Church; Peter Tatchell, "Sunni Muslims Living in Fear in Iran as State-Sponsored Persecution Ramps Up," *International Business Times*, January 22, 2015, http://www.ibtimes.co.uk/sunni -muslims-living-fear-iran-state-sponsored-persecution-ramps -1484673.

35. Paul Coyer, "(Un)Holy Alliance: Vladimir Putin, The Russian Orthodox Church and Russian Exceptionalism," *Forbes*, May 21, 2015, http://www.forbes.com/sites/paulcoyer/2015/05/21/unholy -alliance-vladimir-putin-and-the-russian-orthodox-church/.

36. Mark Mackinnon, "How Vladimir Putin Helped Resurrect the Russian Orthodox Church," *Globe and Mail*, January 15, 2014, http://www.theglobeandmail.com/news/world/how-vladimir-putin -helped-resurrect-the-russian-orthodox-church/article16361650/.

37. Ibid.

38. Ronen Bergman, *The Secret War with Iran*, trans. Ronnie Hope (New York: Free Press, 2008), 7–10.

39. Anna Borshchevskaya, "Russia's Many Interests in Syria," Washington Institute, January 24, 2013, http://www.washington institute.org/policy-analysis/view/russias-many-interests-in-syria.

40. Ibid.

41. Julia Ioffe, "Russia's Game Plan in Syria Is Simple," *Foreign Policy*, September 25, 2015, http://foreignpolicy.com/2015/09/25/russias -game-plan-in-syria-is-simple-putin-assad/.

42. Barnini Chakraborty, "Message to Iran? 3 Years after 'Red Line,' Syria Chem Weapons Charges Unresolved," Fox News, August 20,

2015, http://www.foxnews.com/politics/2015/08/20/three-years
-after-obama-red-line-chemical-weapons-threat-still-in-syria
-iran/.

43. S. A. Miller, "The Knives Are Out: Panetta Eviscerates Obama's
'Red Line' Blunder on Syria," *Washington Times*, October 7, 2014,
http://www.washingtontimes.com/news/2014/oct/7/panetta-decries
-obama-red-line-blunder-syria/.

44. Mario Loyola, "How to Stop Iran's Growing Hegemony,"
National Review, April 10, 2015, http://www.nationalreview.com
/corner/416770/how-stop-irans-growing-hegemony-mario-loyola.

45. Ralph Peters, "The Iranian Dream of a Reborn Persian Empire,"
New York Post, February 1, 2015, http://nypost.com/2015/02/01/the
-iranian-dream-of-a-reborn-persian-empire/.

46. Abdullah al-Thuweini, "Tehran Official: 'Baghdad is Capital of
New Persian Empire,'" *New Arab*, March 10, 2015, http://www
.alaraby.co.uk/english/news/2015/3/10/tehran-official-baghdad-is
-capital-of-new-persian-empire.

47. Ibid.

48. Michael Morell, "Iran's Grand Strategy Is to Become a Regional
Powerhouse," *Washington Post*, April 3, 2015, https://www.wash
ingtonpost.com/opinions/irans-grand-strategy/2015/04/03
/415ec8a8-d8a3-11e4-ba28-f2a685dc7f89_story.html.

49. Samia Nakhoul, "Iran Expands Regional 'Empire' Ahead of
Nuclear Deal," Reuters, March 23, 2015, http://www.reuters
.com/article/2015/03/23/us-mideast-iran-region-insight-idUSK
BN0MJ1G520150323.

50. Zachary Laub, "International Sanctions on Iran," Council
on Foreign Relations, July 15, 2015, http://www.cfr.org/iran
/international-sanctions-iran/p20258.

51. Ibid.

52. "Ukraine Crisis: Russia and Sanctions," BBC, December 19, 2014,
http://www.bbc.com/news/world-europe-26672800.

53. John Simpson, "Russia's Crimea Plan Detailed, Secret and
Successful," BBC, March 19, 2014, http://www.bbc.com/news
/world-europe-26644082.

54. "Crimea Profile—Overview," BBC, March 13, 2015, http://www
.bbc.com/news/world-europe-18287223.

55. Amanda Macias, "A Detailed Look at How Russia Annexed
Crimea," *Business Insider*, March 24, 2015, http://www.business
insider.com/how-russia-took-crimea-2015-3; Matt Smith and Alla

Eshchenko, "Ukraine Cries 'Robbery' as Russia Annexes Crimea," CNN, March 18, 2014, http://www.cnn.com/2014/03/18/world/europe/ukraine-crisis/.

56. "Ukraine Crisis: Russia and Sanctions," BBC, December 19, 2014, http://www.bbc.com/news/world-europe-26672800.

57. Andrew T. Price-Smith, *Oil, Illiberalism, and War* (Cambridge, MA: MIT Press, 2015), 111.

58. Michael Sharnoff, "The Syria-Soviet Alliance," Jewish Policy Center, http://www.jewishpolicycenter.org/833/the-syria-soviet-alliance.

59. Ibid.; see also Fred Haley Lawson, *Global Security Watch—Syria* (Santa Barbara, CA: Praeger, 2013), 161–62.

60. Sharnoff, "The Syria-Soviet Alliance"; Lawson, *Global Security Watch—Syria*, 161–62.

61. Edward Delman, "The Link Between Putin's Military Campaigns in Syria and Ukraine," *Atlantic*, October 2, 2015, http://www.theatlantic.com/internatinoal/archive/2015/10/navy-base-syria-crimea-putin/408694/.

62. "Russia Backs Syria, Last Friend in Arab World," *Moscow Times*, January 30, 2012.

63. Matthew Bodner, "Why Russia Is Expanding Its Naval Base in Syria," *Moscow Times*, September 21, 2015, http://www.themoscowtimes.com/news/article/russia-backs-syria-last-friend-in-arab-world/451931.

64. Frank Gardner, "How Vital Is Syria's Tartus Port to Russia?," BBC News, June 27, 2012, http://www.bbc.com/news/world-middle-east-18616191; see also Ron Synovitz, "Explainer: Why Is Access to Syria's Port at Tartus So Important to Moscow?," Radio Free Europe/Radio Liberty, June 19, 2012, http://www.rferl.org/content/explainer-why-is-access-/24619441.html.

65. See, e.g., "Russia Backs Syria, Last Friend in Arab World."

66. Jonathan Saul, "Exclusive: Russia Steps Up Military Lifeline to Syria's Assad—Sources," Reuters, January 17, 2014, http://www.reuters.com/article/2014/01/17/us-syria-russia-arms-idUSBRE A0G0MN20140117.

67. Ibid.

68. Ibid.

69. Thomas Grove, "Syria Reaches Oil Deal with Ally Russia," Reuters, August 3, 2012, http://www.reuters.com/article/2012/08/04/us-russia-syria-oil-idUSBRE8720WC20120804.

70. Ibid.

71. Ibid.

72. Ibid.

73. See, e.g., Monica Crowley, "Vladimir Putin's Real Target: The World's Oil Supply," *Washington Times*, October 14, 2015, http://www.washingtontimes.com/news/2015/oct/14/monica-crowley -vladimir-putin-targets-world-oil-su/?page=all.

74. Ibid.; "Russia Steps up Military Lifeline."

75. Dominic Tierney, "The Danger of Putin Losing in Syria," *Atlantic*, January 8, 2016, http://www.theatlantic.com/international /archive/2016/01/putin-russia-syria-war/423309/.

76. See, e.g., "Iranian Troops Prepare to Aid Russia with Syrian Ground Assault, Officials Say," Fox News, October 1, 2015, http:// www.foxnews.com/world/2015/10/01/cia-backed-rebels-civilians -reportedly-targeted-by-russian-airstrikes-in-syria/.

77. Lizzie Dearden, "Russia has 'Substantial' Number of Troops Inside Syria, Says Nato Secretary-General," *Independent*, October 6, 2015, http://www.independent.co.uk/news/world/middle-east/russia-has -substantial-number-of-troops-inside-syria-says-nato-secretary -general-a6681611.html.

78. Will Stewart ande Simon Tomlinson, "Putin Signs Decree Drafting 150,000 Conscripts into the Russian Military . . . as Iran and Hezbollah Prepare Major Ground Offensive in Syria with Air Support from Moscow's Bombers," *Daily Mail*, October 1, 2015, http://www.dailymail.co.uk/news/article-3255876/Russia-pouring -gasoline-fire-Syria-s-civil-war-says-America-Putin-defies-West -drops-bombs-non-ISIS-forces-fighting-Assad.html.

79. "Russian Air Force in Syria Deploying Over 50 Planes & Choppers—Defense Ministry," RT, October 1, 2015, https://www .rt.com/news/317179-russian-airforce-syria-aircraft/.

80. See, e.g., Raziye Akkoc, "Russia Kills US-Backed Syrian Rebels in Second Day of Air Strikes as Iran Prepares for Ground Offensive," *Telegraph*, October 2, 2015, http://www.telegraph.co.uk/news/world news/europe/russia/11903702/Russias-Vladimir-Putin-launches -strikes-in-Syria-on-Isil-to-US-anger-live-updates.html.

81. Jonathan Landay, Phil Stewart, and Mark Hosenball, "Russia's Syria Force Grows to 4,000, U.S. Officials Say," Reuters, November 4, 2015, http://www.reuters.com/article/2015/11/04/us -mideast-crisis-russia-syria-idUSKCN0ST2G020151104.

82. Neil MacFarquhar and Anne Barnard, "Putin Orders Start of Syria

Withdrawal, Saying Goals Are Achieved," *New York Times* (March 14, 2016), http://www.nytimes.com/2016/03/15/world/middleeast /putin-syria-russia-withdrawal.html?emc=edit_na_20160314&nlid =53971021&kref=cta&_r=1.

83. Ibid.
84. Esther Pan, "Syria, Iran, and the Mideast Conflict," Council on Foreign Relations, July 18, 2006, http://www.cfr.org/iran/syria-iran -mideast-conflict/p11122.
85. Ibid.
86. Sam Dagher, "Syria's Alawites: The People Behind Assad," *Wall Street Journal*, June 25, 2015, http://www.wsj.com/articles/syrias -alawites-the-people-behind-assad-1435166941.
87. "Sunnis and Shia in the Middle East," BBC News, December 19, 2013, http://www.bbc.com/news/world-middle-east-25434060.
88. Dagher, "Syria's Alawites."
89. Ibid.
90. Ibid.
91. Anthony H. Cordesman, Aram Nerguizian, and Ionut C. Popescu, *Israel and Syria: The Military Balance and Prospects of War* (Westport, CT: Praeger, 2008), 154.
92. Steven Simon, "Iran Primer: Iran and Israel," PBS, October 28, 2010, http://www.pbs.org/wgbh/pages/frontline/tehranbureau/2010 /10/iran-primer-iran-and-israel.html.
93. Bergman, *The Secret War with Iran*, 58.
94. Ibid., 55.
95. Ibid., 58.
96. Ibid.
97. Ibid., 58–59.
98. Ibid., 59.
99. Ibid.
100. Ibid., 59–60.
101. "The Arab/Muslim World: Iran-Iraq War (1979–1988," Jewish Virtual Library, http://www.jewishvirtuallibrary.org/jsource/arabs /iraniraq.html.
102. Max Fisher, "The Secret Plot Behind the Creation of ISIS," *Vox*, April 20, 2015, http://www.vox.com/2015/4/20/8451627/isis-iraq -saddam.
103. "The Arab/Muslim World."
104. Ibid.
105. Ibid.

106. Ibid.
107. Ibid.
108. Hossein Bastani, "Iran Quietly Deepens Involvement in Syria's War," BBC News, October 20, 2015, http://www.bbc.com/news /world-middle-east-34572756.
109. Dagher, "Syria's Alawites."
110. "Iranian Troops Prepare to Aid Russia."
111. Asa Fitch and Sam Dagher, "Syria's Assad Stresses Importance of Alliance with Russia, Iran, Iraq," *Wall Street Journal*, October 4, 2015, http://www.wsj.com/articles/syrias-assad-stresses-importance -of-alliance-with-russia-iran-iraq-1443967266.
112. Christopher Snyder, "Iran and Russia Use Nuclear Deal to Boost Military Ties," Fox News, August 17, 2015, http://www.foxnews .com/world/2015/08/17/iran-and-russia-use-nuclear-deal-to-boost -military-ties/.
113. Jennifer Griffin and Lucas Tomlinson, "Exclusive: Quds Force Commander Soleimani Visited Moscow, Met Russian Leaders in Defiance of Sanctions," Fox News, August 6, 2015, http:// www.foxnews.com/politics/2015/08/06/exclusive-quds-force -commander-soleimani-visited-moscow-met-russian-leaders-in/.
114. Jennifer Griffin and Lucas Tomlinson, "Iran Confirms Trip by Quds Force Commander to Moscow to Discuss Arms Shipments," Fox News, August 8, 2015, http://www.foxnews.com /politics/2015/08/08/iran-confirms-trip-by-quds-force-commander -to-moscow-to-discuss-arms-shipments/.
115. Laila Bassam and Tom Perry, "How Iranian General Plotted Out Syrian Assault in Moscow," Reuters, October 6, 2015, http:// www.reuters.com/article/us-mideast-crisis-syria-soleimani-insigh -idUSKCN0S02BV20151006.
116. Ibid.
117. Jethro Mullen, "Is Russia Preparing to Move Troops to 2 New Syria Bases?," CNN, September 23, 2015, http://www.cnn.com /2015/09/23/middleeast/syria-russia-military-buildup/.
118. Dion Nissenbaum and Carol E. Lee, "Russia Expands Military Presence in Syria, Satellite Photos Show," *Wall Street Journal*, September 22, 2015, http://www.wsj.com/articles/russia-expands -military-its-presence-in-syria-satellite-photos-show-1442937150.
119. Ibid.
120. Paul Sonne and Nathan Hodge, "Vladimir Putin Says Bashar al-Assad Backs Russian Support to Rebels Fighting Islamic State,"

Wall Street Journal, October 22, 2015, http://www.wsj.com/articles/putin-criticizes-u-s-policy-in-middle-east-1445533121/.

121. Ed Payne et al., "Russia Launches First Airstrikes in Syria," CNN, September 30, 2015, 10:15 PM, http://www.cnn.com/2015/09/30/politics/russia-syria-airstrikes-isis/.

122. Richard Spencer, "Who Are the Russians Bombing in Syria and Why?," *Telegraph*, October 1, 2015, http://www.telegraph.co.uk/news/worldnews/europe/russia/11905279/Who-are-the-Russians-bombing-in-Syria-and-why.html.

123. "'More than 90%' of Russian Airstrikes in Syria Have Not Targeted Isis, US says," *Guardian*, October 7, 2015, http://www.theguardian.com/world/2015/oct/07/russia-airstrikes-syria-not-targetting-isis.

124. Kim Hjelmgaard and Doug Stanglin, "Russian Plane Crash in Egypt Kills All 224 People Aboard," *USA Today*, October 31, 2015, http://www.usatoday.com/story/news/world/2015/10/31/russian-plane-crash-egypt/74934010/.

125. Andrey Ostroukh, "Russia Says Bomb Brought Down Plane in Egypt," *Wall Street Journal*, November 17, 2015, http://www.wsj.com/articles/russia-says-bomb-brought-down-plane-in-egypt-1447750695.

126. Hjelmgaard and Stanglin, "Russian Plane Crash in Egypt Kills All 224 People Aboard."

127. "ISIS Claims Bomb That Downed Russian Jet Fit in Soda Can," *CBS News*, November 18, 2015, http://www.cbsnews.com/news/isis-picture-alleged-bomb-on-russian-plane-blew-up-over-egypt/.

128. Adam Withnall, "Russian Plane Crash: Flight Brought Down over Sinai by Bomb in 'Terror Act,'" *Independent*, November 17, 2015, http://www.independent.co.uk/news/world/africa/russia-confirms-plane-which-crashed-over-sinai-was-bombed-in-terror-act-a6737256.html.

129. Ostroukh, "Russia Says Bomb Brought Down Plane in Egypt."

130. See, e.g., "Syria Crisis: Massive Russian Air Strikes on 'IS Targets,'" BBC News, November 20, 2015, http://www.bbc.com/news/world-europe-34882503.

131. Ibid.

132. Raja Abdulrahim, "Syrian Regime, Backed by Russia, Iran and Hezbollah, Expands Ground Offensive to Allepo," *Wall Street Journal*, October 18, 2015, http://www.wsj.com/articles/syrian-regime-backed-by-russia-iran-and-hezbollah-expands

-ground-offensive-to-aleppo-1445206886; Kareem Shaheen, "Isis Seizes Ground from Aleppo Rebels Under Cover of Russian Airstrikes," *Guardian*, October 10, 2015, http://www .theguardian.com/world/2015/oct/10/russian-airstrikes-help -isis-gain-ground-in-aleppo.

CHAPTER ELEVEN: AN IDEOLOGICAL WAR: WHAT CAN WE DO?

1. Raj Bhala, *Understanding Islamic Law (Shari'a)* (New Providence, NJ: Lexis-Nexis, 2011), xxii.
2. Ibid., 527.
3. Wahhabim is "a strictly orthodox Sunni Muslim sect founded by Muhammad ibn Abd al-Wahhab (1703–92). It advocates a return to the early Islam of the [Qu]ran and Sunna [and] reject[s] later innovations[.]" "Wahhabi," Oxford Dictionaries (2016), http:// www.oxforddictionaries.com/us/definition/american_english /wahhabi?q=Wahabi+.
4. Joni Ernst, "The Danger of the Iran Deal," CNN, September 10, 2015, http://www.cnn.com/2015/09/10/opinions/ernst-iran-nuclear -deal/.
5. A SOFA is an agreement between a host country and foreign nation stationing its military forces and defining their legal status in that country. "Status-of-forces agreement," Free Dictionary, http:// www.thefreedictionary.com/status-of-forces+agreement.
6. President George W. Bush signed the agreement in 2008. It provided for U.S. troops' leaving at the end of 2011. Joshua Gillin, "Obama Refused to Sign Plan in Place to Leave 10,000 Troops in Iraq, Bush Says," PolitiFact, May 18, 2015, http://www.politifact .com/truth-o-meter/statements/2015/may/18/jeb-bush/obama -refused-sign-plan-place-leave-10000-troops-i/.
7. Patrick Brennan, "No, U.S. Troops Didn't Have to Leave Iraq," *National Review*, June 16, 2014, http://www.nationalreview.com /corner/380508/no-us-troops-didnt-have-leave-iraq-patrick -brennan.
8. Peter Allen and Corey Charlton, "Paris Terrorist Ringleader Bragged He Entered France Among a Group of 90 Jihadis and Claimed the Migrant Crisis Had Made It Easy for Them to Travel Freely Across Europe," *Daily Mail*, February 4, 2016, http://www .dailymail.co.uk/news/article-3431479/Paris-terrorist-ringleader -bragged-migrant-crisis-easy-Islamists-travel-freely-Europe -reveals-woman-led-police-him.html.

9. "Section 1: A Demographic Portrait of Muslim Americans," Pew Research Center, August 30, 2011, http://www.people-press .org/2011/08/30/section-1-a-demographic-portrait-of-muslim -americans/.

10. "Muslim Americans: No Signs of Growth in Alienation or Support for Extremism," Pew Research Center, August 30, 2011, http:// www.people-press.org/2011/08/30/muslim-americans-no-signs-of -growth-in-alienation-or-support-for-extremism/.

11. Justin Fishel, Benjamin Siegel, and Emily Shapiro, "Inside the Immigration File of San Bernardino Shooter Tashfeen Malik," ABC News, December 22, 2015, 5:07 PM, http://abcnews.go.com /US/inside-immigration-file-san-bernardino-shooter-tashfeen -malik/story?id=35912170.

12. Ray Sanchez, Jason Hanna, and Shimon Prokupecz, "Police: Suspect in Officer's Shooting Claims Allegiance to ISIS," CNN, January 8, 2016, http://www.cnn.com/2016/01/08/us/philadelphia -police-officer-shot/.

13. Geneive Abdo, "America's Muslims Aren't as Assimilated as You Think," *Washington Post*, August 27, 2006, http://www .washingtonpost.com/wp-dyn/content/article/2006/08/25 /AR2006082501169.html.

14. Steve Almasy, Pierre Meilhan, and Jim Bittermann, "Paris Massacre: At Least 128 Killed in Gunfire and Blasts, French Officials Say," CNN, November 14, 2015, http://www.cnn.com /2015/11/13/world/paris-shooting/; Michael S. Schmidt and Richard Perez-Pena, "F.B.I. Treating San Bernardino Attack as Terrorism Case," *New York Times*, December 4, 2015, http://www .nytimes.com/2015/12/05/us/tashfeen-malik-islamic-state.html?_r =0; Emily Shapiro, "Man Accused of Shooting Philly Cop Pledged Allegiance to ISIS, Police Say," ABC News, January 8, 2016, http:// abcnews.go.com/US/man-accused-shooting-philly-cop-confessed -committing-act/story?id=36169588.

15. Abul Taher, "Revealed: UK's First Official Sharia Courts," *Sunday Times*, September 14, 2008, http://www.thesundaytimes.co.uk/sto /Migration/article235989.ece.

16. G. Patricia de la Cruz and Angela Brittingham, The Arab Population: 2000, U.S. Census Bureau (December 2003), http:// www.census.gov/prod/2003pubs/c2kbr-23.pdf.

17. "Javed Ahmad Ghamidi—June 6th—Dallas, TX, USA," YouTube,

August 21, 2015, https://www.youtube.com/watch?v=NMAaXM
kLVdg.

18. Ibid.
19. Ibid.
20. Ibid.
21. Ibid.
22. Ibid.
23. Ibid.
24. Matthew 5:44.
25. Romans 12:14.
26. Romans 13:3–4.

APPENDIX A

1. Converting from Islam is a form of "apostasy" and is punishable by
   death. Ahmad ibn Naqib al-Misri, *Reliance of the Traveller* (1368),
   trans. Nuh Ha Mim Keller, rev. ed. (Beltsville, MD: Amana, 2008),
   595 (hereinafter *Reliance of the Traveller*) ("When a person who has
   reached puberty and is sane voluntarily apostatizes from Islam,
   he deserves to be killed."); ibid., 596–98 ("Among the things that
   entail apostasy from Islam . . . are . . . to speak words that imply
   unbelief such as 'Allah is the third of three,' or 'I am Allah' . . . to
   revile Allah or His messenger . . . to be sarcastic about Allah's name
   . . . to deny any verse of the Koran or anything which by scholarly
   consensus belongs to it, or to add a verse that does not belong to
   it; . . . to mockingly say, 'I don't know what faith is' . . . to describe
   a Muslim or someone who wants to become a Muslim in terms
   of *unbelief* . . . to revile the religion of Islam . . . to be sarcastic
   about any ruling of the Sacred Law; . . . or to deny that Allah
   intended the Prophet's message . . . to be the religion followed by
   the entire world."); see also Abdullah Yusuf Ali, *The Meaning of the
   Holy Qur'an*, 10th ed. (Beltsville, MD: Amana, 2001), *Surah* 5:33
   (hereinafter *Quran*) ("The punishment of those who wage war
   against Allah and His Messenger, and strive with might and main
   for mischief through the land is: execution, or crucifixion, or the
   cutting off of hands and feet from opposite sides, or exile from the
   land: That is their disgrace in this world, and a heavy punishment
   is theirs in the hereafter"). Muhammad was recorded to have
   said, "If . . . (a Muslim) discards his religion, kill him." *Sahih
   Bukhari*, Vol. 4, Bk. 52, No. 260 (English translation of the hadith

of Sahih Bukhari is available at http://www.sahih-bukhari.com/)
[hereinafter *Sahih Bukhari*].

2. U.S. Constitution, Amendment I ("Congress shall make no law
respecting an establishment of religion, or prohibiting the free
exercise thereof. . . ."); *Cantwell v. Connecticut*, 310 U.S. 296, 303
(1940) (The First Amendment "forestalls compulsion by law of the
acceptance of any creed or the practice of any form of worship.
Freedom of conscience and freedom to adhere to such religious
organization or form of worship as the individual may choose
cannot be restricted by law. On the other hand, it safeguards the
free exercise of the chosen form of religion.").

3. *Quran*, at *Surah* 4:140 ("Already has [Allah] sent you word in the
book, that when ye hear the signs of Allah held in defiance and
ridicule, ye are not to sit with them unless they turn to a different
theme. . . ."; see also *Sahih Bukhari*, Vol. 3, Bk. 46, No. 705 ("The
Prophet said, 'Allah has accepted my invocation to forgive what
whispers in the hearts of my followers, *unless* they put it to action *or
utter it.*'" [emphasis added]); Rudolph Peters, *Crime and Punishment
in Islamic Law: Theory and Practice from the Sixteenth to the Twenty-
first Century* (Cambridge: Cambridge University Press, 2005), 65
("If the apostasy consisted in insulting the prophet (*sabb al-nabi*),
according to most schools the apostate is not given an opportunity
for repentance, but is killed immediately after the sentence.").
Blasphemy is a form of apostasy. Apostasy is punishable by death,
and therefore blasphemy is also punishable by death.

4. U.S. Constitution, Amendment I ("Congress shall make no law . . .
abridging the freedom of speech."). Outside of the "uninhibited,
robust, and wide-open" free speech protection of the First
Amendment, *New York Times Co. v. Sullivan*, 376 U.S. 254, 270
(1964), only several narrow categories of speech are excepted from
constitutional protection, such as fighting words, *Chaplinsky v.
New Hampshire*, 315 U.S. 568, 574 (1942); defamatory falsehoods,
Sullivan, 376 U.S. 254, 279–80 (1964); and obscene materials,
Miller v. California, 413 U.S. 15 (1973). The First Amendment
also protects "expressive conduct," such as burning the American
flag. *Texas v. Johnson*, 491 U.S. 397 (1989). The Supreme Court
has continually held that in regulating expressive conduct, the
"government may not prohibit the expression of an idea simply
because society finds the idea offensive or disagreeable." Ibid., 414.

5. *Quran*, at *Surah* 5:90–91 ("O ye who believe! Intoxicants and

gambling . . . are an abomination—of Satan's handiwork; eschew such (abomination), that ye may prosper. Satan's plan is (but) to excite enmity and hatred between you, with intoxicants . . . , and hinder you . . . from prayer: will ye not then abstain?"). The punishment of forty lashes for consuming alcohol derives from hadith. *Sahih Bukhari*, Vol. 8, Bk. 81, Num. 764 ("The Prophet beat a drunk with palm-leaf stalks and shoes. And Abu Bakr gave (such a sinner) forty lashes."); see also *Reliance of the Traveler*, 617; Peters, 64.

6. U.S. Constitution, Amendment XXI (repealing prohibition); 18 Pa.C.S. § 6308 (2010) (establishing the minimum age for consuming alcohol at twenty-one); see also *South Dakota v. Dole*, 483 U.S. 203, 211–12 (1987) (holding that Congress has authority under the Spending Clause to make receipt of federal funds conditional on whether a state's minimum drinking age was twenty-one).

7. *Reliance of the Traveller*, 59 ("Circumcision is obligatory (O: for both men and women. For men it consists of removing the prepuce from the penis, and for women, removing the prepuce (Ar. bazr) of the clitoris. . . ."); see also Centre for Social Cohesion, *Crimes of the Community: Honour-Based Violence in the UK*, 2d ed. (London: Centre for Social Cohesion, 2010), 69.

8. See, e.g., 18 U.S.C. § 116(a) ("[W]hoever knowingly circumcises, excises, or infibulates the whole or any part of the labia majora or labia minora or clitoris of another person who has not attained the age of 18 years shall be fined under this title or imprisoned not more than 5 years, or both.").

9. *Quran*, at *Surah* 2:223 ("Your wives are as a tilth unto you so approach your tilth when or how you will. . . ."); *Reliance of the Traveller*, 525 (It is "obligatory for a woman to let her husband have sex with her *immediately* when: (a) he asks her; (b) at home . . . ; (c) and she can physically endure it."). If a woman refuses her husband, she is deemed "rebellious" and the husband is permitted to force her to comply. Ibid., 542; see also *Quran*, at *Surah* 4:34.

10. *E.g.*, N.J. Stat. Ann. § 2C:25–17 (2011) et. seq. ("Prevention of Domestic Violence Act of 1991"); Okl. St. tit. 21, § 1111(B) (2010) ("Rape is an act of sexual intercourse accomplished with a male or female *who is the spouse* of the perpetrator if force or violence is used or threatened, accompanied by apparent power of execution to the victim or to another person" [emphasis added]).

11. *Quran*, at *Surah* 4:3 ("[M]arry women of your choice, two or three or four; but if ye fear that ye shall not be able to deal justly (with them), then only one, or (a captive) that your right hands possess, that will be more suitable, to prevent you from doing injustice."); Muhammad Subhi Hallāq, *Fiqh: According to the Qur'ân & Sunnah*, Vol. 2, trans. Sameh Strauch, (Darussalam, 2008), 128 (" 'I embraced Islam and at that time, I had eight wives; I mentioned this to the Prophet and he said' ": " 'Choose four of them.' ") (citing Abu Dawood (no. 2241) and Ibn Majah (no. 1952)). Muhammad had multiple wives, and among his wives was a girl, Aisha, whom he engaged when she just was six years old and with whom he had sexual intercourse when she was only nine years old. *Sahih Bukhari*, Vol. 5, Bk. 58, Num. 236 ("[Muhammad] married 'Aisha when she was a girl of six years of age, and he consumm[ated] that marriage when she was nine years old.").

12. *Reynolds v. United States*, 98 U.S. 145 (1878). In *Reynolds*, the Supreme Court of the United States considered the question of whether a criminal charge against a man in a polygamous union would be excused on the basis of the man's Mormon faith. In holding that the criminal conviction would stand, the Court declared:

> Polygamy has always been odious among the northern and western nations of Europe. . . . [I]t is impossible to believe that the constitutional guaranty of religious freedom was intended to prohibit legislation in respect to this most important feature of social life. . . . [A]s a law of the organization of society under the exclusive dominion of the United States, it is provided that plural marriages shall not be allowed. Can a man excuse his practices to the contrary because of his religious belief? [To] permit this would be to make the professed doctrines of religious belief superior to the law of the land, and in effect to permit every citizen to become a law unto himself. Government could exist only in name under such circumstances.

Ibid., 164–67.

13. *Reliance of the Traveller*, 610 ("If the offender is someone with the capacity to remain chaste, then he or she is stoned to death (def: o12.6), *someone with the capacity to remain chaste* meaning

anyone who had sexual intercourse (A: at least once) with their
spouse in a valid marriage, and is free, of age, and sane. . . . If the
offender is not someone with the capacity to remain chaste, then
the penalty consists of being scourged (def. o12.5) one hundred
stripes and banished to a distance of at least 81 km./50 mi. for one
year.").

14. See note 21.

15. While some states still have laws prohibiting fornication, e.g., Ga.
Code Ann. § 16–6–18 (2011), the Supreme Court, in *Lawrence v.
Texas*, has interpreted the Due Process Clause to allow consenting
adults to have sexual relations in private. 539 U.S. 558, 578 (2003)
("The State cannot demean their existence or control their
destiny by making their private sexual conduct a crime. Their
right to liberty under the Due Process Clause gives them the full
right to engage in their conduct without intervention from the
government.").

16. *Quran*, at *Surah* 4:24 ("Also (prohibited are) women already
married, *except* those whom your right hands possess. Thus hath
Allah ordained (prohibitions) against you: Except for these, all
others are lawful, provided ye seek (them in marriage) with gifts
from your property—desiring chastity, not lust. Seeing that ye
derive benefit from them, give them their dowers (at least) as
prescribed; but if, after a dower is prescribed, ye agree mutually (to
vary it), there is no blame on you." [emphasis added]). The typical
mut'ah marriage resembles a short-term contractual relationship
whereby a man gives something of value to a woman in exchange
for the right to have sex with her for the duration of the contractual
relationship. Shaukat Mahmood & Nadeem Shaukat, *Principles and
Digest of Muslim Law* 55–58 (1993). The concept of Islamic *mut'ah*
derives from Muhammad's early teachings and continues to be a
commonly accepted practice by Shi'ite Muslims to this day. See
Kelly McEvers, *Abuse of Temporary Marriages Flourishes in Iraq*,
NPR (Oct. 19, 2010), http://www.npr.org/templates/story/story
.php?storyId=130350678.

17. Because prostitution is illegal in all states (with the exception of
Nevada), see *U.S. Federal and State Prostitution Laws and Related
Punishments*, ProCon.org (Mar. 15, 2010), http://prostitution.
procon.org/view.resource.php?resourceID=000119, contracts
between parties for which the rendering of sexual services is
consideration are unenforceable as a matter of public policy in most

states because "such a contract is, in essence, an agreement for prostitution and unlawful for that reason." *Marvin v. Marvin*, 557 P.2d 106, 113, 116 (Cal. 1976) (holding that agreements between non-marital partners are unenforceable when they "rest upon a consideration of meretricious sexual services."); see also *Wilcox v. Trautz*, 427 Mass. 326, 332 (1998).

18. *Reliance of the Traveller*, 535 ("A man is obliged to pay a woman the amount typically received as marriage payment by similar brides . . . when a man forces a woman to fornicate with him," i.e., rapes her).

19. *Quran*, at *Surah* 24:2 ("The woman and the man guilty of Zina (fornication) flog each of them with a hundred stripes. . . .").

20. Ibid.

21. *Quran*, at *Surah* 4:15 ("If any of your women are guilty of lewdness, take the evidence of four (reliable) witnesses from amongst you against them; and if they testify, confine them to houses until death do claim them, or Allah ordain for them some (other) way."); see also *Reliance of the Traveller*, 638 ("If testimony concerns fornication or sodomy, then it requires four male witnesses (O: who testify, in the case of fornication, that they have seen the offender insert the head of his penis into her vagina)").

22. E.g., Okl. St. tit. 21, § 1111 (2010) (setting out various circumstances under which rape can occur); Fed. R. Evid. 412(a) (1)–(2) (excluding evidence in criminal and civil cases (subject to minor exceptions) that is "offered to prove that any alleged victim engaged in other sexual behavior" or "to prove any alleged victim's sexual predisposition"). Rule 412 was explicitly instituted to protect women in rape proceedings and help bring offenders to justice by encouraging victim participation. Fed. R. Evid. 412 advisory committee's note, available at http://www.law.cornell.edu/rules /fre/ACRule412.htm ("The rule aims to safeguard the alleged victim against the invasion of privacy, potential embarrassment and sexual stereotyping that is associated with public disclosure of intimate sexual details and the infusion of sexual innuendo into the factfinding process. By affording victims protection in most instances, the rule also encourages victims of sexual misconduct to institute and to participate in legal proceedings against alleged offenders.").

23. *Quran*, at *Surah* 5:38 ("As to the thief, male or female, cut off his or

her hands: A punishment by way of example, from Allah, for their crime."). The hadiths explain that "[a] woman committed theft in the Ghazwa [battle] of the Conquest (of Mecca) and she was taken to the Prophet who ordered her hand to be cut off." *Sahih Bukhari*, Vol. 3, Bk. 48, Num. 816. In another instance, "[t]he Prophet cut off the hand of a thief for stealing a shield. . . ." Ibid., Vol. 8, Bk. 81, Num. 788.

24. See, e.g., Cal. Pen. Code §§ 489, 490 (2011) (specifying that punishment for larceny (theft without force or threat of force) should be fine or imprisonment, depending on the severity of the larceny); Cal. Pen. Code § 213 (2011) (punishing robbery (theft by means of force or fear) by varying terms of imprisonment, depending on the severity of the robbery).

25. *Quran*, at *Surah* 4:34 ("Therefore the righteous women are devoutly obedient. . . . As to those women on whose part ye fear disloyalty and ill-conduct, admonish them . . . refuse to share their beds . . . beat them. . . .").

26. *Quran*, at *Surah* 5:5 ("This day are (all) things good and pure made lawful unto you. The food of the people of the Book is lawful unto you and yours is lawful unto them. (Lawful unto you in marriage) are (not only) chaste women who are believers, but chaste women among the People of the Book, revealed before your time. . . ."); see also *Reliance of the Traveller*, 529 ("It is not lawful or valid for a Muslim man to be married to any woman who is not either a Muslim, Christian, or Jew; nor is it lawful or valid for a Muslim woman to be married to *anyone besides a Muslim*." [emphasis added]).

27. U.S. Constitution, Amendments I, XIV. Specifically, in the landmark anti-miscegenation case, *Loving v. Virginia*, 388 U.S. 1 (1967), the U.S. Supreme Court held that "[t]he freedom to marry has long been recognized as one of the vital personal rights essential to the orderly pursuit of happiness by free men." Ibid., 12. Further, "[t]o deny this fundamental freedom on so unsupportable a basis as . . . racial classifications . . . is surely to deprive all the State's citizens of liberty without due process of law." Ibid. Based on the reasoning of this case, any law forbidding interfaith marriages would be held unconstitutional in the United States.

28. *Reliance of the Traveller*, 550–53 (noting that "[a] woman has no right to custody . . . [if] she remarries" and the person who gets custody must also be a Muslim because a "non-Muslim has no right

to authority and hence no right to raise a Muslim."); *Fiqh*, 201–2 ("The mother has more right to custody of her child, so long as she does not remarry[.]").

29. See, e.g., *Ex Parte Byars*, 794 So. 2d 345, 347 (Ala. 2001) ("The controlling consideration in [an initi] al custody determination] is the best interest of the child."); *Martin v. Martin*, 74 A.D. 2d 419, 425 (N.Y. App. Div. 1980) ("It is familiar law that in a proceeding involving two natural parents custody is to be determined solely by what is in the best interest of the child. . . ."); *In re Marriage of Harris*, 499 N.W. 2d 329, 330 (Iowa Ct. App. 1993) ("In child custody cases, the best interests of the child is the first and governing consideration"). As a general rule, neither the father nor the mother automatically has a paramount right to custody of their children; rather, both parents are deemed to have equal parental rights over their children. 27C C.J.S. *Divorce* § 994 (2005); see also *Ex Parte* Byars, 794 So. 2d at 347 ("Alabama law gives neither party priority in an initial custody determination."); *In re Marriage of Harris*, 499 N.W. 2d at 330 ("Gender is irrelevant, and neither parent should have a greater burden than the other in attempting to gain custody in a dissolution proceeding."); *In re Custody of Townsend*, 427 N.E. 2d 1231 (Ill. 1981); *In re Marriage of Murphy*, 592 N.W. 2d 681 (Iowa 1999); In *Interest of Cooper*, 631 P.2d 632 (Kan. 1981); *Park v. Park*, 610 P.2d 826 (Okla. Ct. App. 1980).

30. Raj Bhala, *Understanding Islamic Law (Shari'a)* 879–80 (2011); *Reliance of the Traveller*, 556–60 (noting that a valid divorce must come from the husband); *Fiqh*, 164.

31. *Fiqh*, 171 (asserting that *"Al-Khul* is dissolution, not divorce").

32. *Quran*, at *Surah* 2:229 (providing that in cases where a wife "fear[s] that [she] would be unable to keep the limits ordained by Allah" by remaining in a particular marriage, "there is not blame on either of [the spouses] if she give something for her freedom"); see also Bhala, 882, 884–85.

33. U.S. Constitution, Amendment XIV ("No state shall . . . deny to any person within its jurisdiction the equal protection of the laws."). In the United States, "[a] divorce proceeding is generally a controversy between a *husband and a wife* to determine who is at fault in causing domestic difficulties," and a divorce is available only as an "extraordinary remedy" for "unavoidable and unendurable" circumstances affecting *either* spouse. 27C C.J.S. *Divorce* § 7 (2005) [emphasis added]. However, most states have adopted some

form of no-fault divorce laws. E.g., Cal. Fam. Code § 2310 (2011) (allowing divorce for "irreconcilable differences"); N.Y. Dom. Rel. Law § 170(7) (2011) (allowing divorce if "[t]he relationship between husband and wife has broken down irretrievably for a period of at least six months. . . ."). Also, a divorce proceeding requires adherence to due process requirements, which require giving both parties notice of the proceeding and opportunity to be heard. See *Farid v. Farid*, No. FA094011049S, 2010 LEXIS 2296, at *7–8 (Conn. Super. Sept. 10, 2010).

34. *Reliance of the Traveller*, 522 (There are two types of guardians over women (and young girls), "those who may compel their female charges to marry someone, and those who may not." Guardians who may force the women or girls under their charge to marry include the girl's father or paternal grandfather.); see also Susan W. Tiefenbrun, *The Semiotics of Women's Human Rights in Iran*, 23 Conn. J. Int'l L. 1, 61 (2007).

35. In the United States, marriages procured by coercion or duress are voidable. See, e.g., *Newman v. Sigler*, 125 So. 666, 666–67 (1930); *Fluharty v. Fluharty*, 193 A. 838, 839–40 (Del. Super. Ct. 1937); *O'Brien v. Eustice*, 19 N.E.2d 137, 140 (Ill. App. Ct. 1937); *Norvell v. State*, 193 S.W. 2d 200, 200–201 (Tex. 1946). Valid marriages require the consent of both parties. See, e.g., *Madison v. Robinson*, 116 So. 31, 35 (Fla. 1928); *Elkhorn Coal Corp. v. Tackett*, 49 S.W. 2d 571, 573 (Ky. 1932); *Davis v. Davis*, 175 A. 574, 575 (Conn. 1934); *Shonfeld v. Shonfeld*, 184 N.E. 60, 60–61 (N.Y. 1933); *Tice v. Tice*, 672 P.2d 1168, 1170–71 (Okla. 1983); *Garrison v. Garrison*, 460 A.2d 945, 946 (Conn. 1983). Marriages may be proscribed under certain limited conditions, such as consanguinity, age of the parties, or special relationships between the parties. See, e.g, N.Y. Dom. Rel. Law § 5 (2011) (banning marriage between certain relatives); Texas Fam. Code § 6.205 (2010) (proscribing marriage if either party is under sixteen years of age and a court order has not been obtained); Texas Fam. Code § 6.206 (2010) ("A marriage is void if a party is a current or former stepchild or stepparent of the other party.").

36. *Quran*, at *Surah* 2:282 ("And get two witnesses, out of your own men, and if there are not two men, then a man and two women, such as ye choose, for witnesses, so that if one of them errs, the other can remind her."). Hadiths explain that the testimony of a woman is equal to half that of a man because of a supposed

"deficiency of a woman's mind." *Sahih Bukhari*, Vol. 3, Bk. 48, Num. 826 ("The Prophet said, 'Isn't the witness of a woman equal to half of that of a man?' The women said, 'Yes.' He said, 'This is because of the deficiency of a woman's mind.' ").

37. U.S. Constitution, Amendment XIV, § I ("No state shall . . . deny to any person within its jurisdiction the equal protection of the laws.").

INDEX

Islamic Republic. *See* Iran
Islamic Revolution, Iran. *See* Iranian
     Revolution (1979)
Islamic Salvation Front, 138
Islamic State of Iraq and Syria. *See* ISIS
Islamophobia, 178–80
Ismail (Muslim conqueror), 96
Israel Defense Forces (IDF), 90
Israel/Israelis
     as al-Qaeda target, 149
     and bombing in Buenos Aires, 128–29
     and clash of Islamic and Western
        culture, 50, 52
     creation of state of, 38
     and *dar al-Islam* vs. *dar al-harb*, 133
     and exportation of Iranian Revolution,
        113, 145
     and Gaza Strip, 143, 144
     Hamas and, 5–6, 8, 11, 140, 141, 142,
        143, 144
     Hezbollah and, 122, 123, 130, 169
     and historical roots of terrorism, 7, 8
     and history of Middle East, 38
     investigation of terrorist organizations
        by, 149
     and Iran, 8, 11–12, 100, 101, 110–12, 121,
        128–29, 130, 131, 134, 135, 140–41,
        143, 145, 154, 166, 170, 173
     Iranian intelligence order (2001) and, 154
     Lebanon and, 110–11, 118–19, 120, 121,
        122, 126, 169–70
     modern Middle East and, 35–39
     Muslim Brotherhood and, 135, 141–42
     and non-Muslim occupation of Muslim
        lands, 50
     and *Open Letter* (1985), 123
     Palestine Mandate and, 37
     Palestinians and, 5–6, 39, 118–19, 169
     and radical Islam, 130
     Soviet Union and, 167
     and Suez Canal Crisis, 7
     Syria and, 166, 167, 169–70
     terrorist organizations as threat to, 145
     and tunnel building, 144
     See also Jews; *specific person*
Istanbul, Turkey: bombings (2016) in, 3,
     4–5

Jacob (Hebrew prophet), 42, 82
Jafari, Mohammad Ali, 142
Jafari (Shiite school of thought), 59
Japan, honor-shame culture in, 49
Jarrett, Valerie, 11
Jasser, Zuhdi, 91
Jerusalem
     Al-Aqsa Mosque in, 50, 132, 142
     and British withdrawal from Palestine,
        37–38

as center of Islamic Caliphate, 132
and goal of all Muslims, 13, 142
Hezbollah and, 122
and history of Middle East, 21, 28, 37–38
Khomeini and, 112, 133
Mahdi as ruler of, 132
Muhammad in, 50, 132
and *Qibla* (direction), 132
Quds as Arabic for, 156
and Sunni-Shiite relationship, 132–33
Jesus, 42, 43, 81, 82, 86, 132
The Jewish State (Herzl), 18
Jews
     and abrogation doctrine, 87
     Arab cooperation with, 29–34, 37–38
     and Bible, 87
     and Meccan *surahs*, 82
     Muhammad as protected by, 83
     and non-Muslim occupation of Muslim
        lands, 44, 49
     as "People of the Book," 86
     as special people chosen by Allah, 82
     unholy alliance as endangering lives of,
        13
     and Young Turks, 19
     See also anti-Semitism; Israel/Israelis;
        Judeo-Christians; nonbelievers;
        Palestine; Zionist movement; *specific
        person*
jihad/jihadists
     and abrogation doctrine, 86, 87
     and Allah's revelations to Muhammad,
        82, 83
     ayatollahs as spreading, 175
     and caliph's authority, 89
     and clash of Islamic and Western
        culture, 45–47, 51–52
     definition of, 77–78, 83
     destruction caused by, 91
     and diversity among Muslims, 92
     and exporting terrorism by Iran, 108
     as fighting for cause of Allah, 83–84
     Germany and, 23–25
     and history of Middle East, 23–25
     how to react to, 182–84
     and influence of Islamic culture on
        West, 177
     as inner struggle, 82
     Iran as spreading, 101–3, 113, 175
     and Iranian Revolution, 101
     and Islam as religion of peace, 80, 82,
        83–84, 85–88, 91
     lone-wolf, 177
     martyrdom and, 45
     and Medinan *surahs*, 83–84
     as misinterpreting Quran, 181
     moderate Muslims and, 83, 85, 91
     and nonbelievers, 85

United States (*cont.*)
    terrorist organizations as threat to, 13,
        145, 149, 153, 154
    and unholy alliance as endangering lives
        of others, 12–15
    See also specific person or topic
Uthman (third caliph), 93

values
    and clash of Islamic and Western
        culture, 41, 42, 46–47, 51–52, 55
    and influence of Islamic culture on
        West, 178
    Obama administration views about,
        51–52
    and reactions to jihadist atrocities, 184
    and Soviet-U.S. relations, 6–7
    and War on Terror, 174, 184
violence
    and abrogation doctrine, 86, 87
    debate about, 56
    and forcing Sharia law on others, 57
    and Islam as religion of peace, 79
    See also domestic violence; jihad/
        jihadists; terrorism/terrorists

Wahhabi culture, 175
wali (bride's legal guardian), 67
Wall Street Journal, 2
Walsin-Esterhazy, Ferdinand, 18
war
    and clash of Islamic and Western
        culture, 40–55
    eternal, 90
    and intergenerational focus, 52–55
    nonbelievers as cause of, 89, 90
    between radical Islam and U.S., 1–2
    See also jihad/jihadists; *specific war*
Weizmann, Chaim, 29–32, 33–34
West
    clash of Islamic culture and, 40–55
    and exporting terrorism, 108
    and goals of terrorism, 6
    influence of Islamic culture on, 176–78
    Khomeini's views about, 101, 108
    radical Islam hatred of, 2–3
    Sunnis' hatred of, 108
    See also specific nation or topic
West Bank, 36, 37, 38
Wilhelm II (kaiser of Germany), 23, 24

women
    and clash of Islamic and Western
        culture, 47–48, 50, 53
    and fighting across multiple generations,
        53
    global terrorism and, 173
    and history of Iran, 98, 101
    honor killings and, 76
    Muhummad comments about, 74
    and prevalence of terrorism, 1
    radical Islam and, 91
    rape of, 47
    rights of, 19
    as sex slaves, 1
    and Sharia law, 57, 60–61, 65, 66–69,
        74, 76
    and Young Turks, 19
    See also divorce; marriage; rape
World War I, and history of Middle
    East, 16, 19, 20, 21, 22, 26, 28, 29, 35,
    36, 39
World War II
    and Churchill speech after Dunkirk,
        14–15
    Germany in, 14, 15
    and Great Britain, 163
    honor-shame culture in, 49
    Iran and, 98, 163
    and Soviet Union, 163
World Zionist Congress (Basel, 1897), 18
worldview
    and clash of Islamic and Western
        culture, 42–44, 55, 182, 183
    and reactions to jihadist atrocities,
        183
Worldwide Expulsion and Boycott Order
    (Sharia Council), 60
Wureshi, Nabeel, 89

Ya'alon, Moshe, 90
Yatom, Dani, 12
Yazid (caliph), 103, 104, 105, 106
Yemen, 22, 150, 161, 166
Young Turks, 19–20

Zakiri, Hamid Reza, 152
Zawahiri, Ayman al-, 149–51, 152, 153
Zechariah (Hebrew prophet), 82
Zionist movement, 17–19, 29–32
Zoroastrianism, 95, 96